Starting with Foucault

Starting with Foucault

An Introduction to Genealogy

SECOND EDITION

C. G. Prado

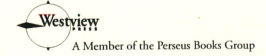
Westview PRESS

A Member of the Perseus Books Group

Published in 2000 in the United States of America by Westview Press, 5500 Central Avenue, Boulder, Colorado 80301-2877, and in the United Kingdom by Westview Press, 12 Hid's Copse Road, Cumnor Hill, Oxford OX2 9JJ

Find us on the World Wide Web at www.westviewpress.com

Library of Congress Cataloging-in-Publication Data
Prado, C. G.
    Starting with Foucault : an introduction to genealogy / C.G. Prado.—2nd ed.
      p. cm
    Includes bibliographical references and index.
    ISBN 0-8133-9078-8 (alk. paper)
      1. Foucault, Michel.   2. Genealogy (Philosophy)   I. Title.

B2430.F724 P73 2000
194—dc21   00-063319

Contents

Preface to the Second Edition

Five years ago I tried to present Foucault's genealogical analytics as clearly as I could in the first edition of *Starting with Foucault: An Introduction to Genealogy*.[1] My targeted audience was philosophers and philosophy students in the Anglo-American analytic tradition. In my experience, too many members of this group simply do not bother to read Foucault, much less engage with his ideas, because of a generally negative impression and the strong tendency to lump him in with various "postmodernists." From what I have been told by students, colleagues, a few readers who have written me, people met at conferences, and not least Westview Press's reviewers, the first edition was quite successful. But after more than five years, I think it needs updating. For one thing, I have used the book in my classes and it is surprising how student response to it has changed since its publication. At that time, few of my students had encountered Foucault. Now students read or read about Foucault in their Political Science courses, Sociology courses, Women's Studies courses, Cultural Geography courses, Film courses, and even Commerce and Business courses. More important is that, like other intellectual innovators, Foucault's ideas have been "appropriated" and are now widely used in diverse contexts and ways. Often they are used with only the most cursory gesture toward their source and with the barest grounding. As a colleague, Bryan Palmer, remarked to me, Foucault is the most referred to and most pirated from but least read contemporary thinker.

The widespread appropriation of philosophical ideas is hardly new. For instance, the notion of a social contract is extensively and variously used without reference to Thomas Hobbes. It is a mark of the importance of new philosophical ideas that they are integrated into common thought and achieve a kind of transparency and anonymity. Foucault's ideas, especially his notion of power, are now taken for granted by many. "Power" may be employed by a cultural geographer concerned with how use of space defines minorities, by a feminist concerned with patriarchal shaping of identities, or by an organizational behaviorist concerned with how institutional hierarchies affect the implementation of policy. What is interesting is that Foucault's notion of power is seldom discussed, much less used, by academic philosophers in the Anglo-American analytic tradition. This has changed little since publication of the first edition. Too many North American universities still offer more courses on Foucault outside their philosophy departments than in them. Even where one would expect serious engagement with Foucault's ideas there tends to be a kind of diminishment of his importance. The main reason for this lack of engagement is perception of Foucault as a radical relativist and irrealist. That is, analytic philosophers see Foucault as leveling all claims and as denying any reality outside of consciousness and language.

What prompted the writing of this second edition were a stylistic and a substantive failing. One reviewer captured the stylistic failing well, saying that the first edition contained too much "Continentalese." The reviewer nicely parodied the style by defining "Continentalese" as "a form of expression in which sentence subjects become monstrously complex and verbs appear so late in the sentence, or in such a subordinate role, that the reader grows weary." I have tried to correct this failing by rewriting the entire book in a more acceptable and accessible style. The substantive failing was that I did not go deep enough in addressing the source of resistance to Foucault on the part of analytic philosophers. I have added a chapter in which I address the issue of perceived irrealism in Foucault. Even more than relativism, apparent irrealism or denial of "external" reality prevents analytic philosophers from giving Foucault's work the attention it merits. It is my hope that these changes will make this introduction to Foucault's genealogical ideas more effective, prompting more of my intended readers to avail themselves of what Foucault offers.

Kingston, 2000

Note

1. Prado 1995.

Chapter One

Foucault: Challenge and Misperceptions

"At the time of his death . . . Michel Foucault was perhaps the single most famous intellectual in the world."[1] So opens James Miller's biography of Foucault. Alan Ryan goes further, asserting that Foucault "was the most famous intellectual figure in the world" when he died.[2] David Macey's biography makes the more modest claim that at his death Foucault "was without doubt France's most prominent philosopher." But Macey adds that Foucault's international reputation had "almost eclipsed his reputation in France."[3] Miller goes on to say that "scholars were grappling with the implications of [Foucault's] empirical research" across the academic spectrum and "pondering the abstract questions [he] raised."[4] Jonathan Arac outdoes Miller in claiming that "Foucault's work . . . changed the basis for the work of all scholars."[5]

This high estimation of Foucault is shared by many North American academics in disciplines ranging from political science and cultural geography through sociology to literary criticism and film studies. Many students in these disciplines consider Foucault a champion in the struggle against what they regard as stultifying disciplinary traditions. The striking exception is "analytic" philosophers, who largely dismiss Foucault. Most philosophers whose post-Kantian canon prioritizes the work of Frege, Russell, Moore, and Wittgenstein do not consider Foucault a philosopher, much less a philosopher who has something to say to them. They regard Foucault as a paradigmatic "Continental" thinker, one whose post-Kantian canon emphasizes the work of Hegel, Heidegger, Husserl, and Merleau-Ponty.[6] Their negative perception of Foucault goes further than seeing him as a member of a different intellectual tradition. They dismiss Foucault as holding "post-

1

modern" views that are inimical to proper philosophizing. Didier Eribon observes in his biography of Foucault that Foucault "drew huge crowds" on his visits to North America[7] but was "completely ignored by most American philosophers."[8] For example, Foucault's visits to the University of California at Berkeley[9] were at the invitation of departments other than philosophy. The philosophers did not consider Foucault to be doing anything relevant to their interests and areas of expertise.[10] Foucault was not just ignored; he was disparaged. Richard Rorty notes that "a distinguished analytic philosopher . . . urged that 'intellectual hygiene' requires one not to read . . . Foucault."[11] Foucault was not only aware of this hostility; he seemed to relish it. He claimed that he was "very proud" that some thought him dangerous for being, in their view, "an irrationalist, a nihilist."[12]

Despite analytic philosophers' disdain, Foucault had a huge influence on North American humanities and social sciences. He raised questions about "the reach of power and the limits of knowledge, the origins of moral responsibility and the foundations of modern government, the character of historical inquiry and the nature of personal identity."[13] Yet despite some of these questions being philosophical by any reasonable standard, Foucault still does not figure in the bulk of the writing and teaching of North American analytic philosophers. They ignored Foucault when he began to achieve global notice and continue to ignore his work. Some of them have taken a belated interest in that work, if only because of its current prominence and its having defied predictions of modish transiency. But when analytic philosophers do consider Foucault's work, treatment of it usually runs more to invective than to sympathetic investigation or exposition. A paper typifying this treatment describes Foucault as not only wrong about nearly everything he did say, but as ultimately having "nothing to say" with respect to "philosophical theories of truth and knowledge."[14]

Foucault remains intellectually distant to most analytic philosophers. This is not only because he is outside their tradition; they also believe his writings belong to a tradition the standards and methods of which fall short of their own.[15] Analytic philosophers see Foucault as in a tradition that is more literary than rigorous and technical. Speaking of Foucault's work, Eribon remarks that North American philosophers "saw no need of this 'literature,' which they ranked in the . . . French tradition of Bergson and Sartre."[16] Analytic philosophers' perception and characterization of Foucault as unrigorous and too literary adversely affects their students. If the students are curious about his work, because of his importance in other disciplines, they are predisposed to find it beyond the pale of technical (read "tough-minded") philosophy. Students then see Foucault as someone whose work does not merit the close study it requires. Alternatively, the exclusionary attitude of their professors prompts other students to revere Foucault as an iconoclastic champion opposed to technical (read "sterile") philosophy. They then are predisposed to find in his work all sorts of ideas supportive of their agendas. The upshot is that the combination of Foucault's importance outside philosophy, and characterization of Foucault's work by analytic philosophers as too problematic in conception and development, elicits opposed and equally unproductive responses. On the one hand, aspirants to orthodoxy ignorantly dismiss Foucault as too literary on the implicit or explicit say-so of their professors. On the other hand, would-be radicals fervently but equally ignorantly embrace various more-or-less popularized versions of Foucault's views. In numerous seminars on Foucault, I have had to work as hard to disabuse ardent students of basic misconceptions as to engage the unresponsive ones.

Foucault's writings are not difficult in the way that Immanuel Kant's are difficult. But his mode of expression and his style are unfamiliar enough to North American readers to mislead and even to irritate them, thereby making what is not inherently difficult nonetheless inaccessible.[17] Style aside, Foucault's work has characteristics that invite misinterpretation. His work exhibits a topical specificity at odds with abstract philosophizing and is deliberately marginal. Foucault employs a measure of provocative intellectual craftiness. Some important shifts in his thinking conspire to invite misunderstanding. There is no single work that adequately represents the complex, variegated, and evolutionary totality of Foucault's philosophical vision. In fact, Foucault's work resists holistic interpretation.[18] In spite of his own avowals about the unity of his project, his books "hardly ever refer back to his previous works."[19] This is why those who read only spottily in his work, basing their impressions on one or two books or articles, invariably form distorted and often astonishingly different ideas of his views.[20] Many are introduced to Foucault through *The History of Sexuality* because of its popularity. They then encounter the concept of "power" as it is used to advance a particular thesis about sexuality. The consequence is that power quite wrongly looks to them like covert manipulation. It is difficult to understand the concept of power without first reading *Discipline and Punish*, where Foucault develops the idea. Reading *The History of Sexuality* first, and then reading, say, the quite differently conceived *Archaeology of Knowledge* poses another interpretive trap. In this case the results are most likely bafflement or misguided dismissal of one or the other work. Unfortunately, even systematic reading of several works does not ensure understanding of Foucault by those who approach his work from outside his intellectual tradition. This is in part because of differences in idiom and tradition and in part because of internal development in his thought. Additionally, Foucault always addresses circumscribed issues and always in opposition to established philosophical and historical scholarship. He leaves it to his readers to make the connections, and the connections often are made in varying ways.

The basic premise of this book is that a special strategy is necessary to read Foucault productively. Not only is it insufficient to read only one or two of his books or articles to get the gist of his thought, one should not begin at the beginning as with most philosophers. To start with *Madness and Civilization* is to risk an erroneous initial impression that Foucault's work is not philosophical enough. To start with the much discussed and in some ways most imposing major "archaeological" work, *The Order of Things*, is to risk misconstruing his middle and last books as less philosophical than they actually are. Despite their originality, *The Order of Things* and *The Archaeology of Knowledge* are methodologically and even thematically closer to traditional philosophy than are the books that follow them. Of greatest importance in Foucault are his challenges to traditional philosophical methods and assumptions and to established conceptions of truth and knowledge. Those challenges are raised most clearly and definitively in his "genealogical" works. It is counterproductive to approach his work in a manner that in any way erodes the philosophical force of these works.

To get a good understanding of Foucault, one must begin in the middle, with the major genealogical works: *Discipline and Punish* and *The History of Sexuality*, Volume 1. That is where we find the most pointed indictments of traditionally conceived truth, knowledge, and rationality. That is where we find the sharpest articulations of the ideas that truth and knowledge are products of power, that the subject is product of disciplinary techniques, and that rationality is itself an historical product. Once the nature and scope of these challenging ideas is appreciated, it is possible to go back to *Madness and Civilization* or *The Order of Things*, and forward to *The Use of Pleasure* or *The Care of the Self*, and productively understand the progression of Foucault's thought. Moreover, the major genealogical works comprise what is most philosophically significant in Foucault's work for my audience: analytic philosophers. It is in those works that Foucault most directly addresses what he describes as of greatest moment: "truth itself."[21]

The aim of this book is to provide those who have not read or have only dipped into Foucault's writings with an accessible introduction to his genealogy. Once readers grasp Foucault's radical ideas concerning truth, knowledge, the subject, and rationality, and understand how these are products of power relations, they will have what is most important in Foucault's thought. This book also has a therapeutic aim. Whether or not because of their philosophical significance, though one would hope because of it, *Discipline and Punish* and especially *The History of Sexuality*, Volume 1, are Foucault's most widely read books. Unfortunately, these also are the most often misinterpreted and misused of his works. The ideas presented in these books are prone to distortion and hasty appropriation. Not only are they difficult ideas, they are Foucault's most revolutionary insights and therefore what is most intellectually exciting in his work. Excitement about the concept of power, in particular, often prompts uncomprehending appropriation and application.[22] My intent, then, is to provide a clear and accessible account of what Foucault is doing in *Discipline and Punish* and *The History of Sexuality*, Volume 1 in order both to provide an introduction to his genealogy and, hopefully, to dispel misconceptions and misinterpretations.

Readers with broad philosophical backgrounds may consider *The Order of Things*, with its emphasis on linguistic and epistemological topics, to be Foucault's most properly "philosophical," and therefore significant, work. They will wonder why that work receives cursory treatment in this book. It is precisely because *The Order of Things* is most recognizable as a philosophical work that one should focus elsewhere to discern the deeper import of the ideas of a most anti-philosophical philosopher. Gilles Deleuze observes that Foucault offers "counterphilosophy" and that his work is most productively read as a counterpoint to established philosophical assumptions and practices, especially analytic ones.[23] There is less to be gained by concentrating on those of Foucault's books that better meet disciplinary expectations than on those that seem to flout good philosophical sense. As will be considered later, Foucault exalts mind-stretching alternity in intellectual pursuits. To achieve alternity of thought, particularly in his genealogical period, he concentrates on the unfamiliar, the enigmatic, the shunned, the obscure, the neglected, and the suppressed. In the spirit of his work, then, if the philosophical tradition prefers *The Order of Things* to *Discipline and Punish* and *The History of Sexuality*, it is the latter two that most deserve our attention.

Necessary Scene-Setting

I need to clarify the reasons for the negative view that analytic philosophers have of Foucault and his work to situate both with respect to my analytic reader's background and expectations. This is necessary to orient my exposition and to make it more accessible, but there is another reason. Beyond exposition, I also try to make a substantive contribution to understanding of Foucault's philosophical vision of truth. To that end I complement the expository chapters with one on truth (Chapter 6) and a related one on realism (Chapter 7). In those two chapters I address the fundamental sources of analytic impatience with Foucault's contentions and work. My objective is not only to make Foucault's work more accessible to analytic philosophers but to interest them in it. Doing so requires disabusing analytic philosophers of the idea that Foucault's thought is hopelessly relativistic and irrealistic.

There are a number of more specific reasons for analytic philosophers' dismissal of Foucault than the general view of his work as unrigorous or too literary. These reasons can be gathered under four headings that have to do with Foucault's predecessors, his peers, his motivation, and his ontology.[24]

Problematic Predecessors

Foucault was trained and worked in the "Continental" or European philosophical tradition. That means that Nietzsche and especially Heidegger loomed very large in Foucault's intellectual development. Foucault recognizes this: "I am simply a Nietzschean"; "Heidegger has always been for me the essential philosopher."[25] Miller quotes Foucault as saying that his "entire philosophical development was determined by [the] reading of Heidegger."[26] Heidegger's influence on Foucault was more than narrowly philosophical, for he was deeply affected by Heidegger's interest in pressing beyond the limits of conventional intellectual inquiry. This legacy is anathema to analytic philosophers. Miller captures the heart of the matter when he notes that someone prepared to "descend into what Heidegger called the 'unthought'" must be prepared to probe "beyond the limits of reason" and to think "without statute or rule, structure or order."[27] For Heidegger and Foucault, this is an intellectual challenge. For analytic philosophers, it is rejection of reasoned inquiry in favor of undisciplined speculation.

Nietzsche often serves as a model of intellectual excess for many analytic philosophers and many do not consider him a philosopher. Bertrand Russell offers a typical assessment: "Nietzsche . . . was a literary rather than academic philosopher. He invented no new technical theories in ontology or epistemology."[28] But if analytic philosophers have their doubts about Nietzsche, they have perceived Heidegger as the paradigm of pretentious obscurity from the time of his initial prominence.[29] Heidegger does not even warrant an entry in the index to Russell's history of philosophy. W. T. Jones's four-volume history also ignores Heidegger and leaves a yawning intellectual gap between the two twentieth-century European figures it does discuss, Edmund Husserl and Jean-Paul Sartre. Wallace Matson's history of philosophy runs to nearly five hundred pages but allots only sixteen lines to Heidegger.[30] There are exceptions to the rule. There have been efforts to link the work of leading analytic philosophers to that of prominent European philosophers, despite Heidegger's strong influence on them. One example is trying to connect Donald Davidson's more recent views on language to the hermeneutics of Hans-Georg Gadamer.[31] Efforts at cross-pollination, however, have had limited success[32] and association with Heidegger remains preclusive of analytic interest.

Problematic Peers

Foucault is not only shunned because of his Heideggerian provenance; he is disassociated from contemporary European philosophers who are taken seriously by analytic philosophers, such as Jürgen Habermas. Foucault instead is ignorantly lumped with Jacques Derrida as a founder of postmodernism and recent French "irrationalism." In the eyes of most analytic philosophers, Derrida inherited Heidegger's mantle of undisciplined speculation and arrogant impenetrability. John Searle, who in effect acted as a spokesperson for analytic philosophers, wrote off Derrida as not being a serious philosopher nearly two decades ago.[33] That dismissal was reiterated in 1992 when Cambridge University awarded Derrida an honorary degree. Nineteen philosophers, including W.V.O. Quine and D. M. Armstrong,[34] wrote to *The Times* in an unsuccessful attempt to block the granting of the degree. They contended that philosophers "working in leading departments throughout the world" judged that Derrida's work "does not meet accepted standards of clarity and rigor."[35] The irony was that those objecting to award of the degree "made themselves . . . absurd because the authority to which they were appealing was none other than themselves."[36] Foucault and Derrida were friends, but their work differs greatly in nature and intent. Nonetheless, analytic philosophers see Foucault as like Derrida in embodying and contributing to the intellectual fragmentation and bankruptcy that supposedly characterize contemporary French philosophy in particular and the last decade of the twentieth century in general.[37] This assimilation is a mistake. As Vasile Munteanu notes, "putting together Foucault with . . . other French contemporaries . . . especially Derrida, is a disservice both to Foucault and to the important ideas that he can bring to North American philosophy."[38]

Problematic Motivation

Foucault's philosophizing is significantly motivated by political considerations, like the work of many European philosophers of our time, such as Sartre and Habermas. What looms largest is the need to come to terms with ideological failures leading to World War II and recent disillusionment with Marxism.[39] Moreover, the developments that culminated in World War II insured that Foucault grew to adulthood with "a particular sense of menace" that heightened his political awareness.[40] Most Europeans perceive political motivation in philosophical thought as legitimate, admirable, and even necessary. However, analytic philosophers perceive political motivation as violating what they understand to be the sacrosanct objectivity of philosophy. Foucault's views are therefore seen not as informed by political considerations but as tainted by nonphilosophical motives and interests.

Problematic Ontology

When analytic philosophers give philosophical reasons for dismissing Foucault, they invariably talk about his relativism. He is perceived as having opted out of serious philosophy by adopting a wholesale relativism diametrically opposed to the Enlightenment values, presuppositions and goals that still constitute bedrock for analytic philosophical thought. The question of Foucault's relativism is labyrinthine in complexity, as we will see, but the important point is that he is wrongly thought to deny truth by relativizing it to discourse and sociopolitical contexts. This is a common misinterpretation that I hope to dispel. Foucault's own comment on it was: "Those who say that for me the truth does not exist are simple-minded."[41] But relativism actually is not the fundamental issue that divides analytic philosophers and Foucault. The real problem is irrealism. Foucault's relativism is taken to entail irrealism. His relativization of truth to discourse is taken as denial of extra-discursive reality. His relativistic pronouncements about truth and discourse are considered to imply that our reality is only a function of discourse.[42]

Despite the foregoing, there undeniably has been some interest in Foucault on the part of analytic philosophers.[43] But widespread perception of Foucault's work as unrigorous, as philosophically compromised by political considerations, and as vitiated by relativism and irrealism has drastically limited such interest. This perception has constrained even those philosophers likeliest to be sympathetic to Foucault's ideas. A case in point is Charles Taylor, who is analytically trained but comfortable with and even proselytic about Foucault's intellectual tradition. Yet Taylor portrays Foucault's work as bad philosophy and discusses it primarily to focus his own criticisms of postmodernist ideas. Taylor casts Foucault as a disciple of Nietzsche's and as having inherited Nietzsche's confusions and reliance on rhetoric. Specifically, Taylor wrongly takes Foucault's conception of power as Nietzschean and argues it is incoherent because it lacks contrast.[44] But proper understanding of Foucauldian power renders Taylor's arguments unpersuasive. I hold no brief for Derrida, but Taylor's treatment of Foucault as doing bad philosophy is comparable to Searle's tendentious reading of Derrida. Rorty tells us that the "weakness of Searle's treatment of Derrida is that he thinks of him as doing amateurish philosophy of language rather than as asking metaphilosophical questions about the value of such philosophy."[45] In a similar way, Taylor treats Foucault's work in a way that precludes its radicalness.

Even more striking than Taylor is the case of Rorty himself. Rorty is the North American philosopher who has the most in common with Foucault. But Rorty has not made as much use of Foucault as one might expect. He invokes his name surprisingly little.[46] Unlike Taylor, Rorty does not think Foucault philosophizes badly, but he is distrustful of what he feels are traditional epistemological implications in Foucault's work. What he does value in Foucault's work he claims to find elsewhere. Rorty maintains that John Dewey waits at the end of the road Foucault travels and that Deweyan pragmatism is capable of yielding "all that is politically useful in the Nietzsche-Heidegger-Derrida-Foucault tradition."[47] Rorty also thinks Foucault offers too bleak a vision of political reality and possibility, a view he shares with a good number of North American academics. Rorty claims that Foucault had a "dangerous" influence on the American political left, prompting "disengagement," and that his lack of a political program produced "profound resentment."[48]

Despite Rorty's ambivalence about Foucault, there are important similarities between the two. I trade on those similarities in exposition of Foucault. Even if the reader is as unfamiliar with Rorty's work as with Foucault's, Rorty's idiom is more immediately accessible to North American readers. Where there is congruence of ideas, Rorty's articulation of those ideas facilitates understanding of Foucault's.

In contrast to most analytic philosophers, many North American feminists have engaged Foucault in serious debate.[49] Feminists have focused on the political implications of Foucault's work and related his ideas on power and the body directly to their own projects. They have rightly concentrated on those parts of Foucault's work that most immediately interest them or affect their own positions. This engagement has yielded mixed results because Foucauldian power is sometimes misrepresented as covert domination. Unfortunately, neither feminist criticism nor sympathetic development of Foucault's views has gained for those views the wider philosophical recognition they deserve.

For the most part, then, analytic philosophers regard Foucault's work as largely external or even inimical to their philosophical projects. This is the case even with respect to his views on the most fundamental philosophical issues. For instance, Foucault said a lot about truth, but to cite him in a discussion of truth conducted by analytic philosophers likely would be seen as facetious. I have observed a great deal of joking dismissal of Foucault in philosophical conversation. The dismissal is not acknowledged as such, but one need only look at one or another feminist work on the negative roles of humor to appreciate how real it is.[50] Foucault's views on truth should be considered relevant to most discussions of the topic, if only because his pluralistic view of truth challenges the traditional unitary conception and may get us past the impasses the latter generates. For example, a pluralistic understanding of truth may resolve our apparent inability to jettison the notion of truth as correspondence in spite of not being able to viably articulate the notion of correspondence. This is why this introduction to Foucault, aimed at readers trained in analytic philosophy, is not only an attempt to win respect for work that is of peripheral interest. The point is to enable a productive dialogue.[51]

Making a Start

Foucault offers historicist views of truth, knowledge, and rationality. He thinks that the most important philosophical projects have to do with understanding how and why we hold some things true, how and why we deem some things knowledge, and how and why we consider some procedures rational and others not. Foucault also offers a historicist view of the subject. Basic to his work is the idea that subjectivity is a complex product rather than a preexistent condition. These views look to many analytic philosophers as at best relativistic sociology of knowledge and at worst absurd. But that perception presupposes just the methodological assumptions and particular conceptions of the nature of truth, knowledge, rationality, and subjectivity that Foucault challenges. If Foucault argues, against the tradition, that there is no Truth but various truths, he may have something more useful in mind than a simple relativism. If, as Todd May puts it, Foucault argues against the tradition that "[t]here is no Knowledge; there are knowledges" and that "[t]here is no Reason; there are rationalities," then Foucault may be contending more than that inquiry and its standards are contextual. If he insists that "it is meaningless to speak in the name of—or against—Reason, Truth, or Knowledge," he may be teaching us a valuable lesson about justification rather than denying its possibility.[52] And if he maintains that subjectivity is manufactured, he may be disabusing us of illusory autonomy.

As to what Foucault does contend, analytically trained or influenced readers will expect exposition of theories and arguments in what follows. However, Foucault mainly offers not so much theories and supporting arguments as persuasive and sometimes compelling characterizations and "pictures." In this his can be compared to the later work of Ludwig Wittgenstein. Many readers will be impatient with claims about the value of views not presented as theoretical claims and supported by arguments. But tolerance of unfamiliar presentation is the price that must be paid to appreciate Foucault's radical thought.

Although Foucault does not proceed in the expected manner of making theoretical claims and offering detailed arguments for them, that should not obscure ideas that are initially startling but ultimately productive. These are many. There are his Nietzschean misgivings about the absolute value of truth. There is his historicist view of knowledge. There is his distrust of the evident, of what manifests itself as obvious. There is his view of truth and knowledge as functions of how we make ourselves certain kinds of subjects for whom the world is then a certain way. There is his querying of how we came to regard ourselves as objects of disciplined knowledge. There's his insightful conception of disciplines as both fields of study and systems of control. And there is his "decentralization" of the subject or his vision of the self, and hence the knower, as emergent from social and discursive relations and practices. All of these ideas are decidedly postmodern in the sense of being opposed to conception of truth as of ultimate worth, as evident to reasoned inquiry, and as objective. They are also opposed to conception of knowledge as possession of truth, and to conception of the self as the unitary condition of cognition. We cannot reasonably expect these radical ideas to be presented in the idiom and style that are the staples of traditional philosophy.

I should add that this introduction to Foucault's genealogy is not an ecumenical exercise. It is not my intent to reconcile diverse traditions.[53] That is far too ambitious a project and almost certainly bound to fail. Neither is this introduction a misguided attempt to present the "real" Foucault—an effort Foucault would have despised.[54] I have no intention of trying to offer either a new interpretation or a comprehensive outline of a body of work that ranges from the brilliant to the possibly incoherent.[55] There are some excellent comprehensive treatments of Foucault's work.[56] As indicated, my objective is to introduce my targeted audience to the most central and productive of Foucault's ideas, and in my view that is to ideas that are most fully developed in his middle works. I offer an introduction that concentrates on Foucault's genealogical analytics. These are his investigations into how the development of discursive practices produces truth and knowledge and so shapes and defines subjects and subjectivity. These are the Foucauldian ideas with the greatest epistemological import; these are also the ideas most perplexing to those trained in analytic philosophy.

Foucault's genealogical contentions represent an extreme point of contrast to the basically Cartesian assumptions and methods that still dominate epistemology. This is especially true with respect to the subject.[57] Foucault does not offer the sort of constructivist alternative to the Cartesian subject that George Herbert Mead offered. Constructivists such as Mead regard the subject as a product of cognition rather than a condition of cognition, but that is basically an ontological thesis about the origin and nature of the subject. Taylor comments on the difference between Mead's and Foucault's conception of subjectivity. He observes that Mead "does not seem to take account of the constitutive role of language in the definition of self."[58] In a sense, Foucault's subject is more emergent than constructed. As I consider in Chapter 4, subjectivity for Foucault is a matter of *saying* and not a matter of *being*. In short, his is not an ontological or metaphysical thesis about the self.

A caution is now necessary. The radicalness of Foucault's ideas should not lead to counterproductive exaggeration of the differences between his thought and more familiar philosophy. I disagree with those who anguish over "the demise of the tradition" and construe Foucault's work as part of some alleged holistic displacement of modernism by postmodernism.[59] Foucault explicitly dismisses the idea that postmodernism constitutes some sort of wholesale intellectual reorientation: "There is no sense at all to the proposition that reason is a long narrative which is now finished, and that another narrative is underway."[60] Rorty admits similarities between his own views and Foucault's. He tolerates the label "postmodern" applied to him, but is "not fond of the term" precisely because he also rejects the idea that it designates a new and systematically different way of thinking.[61] Rorty thinks postmodernism is simply "the gradual encapsulation and forgetting of a certain philosophical tradition."[62] We should try to make productive use of Foucault's ideas rather than misguidedly exaggerate the magnitude of presuppositional and methodological changes and innovations. Some of those ideas pose the most pointed challenges to traditional conceptions of truth and knowledge in the 350 years since *Meditations on First Philosophy* and the two and a half millennia since *Theaetetus*. But they are challenges, not a new and alien way of thinking.

As acknowledged earlier, these challenging ideas are not as accessible as they might be because of idiomatic and background differences. Regretfully, they are made even less accessible by Foucault's own interpretive excursions. Foucault was a highly regarded French intellectual, which means he was a public figure, a celebrity, in a way academics never are in North America. As a consequence, not only must his readers and interpreters contend with his substantial and diversely oriented primary writings, they must also deal with a profusion of interviews, many anthologized, in which Foucault has too much to say about his own work.[63] Foucault had a "revisionist" view of his own work and tended to retrospectively see more coherence and progressive development in it than it actually exhibits. His view of his work as incrementally developmental was in sharp contrast to his often speaking of having changed his mind and of later works superseding earlier ones: "To write a book is . . . to abolish the preceding one."[64] Foucault was also impatient with others' misunderstanding of his work and especially with what he deemed ignorant or ill-conceived criticism. So in addition to his revisionary statements, there are many corrective pronouncements in various secondary writings—commentaries, forewords, afterwords, and annotations that were solicited or volunteered and published in anthologies on his work. There are similar contentions in transcribed lectures that have been published in various collections. A great deal of what Foucault says in these "clarifications" of his work relates to his perspective of the moment. Additionally, a fair bit is ironic, provocative, and, on occasion, has all the earmarks of unconsidered extemporaneous remarks.

The upshot is that, aside from the complexity of his primary writings and whatever problems they may raise, Foucault's secondary writings and interviews, taken together with his primary writings, support too many diverse interpretations.[65] There are passages at odds with some central contentions and comments suggestive of alternative readings of important pronouncements. The breadth of interpretive possibility would be troublesome enough if inadvertent or only a consequence of continuous revision, but a great deal of it was quite deliberate. We will see that providing interpretive possibility is integral to Foucault's conception of philosophizing. Eribon quotes Georges Dumézil, "who knew [Foucault] better than almost anyone else," as saying that Foucault "wore masks, and he was always changing them." Eribon adds, "there are several Foucaults—a thousand Foucaults."[66]

Though Foucault often speaks of his work as of a piece, the integration he saw is problematic. Even a cursory reading of Foucault's claims to unity, found mostly in interviews and pieces like his "Two Lectures" and "The Subject and Power," shows this. The integration he speaks of has more to do with the topics that interest him than with what he has to say about those topics.[67] This is evident in the emphasis put on the formation of the subject, the topic that shows the greatest measure of continuity and consistency in his investigations. Foucault insists that the goal of his work "during the last 20 years" was not to analyze the phenomenon of power but rather "to create a history of the different modes by which . . . human beings are made subjects."[68] He lists as one of the most basic questions he considers that of how "the human subject took itself as the object of possible knowledge."[69]

This question illustrates how many of Foucault's most intriguing ideas are often articulated in uncharacteristically compact ways and as often buried in a mass of detail. The brief way he puts this complex question serves as a warning to those who are tempted by his style to skim over what they think inessential. The question is: How did we come to take ourselves to be the sorts of things that can be studied and known and understood as subjects of broadly scientific or disciplinary investigation? Why did we not continue to see ourselves as known and understood only as friends or adversaries, cooperators or competitors, teachers or students, lovers or enemies? The question is about how we objectified ourselves as the subject matter of various disciplines, and it is perhaps Foucault's most perceptive impulse to wonder about "the objectivizing of the subject."[70]

In the next chapter I will situate genealogy both in relation to my intended readers' philosophical framework and to Foucault's own earlier work. With respect to the former, I try to say just enough to heighten the contrast with Foucault's most challenging ideas in order to avert misunderstandings. With respect to the latter, I try to say just enough about Foucault's mainly archaeological work to give the reader an idea of its character. Chapter 3 is devoted to a single article, the importance of which some think "cannot be exaggerated" with respect to "understanding Foucault's objectives."[71] In Chapters 4 and 5, I consider the two Foucauldian texts that embody the most thorough application of his genealogical analytics and that are, in my estimation, the most central to Foucault's thought.[72] These are *Discipline and Punish*, where Foucault first explicitly addresses the matter of power and its role in the formation of subjects, and *The History of Sexuality*, Volume 1. In the latter Foucault considers how formation of subjects is effected in the area he deemed most central to the formation and development of identity.[73] In Chapter 6, I offer what I believe to be a novel way of sorting out Foucault's views on truth. Chapter 7 is given over to the issue of irrealism, which, I contend, is the real source of analytic philosophers' antipathy to Foucault's work. In Chapter 8, I consider the relation of genealogy to archaeology and Foucauldian ethics and the central question of the cogency of Foucault's philosophical claims. The latter is an instance of the larger issue of how historicist theses could be judged intellectually compelling.

Notes

1. Miller 1993:13.
2. Ryan 1993:12.
3. Macey 1993:xi.
4. Miller 1993:13.
5. Arac 1991:vii.
6. I expand a little on this distinction below.
7. Eribon 1991. Specific reference is to visits by Foucault in the early 1980s to the University of California at Berkeley and at Los Angeles and to the University of Vermont.
8. Eribon 1991:313.
9. These began in 1975.
10. Miller 1993.
11. Rorty 1982:224. I have it on excellent authority that the philosopher in question was D. M. Armstrong.
12. Martin, Gutman, and Hutton 1988:13; compare Allen 1993:181.
13. Miller 1993:13.
14. Nola 1994:3.
15. I recall with regret that because I once shared this view, I failed to go and hear Foucault while I was a Visiting Scholar at Princeton in 1981. He was there while visiting a number of eastern universities. I took advantage of lectures given by visitors such as MacIntyre and Nozick, but at the time thought I had nothing to gain from hearing Foucault.
16. Eribon 1991:313; compare Rorty 1982:223–27; see also Ricoeur 1992: 16–17.
17. Bernauer, J. 1993:2–3.
18. Gutting 1994a:3–4.
19. Gutting 1994a:3.
20. Compare O'Hara 1986.
21. Foucault 1980b:133; compare Allen 1993:149–76.
22. The most common mistake is to read and use Foucauldian power as covert manipulation. A student told me at the end of a course on Foucault that she had not striven to understand Foucault because "his ideas" (in particular, power as covert manipulation) had impressed her as ideally suited to serve the agendas that defined

her life. I knew I was not going to change her mind about power, but did want to ask her how she knew they were *his* ideas.

23. Deleuze 1984:149.

24. I use "ontology" here for want of a better term. The sense will be clarified below.

25. Foucault 1989:327, 326.

26. Miller 1993:46.

27. Miller 1993:49–50.

28. Russell 1945:760.

29. Ryle 1929; Carnap 1931.

30. Russell 1945; Jones 1969; Matson 1987:468.

31. Ramberg 1989; see also Malpas 1992; compare Staten 1984.

32. It is decidedly not philosophers but political scientists, sociologists, literary critics, film theorists, and more specialized disciplinarians such as organizational behaviorists who read and use Foucault extensively in North America. Recently, and surprisingly, professors of accounting have turned to Foucault. See Burrell 1988; Hooper and Pratt 1993; Hopper and Macintosh 1993; Macintosh *et al.* 2000.

33. Searle 1983.

34. See note 11, above.

35. Rée 1992:61.

36. Rée 1992:61.

37. Bell 1992.

38. Munteanu 1998.

39. Miller 1993:17.

40. Bernauer, J. W. 1993:7.

41. Foucault 1989:295.

42. As I consider below, Foucault did make assertions that can be read in this way.

43. Dreyfus and Rabinow 1983; Bernauer, S. J. 1987; Flynn 1989; Schurmann 1989; Seigel 1990; Shumway 1992; May 1993; Gutting 1994a.

44. Taylor 1984, 1987; compare Allen 1991; Bové 1988.

45. Rorty 1991b:94n.

46. In an e-mail (Nov. 1999) Rorty said that at the end of his last seminar on Foucault and Habermas he told the students he would not teach Foucault again.

47. Rorty 1982:xviii; 1991c:3, 1991b.

48. Borradori 1994:111.

49. Diamond and Quinby 1988; Bartky 1990; Hartsock 1990; Code 1991; Sawicki 1991; Ramazanoglu 1993. See especially Sawicki 1994.

50. Mackie 1990.

51. James Bernauer's Foreword to Carrette 1999 is one of the most moving examples I have read of how productive philosophical dialogue can be established with aspects of Foucault's thought.

52. May 1993:2.

53. Compare Rorty 1982:225–26.

54. Eribon 1991:xi.

55. Compare Gutting 1994a:3–4.

56. Dreyfus and Rabinow 1983; Bernauer, J. W. 1993.

57. Prado 1992.
58. Taylor 1989:525, n12.
59. Nielsen 1989; Nielsen and Hart 1990; compare Latour 1993.
60. Foucault 1988b:35; compare Bernstein 1992.
61. Rorty 1991c:n18.
62. Rorty 1992:71.
63. Foucault 1980b, 1988b, 1989.
64. Foucault 1989:303; compare Foucault 1991a:27; Gutting 1994a:1–27.
65. For a unified and somewhat metaphysical reading of Foucault, see Deleuze 1988. For a decidedly political reading, see Fink-Eitel 1992. For a more literary reading, see Mahon 1992. For an epistemologically and psychologically oriented reading, see May 1993. For a somewhat ethically oriented reading, see Bernauer, J. 1993. For a more historiographical reading, see Gutting 1994a. See also O'Hara 1986 and Polan 1982.
66. Eribon 1991:xi; compare Macey 1993; see also Foucault 1989:193–202.
67. Foucault 1989, 1976, 1983a.
68. Foucault 1983a:208.
69. Foucault 1988b:30.
70. Foucault 1983a:208.
71. Bouchard 1977:139n.
72. Compare May 1993.
73. Miller 1993:15–16.

Chapter Two

The Domains of Analysis

Understanding Foucault requires heightened awareness of important differences between his presuppositions and methods and those that structure philosophy in North America. Deleuze is quite right in saying that what Foucault offers runs counter to established philosophical practices and objectives.[1] The trouble is that one's own presuppositions and methods are usually transparent. Just what it is that Foucault opposes is not always obvious. A necessary prelude to consideration of Foucault's work and ideas is a brief recapitulation of what his genealogical views most sharply counter.

In the previous chapter I contrasted analytic philosophy with Continental or European philosophy, implying that the bulk of North American philosophers are analytic philosophers. The people I have in mind share presuppositions, priorities, techniques, methodologies, interests, and goals that have defined philosophy in the United States and Canada for most of this century. Philosophy in Great Britain, Australia, and Scandinavia is also largely analytic.[2] What this means is that the philosophy practiced in these countries is generally a dissective or taking-apart style of intellectual inquiry as opposed to a more synthesizing or putting-together sort of inquiry. This contrast is often drawn in histories of philosophy, as in comparing philosophers like Hume and Russell on the one hand and G. W. Leibniz and Henri Bergson on the other. The former are described as analytic because they try "to understand complexes by reducing them to their . . . parts and to the relations in which these parts stand." The latter are then described as "integrative" because they believe the things we try to understand "are parts of larger unities" and can be fully understood only when fitted into those unities.[3]

The analytic approach to intellectual inquiry began in earnest with Plato's *Theaetetus* and *Sophist* and Aristotle's *Prior Analytics*. It is paradigmatically illustrated in René Descartes's *Discourse on Method* and *Medita-*

tions on First Philosophy and in Hume's *Treatise on Human Nature*. It became the definitive methodology for Anglo-American philosophers with the work of Russell and Moore. The Logical Positivists gave "analytic" a technical sense in redefining philosophy as concerned with the analysis of meaning and hence as prior to science's assessment of empirical claims. This technical sense still has a good deal of currency, but more important is that it captures something essential about mainstream analytic philosophy. Philosophical analysis, rigorous reduction to elements, must precede whatever positive thesis philosophers may propose on a given topic. Searle's ridicule of Derrida exhibits this priority in contrast to literary and politically colored philosophizing that focuses on the "larger unities."

The trouble is that the contrast between dissective analysis and integrative speculation has in effect metamorphosed. It has become a contrast between "real" philosophy, conceived as rigorous and ahistorical, and a kind of philosophy *manqué*. Real philosophy is taken to be what it is because of the ultimacy of its subject matter. Against this, the other sort is deemed to be basically frivolous historicist reflection deeply embedded in its time and culture and characterized more by modishness than real significance. This contrast, and the self-image it reflects, has more to do with dismissal of postmodernism than relativism as such. Relativism is unpopular with analytic philosophers, but relativistic positions vary and their adherents are not all disdained in the way Foucault is disdained.[4] Postmodernists are seen as simply not serious, and Foucault, along with Derrida, is the best known postmodern. As Rorty says in his remark about Searle's assessment of Derrida, he and Foucault are seen as "doing amateurish philosophy."[5] However, the "amateurish" philosophy is perceived as pernicious. There is a normative base for the dismissal of Foucault. Deep disapproval of historicism drives rejection of Foucault's work. Historicism is the view that our ideas of truth, knowledge, and rationality, and all other canonical or authorizing principles, are products of social and cultural developments.[6]

The wellhead of Foucault's historicism is the Hegelian idea that philosophy is its time held in thought. This idea is turned on its head by analytic philosophers who see Foucault's thought and postmodernist thought generally, as our time imprinted on philosophy. What they most reject in Foucault is not so much relativism as historicism. Historicism subordinates truth and knowledge to history. It makes truth, knowledge, and rationality itself what our time and culture deem them to be. Claims to objectivity then reduce to expressions of consensus among social, disciplinary, and political groups. All of this is taken as abandonment of governing standards for intellectual inquiry. And there is more. As important is that once truth and knowledge are made historical, irrealism is seen to follow because historicism precludes access to ahistorical or mind-independent reality. The point can be put in this way: historicism is perceived as an abandonment of objective standards for intellectual inquiry, less because historical or contextual standards are thought preferable, but because recourse to anything else is thought impossible. For philosophers, as opposed to, say, intellectual historians, the fundamental problem with Foucault's claims is that they are seen as entailing denial of "external" reality.[7]

Foucault's views are unquestionably historicist. He maintains that "forms of rationality are created endlessly" and rejects as fundamentally misconceived the conception of any form of intellectual inquiry as having access to objective external correctness-criteria.[8] This is the basic similarity between Foucault and Rorty, who contends that there is "no criterion that we have not created in the course of creating a practice." Hence there is no rationality "that is not obedience to our own conventions."[9]

Ahistorical conception of rationality is the most fundamental presupposition Foucault challenges. Analytic philosophy is characterized by a conception of rationality as ahistoric in being necessarily prior to all intellectual inquiry and as transcending disciplinary, temporal, and cultural contexts. Against this, it is part of Foucault's project to "isolat[e] the form of rationality presented as dominant, and endowed with the status of the one-and-only reason." He wants to demonstrate that our rationality "is only *one* possible form among others."[10] As for the tradition he opposes, he charges that it "operates as though a rational critique of rationality were impossible, or as though . . . a contingent history of reason were impossible."[11] The furor over Derrida's honorary Cambridge degree provides a practical example of what Foucault has in mind. David-Hillel Ruben claimed in *The Times* correspondence that although "philosophers love a good argument about anything," Derrida disqualified himself from participation in such arguments. The reason was that he questioned philosophers' rules for "clear, rigorous, rational discussion."[12] Evidently "anything" does not include the rules by which argument is conducted, so if one questions those rules, one is being irrational.

The ahistoricist/historicist contrast between analytic philosophers and Foucault can be summed up in this way. On one hand we have philosophers committed to real progress in intellectual inquiry governed by ahistoric rationality; on the other we have a philosopher who sees such notions of progress and rationality as themselves subjects for historical explication. The contrast is one between those who conceive of themselves as employing a methodology governed by objective standards, and someone who considers appeals to objective standards to be constitutive moves in the production of a set of norm-setting practices.

Foucault's rejection of the idea that objective standards govern intellectual inquiry and enable us to attain perspective-neutral knowledge poses a paradox of reflexivity. Hilary Lawson describes this as the inescapable "turning back" on ourselves—on our beliefs, language, and practices—in the conduct of intellectual inquiry.[13] The acknowledgment of reflexivity is perhaps post-modernism's defining feature and its biggest problem. Such acknowledgment amounts to reconceiving inquiry as only a highly complex form of self-awareness. Rorty makes a remark about the unviability of the correspondence theory of truth that can be generalized to make the point. We are unable "to step outside of our current theory of the world" in order to evaluate whether it fits the world, so we have no standard to appeal to in checking the soundness of our methods of inquiry.[14] Two other North American philosophers who concur with Foucault regarding the internality of standards are Thomas Kuhn and Paul Feyerabend.[15] But Foucault's conception of power relations makes his rejection of objective standards unique. His is not only a critique of philosophical inquiry, conceived as governed by ahistorical standards and capable of discerning "conceptual" truths, or of scientific inquiry conceived as capable of limning empirical truths. In his genealogical analyses Foucault offers detailed accounts of how such conceptions themselves have their genesis and come to achieve regulatory dominance. He tries to "make visible" the interrelatedness of power and knowledge, especially their mutually determining and enabling roles. He tries to show that rather than knowledge yielding power through accurate description and the enabling of manipulative control, "power perpetually creates knowledge and, conversely, knowledge constantly induces . . . power."[16]

The philosophers Foucault most directly opposes see themselves as having advanced on their predecessors, as being at a contemporary intellectual pinnacle that they have hopes of raising higher. They attribute the progress made to methods that conform to ahistoric inquiry-governing rationality. For Foucault, power relations determine what they think they find when they review claimed progress in achievement of knowledge. As for inquiry-governing rationality, he contends that "reason is self-created." He maintains that rather than rationality being unitary and ahistoric, "rationalities engender one another, oppose and pursue one another."[17] Foucault thinks the histories of philosophy, science, and other disciplines are interpretive constructs imposed on a number of events selectively identified and described. Those histories are not chronicles of events that are independent of construal and that constitute an objectively progressive sequence irrespective of our historical stories. Rorty makes the point in saying that it's only after a given vocabulary has become established that we "can tell a story of progress."[18] The establishment of a vocabulary or idiom is not achieved on the basis of discernment of ahistoric truth. It is simply that the idiom becomes "normal" in the Kuhnian sense of being generally accepted by a community of inquirers.

Foucault's denial that the historical accounts we give of disciplinary knowledge do or could capture objective progress is fundamental to his genealogical analytics. There is no story-independent progress that historians discern and describe. Historians record sequences of occurrences that power relations determine to be significant. This denial perplexes many. They do not see how he can deny there is an independent subject matter for history, a subject matter that historians might or might not correctly trace. Often the perplexity forces adoption of dubious interpretations of Foucault to make his genealogical accounts more manageable and to mold them to disciplinary expectations. But Foucault's denial must be taken together with the mechanisms he describes as explaining why we have the histories we do have. The great challenge Foucault's work poses is in his accounts of how power has defined both disciplines and their contents. That is why Jonathan Arac says "to defend a subject against Foucault requires redefining the subject."[19]

The Three Domains

The dominant elements in Foucault's intellectual milieu were phenomenology, hermeneutics, and structuralism. Phenomenology originated with Husserl and was further developed by Merleau-Ponty. Heidegger reconceived hermeneutics; he generalized an interpretive methodology focused on sacred texts into a theory of understanding. Gadamer refined hermeneutics and "popularized" it among academics in various disciplines. Structuralism arose from Saussure's semiotics and was developed in diverse ways by Claude Lévi-Strauss, Louis Althusser, and Roland Barthes. What is significant is that Foucault's intellectual growth took place in a context rich in philosophical alternatives.[20] Hubert Dreyfus and Paul Rabinow argue that in order to understand Foucault one must triangulate him among phenomenology, hermeneutics, and structuralism. But they correctly contend that Foucault's "interpretive analytics" goes beyond all three to constitute a novel way of grasping "how in our culture human beings have become the sort of objects and subjects structuralism and hermeneutics discover and analyze."[21] Miller paints a more adversarial picture. He sees existentialism, personified in Sartre, as having a stranglehold on philosophy in France. He then sees structuralism as an oppositional movement that attracted Foucault and provided the springboard for the phenomenal success of *The Order of Things*.[22]

Foucault's early work was structuralist in character despite his denials that he was ever a structuralist.[23] In his "Foreword to the English Edition" of *The Order of Things*, Foucault complains that "half-witted" commentators label him a structuralist. He adds that he has been "unable to get it into their tiny minds" that he used "none of the methods, concepts, or key terms that characterize structural analysis."[24] However, these remarks are at odds with Foucault's own statement of purpose in *The Order of*

Things.[25] Miller, speaking of the reception of *The Order of Things*, says that the reviewer for *L'Express* "never used the magic word 'structuralism' because she did not need to." Foucault's "structuralist sympathies" were evident in his talk of "system" and his references to Lévi-Strauss.[26] *The Order of Things* and *The Archaeology of Knowledge* certainly seem to be contributions to a successor discipline to epistemology, which is precisely what structuralism was supposed to be.[27] Foucault's position in those works clearly is that while philosophical inquiry cannot justify knowledge claims, as the tradition would have it, such inquiry can successfully investigate the role of "discourse." The key point is that discourse is conceived as an autonomous determinant of cognitive and social practices, and that is the heart of structuralism.

However, in the late 1960s Foucault abandons the sort of theorizing that aims at discerning underlying epistemological determinants. He does so less explicitly than by a change of emphasis. Dreyfus and Rabinow say that early in his career Foucault "used variants of a strict analysis of discourse," but that particularly after 1968 "Foucault's interests began to shift away from discourse."[28] Foucault begins to focus on power relations, which in 1968 "had not been previously thematized."[29] Foucault admits that his work lacked "the problem of 'discursive regime,' the effects of power."[30] In focusing on power Foucault discards his inclination "to treat language as autonomous and as constitutive of reality," and so rids himself of the traces of idealism that "lurk in the structuralist suggestion that discourse organizes . . . all social practices and historical epochs."[31]

Because of the move away from conception of discourse as an autonomous determinant of cognitive and social practices, Foucault is thought of as a poststructuralist by most of his European peers.[32] The poststructuralist characterization seems justified. The structuralists see cultural phenomena as determined by underlying structures best understood on the model of rule-bound systematic interrelations of signs. Foucault sees cultural phenomena as the results of power relations. The structuralists see the individual subject as a product of constitutive logical relations. Foucault sees the subject as emerging from discursive and behavioral practices and from interactions with equally emergent others. But Dreyfus and Rabinow are right to stress that Foucault is a truly innovative philosopher ill served by modish intellectual labels. Certainly facile characterization of Foucault as a postmodern or Derridean deconstructivist is quite mistaken.

With respect to his originality, perception of Foucault as a disciple of Nietzsche is too simple if not altogether wrongheaded. It is also prejudicial if used to dismiss Foucault on moralistic grounds or as too unrigorous to be taken seriously. In Chapter 3 we will consider Foucault's most concentrated discussion of Nietzsche, but not with a view to portraying Foucault as owing most of his ideas to Nietzsche. It is with regard to truth that Foucault owes the most to Nietzsche. I do not believe, as many do, that Foucault owes his notion of power to Nietzsche's "will to power." Nietzsche's sister compiled a book on the will to power from a mass of notes of dubious importance and intent and very likely did Nietzsche a disservice. But it is decidedly a disservice to trace Foucault's notion of power relations to that book. Foucault himself tells us that his debt to Nietzsche had to do with the question of the value of truth: "What I owe Nietzsche, derives mostly from the texts of around 1880, where the question of truth, the history of truth and the will to truth were central to his work."[33]

Whatever intellectual debts he may owe to Nietzsche, Heidegger, and others, Foucault is an innovative thinker whose stock-in-trade is the overturning of established "knowledges." In his first major work, *Madness and Civilization*, he shows himself possessed of a disturbing originality by articulating his initial "central intuition" that madness is an invention.[34] He portrays psychiatric reforms, such as those of Samuel Tuke and Philippe Pinel, as an "insidious new form of social control" that created a class of malady and then assigned it a negative moral status.[35] As we will see in subsequent chapters, in *Discipline and Punish* Foucault recasts penal reform as the imposition of insidious control, and in *The History of Sexuality* he rethinks sexuality as a deployed subject-defining and regulating "regime."

Foucault's originality was wrapped up with his Heideggerian ambition to think the "unthought" and a Nietzschean interest in the daimonic. His goal was to come to terms with the Nietzschean question: "How did I become what I am and why do I suffer from being what I am?"[36] Foucault's efforts in this direction go well beyond academic philosophy to interests in death and sadomasochism, which appear to many as pathological. But it is precisely one of Foucault's aims "to disarm this reflexive response" to what is deemed unnatural and to have us rethink the limits of reason.[37]

Foucault's intellectual career includes fairly distinct stages characterized more by different emphases on topics of interest and diverse approaches to them than by the radical shifts that marked careers such as Wittgenstein's. Hinrich Fink-Eitel describes Foucault's career as divisible into four stages that correspond very roughly to the 1950s, 1960s, 1970s, and 1980s. In the first stage Foucault "was especially oriented to Heidegger's philosophy." In the second stage Foucault "became an archaeologist of knowledge and wrote a 'theoretical' philosophy of objective, autonomous . . . discourse and knowledge formation." In the third stage he "became an archaeologist for the genealogy of power." And in the fourth stage Foucault "became an ethical writer."[38] So long as we are careful not to take useful but rough distinctions too seriously, we can set aside the first stage, during which Foucault was still forging his philosophical identity, and work with the three remaining more-or-less standard divisions of Foucault's work. These may be called "domains of analysis," following Arnold Davidson.[39] The first domain of analysis is *archaeology*, which most characterizes Foucault's earlier books, published from 1961 to 1969. The second is *genealogy*, which most characterizes the books published from 1971 to 1976. The third domain of analysis is *ethics*, which most characterizes Foucault's last two books, both published in 1984, the year of his death. These domains should not be thought of as separate or as superseding one another, as Dreyfus and Rabinow correctly and emphatically insist: "*There is no pre- and post-archaeology or genealogy in Foucault.*"[40]

As indicated in Chapter 1, it is not my intention to try for comprehensiveness in this introduction to Foucault. Therefore, I do not consider the domain of ethics, except briefly in Chapter 8. What I can say here is that, for Foucault, ethics was self-directed rather than other-directed. Davidson describes Foucault's ethics as analysis "of the self's relationship to itself."[41] Foucault was closer to the Greeks and Romans he discusses in the second and third volumes of his history of sexuality (and from whom he also sought inspiration) in his approach to ethics, than he was to his recent predecessors and contemporaries. Nonetheless, his ethical investigations do bear a family resemblance to those of Paul Ricoeur, whose recent work has concentrated on determining the precise nature of the ethical subject.[42]

With respect to the domain of archaeology, my interest is limited to providing a backdrop for discussion of genealogy. I can situate genealogy relative to archaeology by citing Davidson's succinct descriptions of these two domains of analysis. Davidson describes archaeology as "analysis of systems of knowledge" and genealogy as analysis "of modalities of power."[43] Foucault himself offered something akin to Davidson's tripartite characterization with specific reference to the social sciences. He says that his work included investigation of the sorts of forms of inquiry "which try to give themselves the status of sciences," investigation of "the objectivizing of the subject," and investigation of "the way a human being turns him- or herself into a subject."[44] The shift from archaeological analysis, in which discourse is deemed to shape practice, to genealogical analysis, in which discourse and practice are deemed to shape one another, is the main reason to briefly consider archaeology.

Archaeology

We can characterize archaeology as a form of inquiry primarily focused on the human sciences as systems of knowledge. Archaeology is a critical investigation of disciplinary systems of knowledge with the goal of understanding the discursive practices that produced those systems of knowledge. The archaeologist's interest, therefore, is in disciplinary discourse, in expert pronouncements and idioms. But it must be kept in mind that, as noted earlier, for Foucault a "discipline" is both a field of study and a system of control. The concern with expert pronouncements and idioms, then, involves both understanding how they constitute a learned practice and how that practice shapes behavior. What needs to be stressed is that archaeological investigation proceeds without concern as to whether what its target systems "say is true, or even . . . make[s] sense." Archaeology "must remain neutral as to the truth and meaning of the discursive systems it studies." Archaeology is concerned with mapping "all disciplines with their accepted concepts, legitimized subjects, taken-for-granted objects, and preferred strategies, which yield justified truth claims."[45] The aim is not to assess the truth of knowledge-systems' claims, but to understand how those claims come to be claims, how they are deemed justified or otherwise within knowledge-systems, and how some of them come to constitute knowledge within those systems.

As to how archaeology actually proceeds, Foucault makes a crucial point when he says, "[a]rchaeological comparison does not have a unifying but a diversifying effect."[46] Though archaeology also unearths hidden similarities, it is of paramount importance—with respect to archaeology itself and perhaps more so with respect to genealogy—that it undermines accepted continuities even while establishing connections between practices previously thought disparate. Archaeology is always diversifying in the sense that even in establishing surprising similarities it disrupts conventional views. Archaeology is comparative, but in the sense that its focus is not accepted similarities but neglected or suppressed similarities and differences between an established system of knowledge and superseded or suppressed ones. Archaeology has a diversifying effect in that its objective is to fracture the smooth totality of a disciplinary tradition's picture of itself or of one of its constitutive elements. The objective is to unearth, to excavate factors and events, overlooked likenesses, discontinuities and disruptions, anomalies, and suppressed items. These yield a new picture of whatever has previously gone unquestioned and has been taken as definitive knowledge and truth with respect to a particular subject matter. Foucault is everywhere concerned with exhuming the hidden, the obscure, the marginal, the accidental, the forgotten, the overlooked, the covered-up, the displaced. His subjects for investigation are whatever is taken as most natural, obvious, evident, undeniable, manifest, prominent, and indisputable.

Shored up by meticulous empirical research, Foucault's basic strategy in both archaeology and genealogy is to retell the history of a discipline or institution or practice. He highlights and connects previously marginal and obscured elements and events, thereby presenting a very different picture of that discipline, institution, or practice. In archaeology, Foucault's targets are disciplines or sciences, but his method is not to engage in abstract debate about operant theories. Instead he probes the subject matters of disciplines or sciences as delineated and treated in institutional establishments. Cases in point are madness, the subject matter of psychiatry as dealt with in the asylum, and illness, the subject matter of medicine as dealt with in the clinic.

The diversifying effect of archaeological investigation is not limited to particular disciplinary practices. It is also operant on a grander scale in what Foucault calls "epistemes." These are essentially conceptual frameworks.[47] Epistemes are holistic frameworks that define problematics and their potential resolutions and constitute views of the world comprising the most fundamental of identificatory and explanatory notions, such as the nature of causality in a given range of phenomena. As much of Foucault's effort was directed at understanding shifts between these frameworks as to discern their patterns and limits.

An example of different epistemes, and of the shift from one to another, comes early in *The Order of Things*. It is Foucault's discussion of the difference between the "Renaissance" and "Classical" conceptions of language, specifically the difference between "trinary" and "binary" conceptions of the relation of signs to what they signify. In making out the nature of the shift at issue, Foucault provides a good instance of his ability to occasionally season his often prodigal prose with beautifully compact statements the length of which are inversely proportional to their importance. Speaking of the shift to the "Classical" or modern episteme and the reconception of language, Foucault remarks that "knowledge that divined, at random, signs that were absolute" came to be replaced by "a network of signs" that was developed "in accordance with a knowledge of what is probable." The superbly tight addendum is: "Hume has become possible."[48]

Foucault's point is that in the episteme in place prior to Descartes, the conception of the relation between signs and what they signify was trinary. The relation comprised the sign, the thing signified, and an essential resemblance between the two. This was a conception of language as naturally, as opposed to conventionally, connected to its referents. It also was a conception that distinguished among "that which was marked, that which did the marking, and that which made it possible to see in the first the mark of the second."[49] This last is what makes (Renaissance) language inherently *resemble* the world, as opposed to representing the world. Resemblance is a matter of signs being natural correlates of things rather than arbitrarily assigned labels. For Descartes, words and things "were separated from one another." Though discourse "was still to have the task of speaking that which is, [it] was no longer to be anything more than what it said."[50] For Descartes, the conception of signification became binary and comprised only the sign and the thing signified. When Descartes recast consciousness as awareness of internal ideas, he detached language from the world. In doing that, he did not only construe language more or less as Aristotle did in

Posterior Analytics—as so many signs the assignation of which is essentially arbitrary and is regulated by convention. Descartes made the assignation of signs contingent on an epistemologically problematic relation between ideas and their putative causes, thus enabling Humean skepticism.

The enabling of Humean skepticism, as well as the recasting of truth as something about the content of utterances rather than about utterings, are philosophical points that, even though illustrating radical conceptual changes, fall short of conveying the scope of a shift from one episteme to another. Foucault's notion of this epochal change is more evident in less philosophically significant passages, such as one where Foucault quotes Claude Duret. Writing in 1613, Duret describes how various people write from right to left (Hebrews and Arabs), from left to right (Europeans), from top to bottom (Chinese and Japanese), and from bottom to top or in "spiral lines" (Mexicans).[51] The right-to-left movement follows "the course . . . of the first heaven." The left-to-right movement follows "the course . . . of the second heaven, home of the seven planets." The top-to-bottom movement conforms to "the order of nature" evident in how people have "heads at the tops of their bodies." And the bottom-to-top or spiral movement conforms to the sun's "annual journey through the Zodiac." For Duret, these four diverse manners of writing reveal not only "the world's frame" but also "the form of the cross."[52] What is important here is not the particulars of the example, but how language was seen as related to the world. Language was not a mere convention-governed invention, but something integral to nature and use of which constituted a natural reflection of what there is and the structure of reality. We see how language had to intrinsically mirror reality only when conception of language as an integral part of a God-created world is appreciated. We understand the magnitude of the change to language, conceived as conventional, when the apparent absurdity of the example is dispelled by comprehension of language as *in* the world rather than as merely *about* the world.

Archaeology, then, is investigation of the discontinuities and newly established similarities that reveal abandonment of one conceptual framework and adoption of another. It is the unearthing of abandoned frameworks and the comparing of them with presently dominant ones; it is the meticulous mapping of established and excavated frameworks with a view to understanding the means of their production and their operation. Perhaps as illuminating as any positive characterization of archaeology is a negative one that says what happens when archaeology goes wrong. Archaeology goes wrong when it turns into a theory about how things are and pretends to transcend its historical situatedness and to discover hidden determinants underlying phenomena. These pretensions are just what Foucault rejects in structuralism and the vestiges of which he disavows in his own work. When archaeology takes a structuralist turn its focus is "deflected from an interest in the social practices that [form] both institutions and discourse to an almost exclusive emphasis on linguistic practices." One consequence is ill-conceived objectivization of discourse as a holistic determinator of cognitive and social practices. Another is "neglect of the way discursive practices are themselves affected by the social practices in which they and the investigator are embedded."[53]

When archaeology claims objectivity for itself, it wrongly casts itself as capable of discerning underlying objective realities. It also wrongly casts discursive practices as autonomous, as unilaterally determining the character and direction of social and institutional behavior while themselves remaining unaffected by that behavior. Archaeology then becomes a form of bad idealist metaphysics. Properly done, archaeology is "an inquiry whose aim is to rediscover on what basis knowledge and theory became possible."[54] The intent is to unearth the contexts in which truth and knowledge are produced, the activities and practices that manufacture and develop the methods we dub scientific and that fabricate the bodies of judgments and beliefs we dub sciences. Archaeology is the mapping of the enabling conditions for the production of truth and knowledge. It cannot be a method for discerning objective determinants, such as practice-determining discursive structures, lurking behind the appearances they supposedly produce. To do archaeology is precisely to understand how something like a discursive structure comes to be considered an underlying reality.

Nonetheless, for a time Foucault did seem to take archaeology as capable of discerning underlying appearance-determining realities. At least his interest was deflected onto discourse in a way that gave to discourse the status of an autonomous determinant of practices. Even more problematic than this misconceived focus on discourse was Foucault's erstwhile ambition to get beyond practices and construals to something primitive that underlies even discourse. In 1961 he wrote that we "must try to return to that zero point . . . at which madness is an undifferentiated experience" before it is shaped and categorized by discourse and practices.[55] Though made at the very start of his archaeological period, this sort of remark causes Rorty to think Foucault was mistakenly trying "to make archaeology the successor subject to epistemology."[56] But no trace of archaeology so conceived is found in *Discipline and Punish* and *The History of Sexuality*. Even as early as *The Archaeology of Knowledge* Foucault warned that archaeology does not attempt to return to some zero point, that it "does not imply the search for a beginning."[57] By 1977 Foucault is openly scornful of vestigial epistemological ambitions to "rediscover the things themselves in their primitive vivacity."[58]

To reiterate, archaeology is supposed to be detailed, descriptive, assessment-neutral investigation of disciplines, of expert idioms, of truth and knowledge-determining systems. It cannot claim to get behind appearances to ahistoric determinants. It aims to exhaustively track down and disinterestedly describe factors and events that enabled the emergence of the discipline or institution that is the subject of its inquiry. Archaeology begins by discounting received opinion, by rendering problematic what is least questioned, by reconstruing the apparently obvious and natural as suspect. It then searches out the discontinuities that mark shifts between conceptual frameworks. It searches out the disparate and accidental factors that result in the formation of such frameworks and the acceptance of something as knowledge.

The archaeologist, then, looks beyond the image of a discipline or a science or an institution projected by its practitioners and adherents into the component practices. The archaeologist recounts a restructured history of the targeted discipline, science, or institution by taking actions and events and interpreting them in light of data that "hardly anyone else . . . noticed."[59] The result is "a reordering of events . . . not perceived before."[60] The aim of the reordering is to lay bare "the empirical conditions under which [expert] statements come to be counted as . . . true." This is achieved by providing an alternative account in which the accepted truth of those expert statements is revealed as one possible set of construals rather than being unique and hard-won objective correctness.[61]

The heart of Foucault's archaeological and genealogical investigations is what Ian Hacking describes as an effort "to rethink the subject matter." In archaeological investigation this means beginning "from the ground up, at the level of tiny local events where battles are unwittingly enacted by players who do not know what they are doing."[62] What Hacking means about the players not knowing what they are doing is not that the particular things they do are done blindly or without thought, or that they are lacking intention. Foucault himself put the point quite effectively. He tells us: "People know what they do; they frequently know why they do what they do; but what they don't know is what what they do does."[63] In other words, they do not know the consequences of their actions. It is the actual consequences of action that are the building blocks of archaeology's epistemes and of genealogy's disciplinary techniques.

It may seem that archaeology would be the Foucauldian domain of analysis of most interest to epistemology-oriented analytic philosophers. Archaeology deals, if not quite with the justification of knowledge, then with the origins of what is deemed knowledge.[64] Given my intended audience, this introduction to Foucault might seem better focused on archaeology than on genealogy, regardless of how much these domains of analysis may overlap. However, as indicated, it is in Foucault's genealogical analytics that we find the most direct challenges to analytic philosophical assumptions and methodology. It is in the genealogical works that we find truth, knowledge, and rationality reconceived as products of power. It is also in those works that Foucault develops what he describes as his greatest debt to Nietzsche, namely, the question about the value of truth.[65] Genealogy, then, takes priority over archaeology. An additional reason to give precedence to genealogy is that genealogy's own importance is clearer than why Foucault himself found it important to shift his focus from archaeology to genealogy.[66]

Though not of immediate concern, one possible explanation for the shift of focus is that over time Foucault became more concerned about the problem regarding the status of archaeological claims. Some see the problem as fatal to Foucault's position. The problem is not, as some might expect, that all the talk about "unearthing" suggests an inconsistently implied existence of underlying realities. The problem instead has to do with the paradox of reflexivity. All possibility of methodological objectivity evaporates with the contention that everything theories postulate as external to themselves can be redescribed as internal by providing a suitable originative story. David Couzens Hoy notes that, on the one hand, Foucault's archaeology "makes truth relative to an episteme, that is, to what in Anglo-American philosophical vocabulary could be called a . . . paradigm or conceptual framework."[67] But on the other hand, it looks as if in spite of abandoning attempts to unearth realities, archaeology inescapably exempts its own pronouncements from the relativization of truth and knowledge. In tracing what generates a discipline, an expert perspective, or knowledge, the archaeologist offers an account of the conditions within which one set of judgments and statements is deemed true. It then looks as if archaeology must be done outside such conditions or be merely more of the same sort of knowledge produced within a different set of conditions. As we will see in the following chapters, this problem about the point from whence archaeology speaks plagues genealogy as well.

I turn now to genealogy, which Dreyfus and Rabinow define as Foucault's investigation of "that which conditions, limits, and institutionalizes discursive formations."[68]

Notes

1. Deleuze 1984:149.
2. Note that "analytic" is not used here in the pejorative sense currently favored by critics to describe all philosophizing that is not postmodern.
3. Matson 1987:403.
4. Krausz 1989.
5. Rorty 1991b:94n.
6. This current use of "historicism" is quite different from Karl Popper's sense of a belief in large-scale laws of historical development. It is basically the earlier (late nineteenth century) sense that "maintained that each age should be interpreted in

terms of its own ideas and principles." Bullock and Stallybrass 1983:285–86. *The Cambridge Dictionary of Philosophy* says of this sense that it refers to "the doctrine that knowledge of human affairs has an irreducibly historical character and that there can be no ahistorical perspective." Audi 1996:331.

7. This point is the focus of Chapter 7.

8. Foucault 1988b:35.

9. Rorty 1982:xlii.

10. Foucault 1988b:27.

11. Foucault 1988b:27.

12. Rée 1992:61.

13. Lawson 1985.

14. Rorty 1979b:85.

15. Kuhn 1970; Feyerabend 1978.

16. Foucault 1980b:51.

17. Foucault 1988b:29.

18. Rorty 1989:55.

19. Arac 1991:vii.

20. It is important to note, though, that Marxism inevitably colored phenomenological, hermeneutic, and structuralist positions.

21. Dreyfus and Rabinow 1983:xii; also xi–xxvii; but see Gutting 1994a:3–5.

22. Miller 1993:123–64, esp. 147–51.

23. Hoy 1986:4.

24. Foucault 1973:xiv.

25. Foucault 1973:xx–xxii.

26. Miller 1993:148.

27. Hoy 1986; Dreyfus and Rabinow 1983.

28. Dreyfus and Rabinow 1983:104.

29. Dreyfus and Rabinow 1983:104.

30. Foucault 1980b:105.

31. Hoy 1986:4.

32. As noted, in North America Foucault usually is thought of as a Derridean postmodern deconstructionist.

33. Foucault 1988b:32; Allen 1991.

34. *Madness and Civilization* was Foucault's doctoral dissertation.

35. Miller 1993:103, 113; note that Miller erroneously gives Tuke's name as "William."

36. Miller 1993:109.

37. Miller 1993:112.

38. Fink-Eitel 1992:72.

39. Miller 1993:37–65; Davidson, A. 1986:221.

40. Dreyfus and Rabinow 1983:104.

41. Davidson, A. 1986:221.

42. Ricoeur 1992.

43. Davidson, A. 1986:221.

44. Foucault 1983a:208–9.

45. Dreyfus and Rabinow 1983:xxiv.

46. Foucault 1972:159–60.

47. Readers with an analytic background will immediately think of Donald Davidson's rejection of "the very idea" of conceptual schemes as incoherent. Davidson, D. 1973/1974. Whether Foucault conceived of epistemes as incommensurable in a way making them vulnerable to Davidson's arguments is an interesting question, but not one I can pursue here.

48. Foucault 1973:60.

49. Foucault 1973:64.

50. Foucault 1973:43.

51. All I can suggest, regarding Duret's choice of Mexicans for his fourth example, is that the Aztec calendar is a spiral and can be imagined as spiraling upward.

52. Foucault 1973:37.

53. Dreyfus and Rabinow 1983:xii.

54. Foucault 1973:xxi–xxii.

55. Foucault 1965:ix.

56. Hoy 1986:3.

57. Foucault 1972:131.

58. Foucault 1988b:119.

59. Hacking 1981:28.

60. Hacking 1981:29.

61. Hoy 1986:3.

62. Hacking 1981:29.

63. Dreyfus and Rabinow 1983:187.

64. Machado 1992.

65. Foucault 1988b:32; but see Mahon 1992.

66. It must be kept in mind that we here are dealing with matters of emphasis rather than wholly disparate methods.

67. Hoy 1986:5.

68. Dreyfus and Rabinow 1983:104.

Chapter Three

Genealogical Analytics

Nietzsche's inversion of the particular over the universal was a philosophical revolution as momentous as Kant's "Copernican" inversion of the subjective over the objective. Foucault emulates Nietzsche with three inversions of his own. He inverts interpretive significance of the marginal over the ostensibly central; he inverts the constructed over the supposedly natural; and he inverts the originative importance of the accidental over the allegedly inevitable. At a very abstract level, these inversions constitute the core of what is novel in Foucault's thought. In contrast, the social and conceptual mechanisms he painstakingly describes, most notably the workings of power, are the details of how these inversions function.

Foucault acknowledges his intellectual debt to Nietzsche in his exposition of Nietzschean genealogy in "Nietzsche, Genealogy, History." The article is exegetical, but Foucault effectively articulates the basic conception of his own genealogy in expounding Nietzsche's. This is why commentators like Donald Bouchard think "Nietzsche, Genealogy, History" is so important.[1] The article serves as a prolegomena to Foucault's implementation of genealogy in *Discipline and Punish* and *The History of Sexuality*.

Foucault develops Nietzsche's idea that history is misconceived as "an attempt to capture the exact essence of things." He argues that history is inherently flawed if conducted as a search for "origins" in the sense of essential beginnings.[2] Genealogy is the alternative to history so conceived and "opposes itself to the search for origins."[3] The heart of the concept is that there are no essences to be discerned behind historical developments, that there are no essences that explain why things developed as they did. A paradigm of what genealogy opposes is the Augustinian view of history as recording a divinely scripted linear and teleological sequence of events. For Augustine, history is an unfolding story with a beginning (the Creation), a middle (the Incarnation), and an eventual end (the Last Judgment).[4] In this conception the historian's task is to integrate what are apparently unconnected events by discerning the hand of God behind those events. Geneal-

ogy repudiates this idea that there is behind events a guiding hand or set of
regulating principles that determines how things progress and explains why
the present is as it is. Genealogy "does not pretend to go back in time to re-
store an unbroken continuity." It does not try to make out a harmony in
past events that reveals hidden forces that "animate the present, having imposed a predetermined form [on] all its vicissitudes."[5]

Foucault insists with Nietzsche that "if the genealogist refuses to [do]
metaphysics" what he or she finds underlying historical events is "not a
timeless and essential secret, but . . . that they [events] have no essence or
that their essence was fabricated."[6] Elsewhere Foucault speaks of "evental-
ization" in describing a "breach of self-evidence." What he means is that
there is a need to focus on particulars and not to gloss over them, to make
"visible a singularity . . . where there is a temptation to invoke . . . an obvi-
ousness that imposes itself uniformly."[7] Genealogy does not operate on a
murky field of elusive but objective events, trying to sift out the continuities
that reveal the causes of a sequence of pasts and of the present. Genealogy
does not claim to mine a continuous vein in which determinants of later
events can be found if research is good enough. Instead genealogy "operates
on a field of entangled and confused parchments, on documents that have
been scratched over and recopied many times."[8] What genealogy unearths is
the antithesis of essences. What it finds are happy and unhappy accidents
and coincidences that are united only by essentialist interpretation. As Rorty
might put it, what genealogy does is map the "reinterpretation[s] of our predecessors' reinterpretation[s] of their predecessors' reinterpretations.[9]

The core of the genealogical inversion of the accidental over the allegedly
inevitable is that rather than providing discernment of unity, history only
tracks complexity and disparity. Rather than history being a searching
through the past's myriad details for future-determining continuities, it is
only a tireless sifting out of disparate components that our interests and
priorities turn into episodes in an imposed progression. But the contrast
here is not simply one between striving to find universal, teleological determinants, on the one hand, and attending to micro-particulars on the other.
Universalist accounts may require attention to particulars and some anti-
universalist accounts may not. The contrast is between conceiving of micro-
particulars as components of some broader process, and seeing those particulars as exhaustive of history's subject matter.

It is worth stressing the broader implications of Foucault's endorsement
of Nietzsche's rejection of the quest for origins before we look more closely
at "Nietzsche, Genealogy, History." It is not just history that is considered.
Reason or what might be better described as the nature and development of
reasoned inquiry is also at issue. Foucault contends that an examination of
reason's own history reveals that it "was born . . . from chance." He denies
that reasoned inquiry developed progressively through the honing of in-

creasingly successful investigative principles. Foucault's claim is that it was the haphazard compilation of complex practices and maneuvers that "slowly forged the weapons of reason."[10] The discussion, then, is not just about history as a discipline; it is about history as a paradigm of reasoned inquiry.

Foucault begins "Nietzsche, Genealogy, History" by considering Nietzsche's use of a number of terms denoting origin, emergence, beginning, and descent-from. These are *Ursprung*, or origin; *Herkunft*, or descent, origin; *Entstehung*, or emergence; *Abkunft*, or descent; and *Geburt*, or birth. His point is to show how Nietzsche introduced a contrast between a search for origins, in the humdrum sense of causes and sources, and a quest for Capital-O Origins as "an attempt to capture the exact essence of things."[11] But the contrast is reductive; it is not merely one between a pair of aims and methods. Nietzsche and Foucault want to show that the quest for essences is wholly misconceived. They seek to show that rather than determinative origins, what "is found at the historical beginning of things . . . is disparity." Foucault describes historical beginnings as "lowly: not in the sense of modest . . . but derisive and ironic, capable of undoing every infatuation." He adds that it is a "cruelty of history that compels . . . abandonment of 'adolescent' quests: behind the always recent . . . truth, it posits the ancient proliferation of errors."[12] To illustrate his point Foucault quotes a biting remark from Nietzsche that captures the irony of the quest for essences: "We wished to awaken the feeling of man's sovereignty by showing his divine birth: this path is now forbidden, since a monkey stands at the entrance."[13]

In clarifying the distinction between the search for origins and genealogy, Foucault considers Nietzsche's attempt to make the notion of descent (*Herkunft*) capture not only likenesses, such as familial traits, but differences within general likeness. Descent normally is used to speak of extraction or lineage. Foucault notes that "analysis of descent permits . . . dissociation" and that by unearthing lost details it enables "recognition and displacement [of] empty synthesis."[14] Genealogy attempts to "identify the accidents, the minute deviations . . . the reversals . . . the errors, the false appraisals, and the faulty calculations that gave birth to those things that . . . have value for us."[15] It is through dissociative analysis of descent that genealogy reveals the miscellaneous and discontinuous nature of beginnings. The thrust of genealogical strategy is that the more discontinuous and disassociated details are excavated, the harder it is to impose some grand synthesis or design on past events. The point is also to bring out how the designation of something as a significant event requires imposition of a holistic interpretation.

In discussing descent Foucault makes a point important to understanding both the role of and the emphasis on the body in *Discipline and Punish* and

The History of Sexuality. He asserts that analysis of descent applies also to the body, that the body "and everything that touches it . . . is the domain of *Herkunft*." This is because the body "is the inscribed surface of events (traced by language)." It is the body that bears and manifests the effects of regulating discourses in its habits and gestures, in its postures, in its speech. A major task of genealogy is "to expose a body totally imprinted by history."[16] It is also genealogy's task to show how the body is "the locus of a dissociated self (adopting the illusion of a substantial unity)."[17] The body supports a self, a subject, which does not recognize itself as emergent but takes itself as prior to the effects of discourse. Genealogy, as the analysis of descent, carefully exposes the tiny influences on bodies that, over time, produce subjects defined by what they take to be knowledge about themselves and their world. As important, genealogy exposes how those subjects come under the illusion that they are individually substantial, autonomous unities.

Here we have another passage in which Foucault compactly articulates a fundamental philosophical point. The body is the "inscribed surface of events (traced by language)" and supports an emergent self that believes itself to be a "substantial unity." In doing so he encapsulates much of what is central to *Discipline and Punish* and *The History of Sexuality*. The parenthetical amplification "traced by language" alludes to what was mentioned in connection with archaeology and is evident in *Discipline and Punish* and *The History of Sexuality*. This is the point that it is expert discourse, disciplinary discourse, that shapes subjectivity and establishes regimes of truth. Foucault is not concerned with ordinary talk; he is concerned with expert or learned talk, with the idioms of science, of the academy, of authority. Foucault gives full weight to practice's reciprocal enabling and shaping of discourse in his genealogical analyses, in contrast to his earlier inclination to construe discourse as a unidirectional determinant of practice.

However, in tracing descent it is not enough to mark likenesses and differences within likeness. The analysis of descent is incomplete without the complementary analysis of emergence (*Entstehung*) in the complex sense of both initial appearance and achieved dominance. In the analysis of descent the aim is to understand the miscellany of beginnings; in the analysis of emergence the aim is to understand catalytic coming to be. Analytic complementarity is achieved with understanding of originative diversity or miscellany and of how the items discerned come together to produce a particular result. As in the analysis of descent, the point of analysis of emergence is to produce accounts that show the variety of generative factors and thus belie the idea that history traces underlying determinative continuities. Analysis of emergence produces accounts of whatever comes to be as not "the final term of a historical development."[18] The analysis denies historical progressive evolution by showing that what comes to be "is always produced through a particular stage of forces" and not a result of teleological processes. What emerges or comes to be does so because of a compilation of disparate factors. What emerges is not the culmination of anything but is a consequence of an accumulation of factors with no inherent interrelatedness. It is only the retrospective imposition of some historical interpretation that makes those factors appear to be more than coincidentally related.

The message here is that we misconceive history if we think of it as discerning objective continuities. We also misconceive history if we think of it as discerning goal-directed processes. The analysis of emergence traces the unknowingly combative campaigns that accidentally constituted forces "wage against each other." It shows how something comes to be as a result of blind conflict instead of as a product of an "obscure purpose that seeks its realization at the moment it arises."[19]

At this point we approach the notion of Foucauldian power. In describing the interplay of forces that result in emergence, Foucault speaks of it as "the endlessly repeated play of dominations."[20] This is not to say that power is domination. The instances of domination that are endlessly played out are the constitutive elements of power. As I explain in the next chapter, Foucauldian power is not domination. It is the complex network of acts of domination, submission, and resistance. Power constrains *actions*, not individuals. Power is a totality made up of individuals being dominated, coerced, or intimidated; of individuals submitting to domination, coercion, or intimidation; and of individuals resisting domination, coercion, or intimidation. Power is all about people acting in ways that blindly and impersonally condition the options and actions of others.

At this point we also see the divergence between the Nietzschean and Foucauldian views. Alluding again to Nietzsche, Foucault offers as examples of the play of dominations the mastery or influencing of some individuals by others. This control "generates the idea of liberty."[21] His point is that objectification and awareness of control prompts the thought that one might live *un*controlled, free. For Nietzsche freedom is real enough, though difficult to attain. Unlike Nietzsche, Foucault does not think of domination only in terms of control exercised by one individual or class over another, and which might be escaped. There is nothing that we can escape to be free because, as we will see in Chapter 4, power relations are all-pervasive and define the contexts in which human agents act.

Emergence is appearance or advent enabled by collisions of forces, some of which enhance, nullify, or redirect others, and some of which combine with others to form new forces. The list of what emerges is diverse. It includes value-sets, institutions such as representative government, disciplinary constructs like "human sexuality," and concepts such as that of inalienable rights and of historical inevitability. What emerges and gains dominance is everything that orders our lives and which appears natural to us in those lives. What emerges and gains dominance then looks to be pre-

determined and is legitimized by its apparent inevitability. The first task of
adherents of what emerges, whether it is an idea, a value, a discipline, or
an institution, is to establish it as natural, as inevitable, as truth that has
been discerned. It is the task of genealogy to counter the view of the emergent as inevitable by recording its lowly beginnings. Genealogy proceeds
by tracing "the history of morals, ideals, and metaphysical concepts, the
history of the concept of liberty or of the ascetic life."[22] Genealogy ana-
lyzes the descent and emergence of morals, ideals, metaphysical concepts
and all manner of institutions to show them to be the products of happen-
chance meetings of blind forces and not discovered truths or preordained
developments.

Foucault describes genealogical tracing of the descent and emergence of
concepts, ideas, and institutions as "gray, meticulous, and patiently documentary."[23] But genealogy's claimed meticulously documentary nature
poses a problem that we encountered earlier. Foucault's critics pose the
question: How can genealogy be documentary in nature without violating
its historicist conception? The problem is the same as that noted in connection with archaeology. Foucault can be read as implicitly but inconsistently
contending—or as committed to contending—that genealogy can get things
right. It then looks as if genealogy must be exempted from its own contentions about happenstance and lowly beginnings. (It will emerge in Chapters 6 and 7 that Foucault's complex conception of truth in fact limits his
skepticism about objective knowledge.) It is difficult to see how genealogical analyses themselves remain historicist in nature while exposing the constructed nature of all other disciplinary truths. It does look as if the way genealogy exposes alleged event-determining essences as constructed is by
tracing objective sequences of events that have been distorted by ideological
or other factors. The claim that those sequences have been misinterpreted,
in being made to look integrated and teleological, seems to entail that the
genealogical account of those events is the correct one. The alternative, as
we saw with archaeology, is to accept that genealogical accounts are just so
many more stories on an equal footing with the stories genealogy opposes.

At this juncture one feels the threat of the Nietzschean nihilism that
haunts Foucault's work. The threat is that intellectual inquiry is hopeless
because it is incapable of yielding anything but preconceptions and favored
illusions. The fear is that intellectual inquiry cannot provide a ground for
progressive change in any area of human activity because it is always ratio-
nalizational rather than rational. This is the bleakness Rorty sees in Foucault's work and what is so regularly softened or denied in North American
interpretations of that work. Rorty maintains that it is the French Foucault
that "is the fully Nietzschean one," whereas the threatening nihilistic ten-
dencies are "drained away" in the Americanized Foucault.[24] But there is a
reason for this transatlantic interpretive softening beyond intellectual

squeamishness. When North Americans turn to European thinkers, they often do so looking for productive ideas to revitalize their own philosophical projects. They then are unprepared to accept some aspects of what they find. North American philosophers who take an interest in Foucault's work tend to assume that his eminence is due to success in proffering positive theories. They are reluctant to accept Foucault's essentially negative historicization of philosophical methods and assumptions. North American philosophers try to see the Nietzschean element in Foucault as only provocative, as challenging hyperbole. This is to distort Foucault in order to avoid the nihilism. Foucault did not seek absolutes of any sort in his most critical phase. He was not trying to overcome what Richard Bernstein calls "Cartesian anxiety" by seeking certainty in power relations when he could not find it in epistemological arguments.[25] Many, including Rorty, think that, at some level, Foucault intended genealogical analytics to be a successor to epistemology. This is not the case, and the nihilism, or at least the threat of nihilism, is real.

Questions about the historicist nature of genealogy (and archaeology) suggest that genealogical accounts of how power produces truth, knowledge, and criterial concepts like rationality, are themselves only more products of power. It seems that genealogy can be fully historicist only if its supposedly documentary accounts are acknowledged to be only so many more productions of power. Foucault's genealogical accounts, then, seem to be only interest-determined interpretations that we have no definitive way of judging better or worse than their competitors. If we prefer them to others, it likely is only because of how power relations have shaped our interpretive inclinations. Doubts can be raised about any given account just to the extent that an alternative attracts us. If we apply this nihilistic view beyond the strictly theoretical sphere to the political arena, it seems that struggle against domination is pointless since it can result only in establishing different forms of domination. No political analysis can yield discernment of objective conditions, so no activism can establish objectively better conditions. Foucault's own political activism was often challenged on this basis, because it seemed he could not endorse any political alternative as inherently better than any other.

Rorty uses what he calls "irony" to deal with the threat of nihilism. This is ironic acceptance of the incongruity that we feel a need to ground our highest values in something other than ourselves. He advocates admitting that we have "radical and continuing doubts" about our vocabularies—our established discourses—because we often are "impressed by other vocabularies."[26] Rorty advocates the additional but harder admission "that argument phrased in [our] present vocabulary can neither underwrite nor dissolve those doubts."[27] Rortyan ironists claim to understand that "there is nothing beyond vocabularies which serves as a criterion of choice between them."[28] This solution will not satisfy many and is not Foucault's solution. He puts his faith not in irony but in novelty of thought, as we will see later. Fortunately, an introduction to Foucault's genealogy is not the place to attempt to deal with the huge question of nihilism.

Once he has characterized genealogy, Foucault addresses the question of how to best understand the relation between genealogy and traditional history. The denial of origins, of course, is not a rejection of history as such. Genealogy is opposed to history only as a quest for originative determinants. Genealogy itself requires history in the mundane sense of annals of the past. The genealogist "needs history to dispel the chimeras of the origin."[29] We need to think of history neutrally as just so many extant chronicles and records of past times. We then can appreciate that history so conceived is the only raw material available to both genealogists and origin-seeking historians. Genealogy, if anything, is more deeply concerned with historical data than is the quest for origins. The latter, history as traditionally conceived, may take a broad view of historical data in trying to discern large-scale patterns supposedly revelatory of great forces at work. In contrast, genealogy can only focus on minutia; it "depends on a vast accumulation of source material" and "demands relentless erudition."[30] The genealogist needs archives, chronicles, diaries, journals, logbooks, letters, memoirs, official records, and registries more than any traditional historian does. Unearthing lowly and accidental beginnings requires sifting through details.

Genealogy even needs the historians' grand narratives because without them it would lack a counterpoint. Genealogy's unearthing of marginal and neglected items is done to offer alternative accounts to epics that claim to depict underlying continuities. It is this contrast with traditional grand-narrative history, then, that needs to be fleshed out. In order to do so Foucault continues his consideration of Nietzschean genealogy by contrasting Nietzsche's notion of *wirkliche Historie* ("effective history") with history that claims "a suprahistorical perspective" and takes its task to be reshaping the "diversity of time into a totality."[31]

Totalizing history can only be done on the basis of belief in ahistorical absolutes, like Capital-R Rationality and cross-cultural and trans-epochal values and ideas. Nietzsche saw that historians seeking Capital-O Origins assume such things as that "words kept their meaning, that desires still pointed in a single direction, and that ideas retained their logic."[32] Totalizing history requires something that is able to unify disparate historical events, to mold those events into coherent progressions and to do so from outside those progressions. Against this, Nietzsche's effective history eschews such absolutes. Instead of attempting to unify, effective history "distinguishes, separates, and disperses" and focuses on "divergence and marginal elements."[33] Effective history "differs from traditional history in being without constants." It discards traditional concepts and methods designed to achieve comprehensiveness and the attempt to retrace "the past as a patient and continuous development."[34]

The contrast between effective and totalizing history turns on totalizing history's need to assimilate or "dissolv[e] . . . singular events into an ideal continuity." Effective history "deals with events in terms of their most unique characteristics."[35] For the genealogist, the events that make up history are not so many determinate assassinations, battles, coronations, decisions, elections, revolutions, and treaties, as they are for the traditional historian. Instead the events that make up history for the genealogist are changes in force relationships. They are such things as "the reversal of a relationship of forces, the usurpation of power, the appropriation of a vocabulary turned against those who had once used it."[36] These events are not so much delineated occurrences as they are relational changes. Their particularity is crucial, for each relational change must be understood in terms of specific, detailed accounts of as many as possible of the factors that contribute to its coming about. Effective history "shortens its vision to those things nearest to it"; effective history reverses historians' "pretension to examine things furthest from themselves."[37]

Foucault turns to consideration of perspectivism in ending his discussion of how effective history relates to traditional history. The "final trait of effective history is its affirmation of knowledge as perspective."[38] In contrast to traditional history's conception of its inquiries as aiming at objective knowledge, effective history is avowedly perspectival. Effective history never forgets or obscures its own temporal and cultural situatedness. It rejects as absurd the idea that history can be done objectively, that it can be conducted from no particular point of view. Effective history goes further than rejection. It casts traditional history's invocation of "objectivity, of the accuracy of facts and of the permanence of the past" as a mask for vested interests operant in the production of holistic narratives.[39]

Foucault pursues the contrast between effective and traditional history, near the end of "Nietzsche, Genealogy, History." He discusses how history must be mastered "so as to turn it to genealogical uses, that is, strictly anti-Platonic purposes."[40] Foucault offers a three-way characterization of uses of history that correspond to but oppose Platonic "modalities." These are the parodic, dissociative, and sacrificial uses. The first use of history is parodic in being "directed against reality, and [opposed to] the theme of history as reminiscence or recognition." The second use is dissociative in being "directed against identity, and [opposed to] history given as continuity or representative of a tradition." The third use is sacrificial in being "directed against truth, and [opposed to] history as knowledge."[41]

The parodic use of history opposes the traditional historian's imposition of singular, integrated identities by offering "alternative identities" to defeat essentialist notions. The targets are ideas such as that of human beings as embodying ahistoric rationality or as the products of divine creation. The point of the parodic use is to impugn preferred images by providing alternatives that serve their purpose all the better if tinged with absurdity. The passage cited earlier, in which Foucault quotes Nietzsche, provides a pithy example of the parodic use. Our self-description as the children of God is challenged by evolutionary theory's replacement of Adam as a God-created communal father with "a monkey."[42]

The dissociative use of history differs from the parodic. Instead of only furnishing challenging possible alternatives to imposed identities, it systematically impugns imposed identities from within those identities. The dissociative use proceeds by discovering and highlighting discontinuities and inconsistencies. The dissociative use, like the parodic, is directed against traditional history's imposition of images such as human beings as the children of God. The point of the dissociative use is to demonstrate that history does not "discover a forgotten identity" but instead unearths "a complex system of distinct and multiple elements" that defies synthesis.[43] Rather than history discerning a solid basis for thinking ourselves the children of God, it roots out a disparate collection of happenstance factors that combined to produce that idea.

The sacrificial use of history counters traditional history's pretensions to neutrality and objectivity by showing the interest-dependent nature of invented subjects of alleged knowledge.[44] This use exposes as false traditional history's claimed discernment of delineable subjects such as archetypes or eras. For Foucault these supposedly discerned subjects are only the manufactured products of "the will to knowledge" or the quest for essential natures and absolute truth. Additionally, the sacrificial use reveals how the quest for objective knowledge strips away every aspect of a subject's temporal, historical, and cultural situatedness as only incidental to its imagined essence. This is why Nietzsche "reproached critical history for . . . sacrificing the very movement of life to the exclusive concern for truth."[45]

The parodic, dissociative, and sacrificial uses of history are designed to prevent Platonistic reification, or what Foucault speaks of as consecration of the past. The uses in question foil claimed discernment of teleological development. That is, they thwart "Whiggish" interpretation that reads prior events as incrementally progressive and as culminating in the present state of affairs. History is not allowed to pretend that it is an exercise in recollection, that it goes back in time to recover something determinate and objective. In this way genealogy achieves nothing less than "a transformation of history into a totally different form of time."[46] In other words, the past ceases to be a sort of frozen sequence of integrated, determinate events. Our historical narratives cease to be reports on such events made possible by the communal memory of written and oral records. Instead history becomes a present-tense exercise: Doing genealogy "means that I begin my analysis from a question posed in the present."[47]

It is important to understand that the foregoing has as much to do with conception of intellectual inquiry as with conception of history. Genealogy reconceives intellectual inquiry as a series of diverse practices governed by thoroughly historical standards. The corollary to this view is that the actual workings of these practices are masked from those who participate in them. Participants see their activities as regulated not by historical standards but by ahistorical principles. They see the fruits of their activities as ongoing discernment of truth and therefore as the acquisition of objective knowledge. Nor is that acquisition of knowledge deemed mere fact gathering. It is taken to be gradual augmentation of a growing and increasingly integrated accumulation of related discoveries. These discoveries are then seen as falling into various categories that correspond to and delineate proper subjects of inquiry. These subjects in turn demand and support certain disciplinary methods and procedural standards. The result is a steadily increasing number of expert disciplines devoted to an equally increasing number of "natural" topics. Genealogists try to show that these disciplines discern nothing, discover nothing. Rather than discerning truths and subjects of possible knowledge, they manufacture their own content. The genealogist's main claim is that these disciplines never get beyond their own idioms and self-generated topics. Genealogists try to show that rather than being ways of limning reality, these disciplines are interwoven collections of individual maneuvers that had their beginnings in varying responses to diverse situations. What weaves these maneuvers into established practices is expert discourse. Expert discourse provides the medium in which these maneuvers congeal into learned fields and their respective procedures. Expert discourse also enables expansion of the ranges of those fields and of the jurisdictions of their procedures.

The picture that emerges from "Nietzsche, Genealogy, History" is one where truth is not how things are. Instead, truth is the highest-order value in a given practice or set of practices. And knowledge is not the learning of how things are. Instead, knowledge is the highest-order category in a practice or set of practices. In like manner, rationality is not an ahistorical absolute that governs the discernment of truth and acquisition of knowledge. It is not a set of objective standards that determine coherence and cogency. Much less is it an absolute nature we instantiate. Instead, rationality is a notion that functions as a touchstone for a set of practices. The generative sources of truth, knowledge, and rationality are lowly, as in the case of all other historical beginnings.[48] Most important is that according to genealogy truth, knowledge, and rationality *have* generative sources. They are not timeless; they are historical in having their beginnings in things we have said and done.

A New Analytic or an Old Relativism?

The focus in Chapters 4 and 5 in effect is the second and third of the inversions mentioned earlier, namely, of the constructed over the supposedly natural and of the accidental over the allegedly inevitable. The latter is evident in description of how disciplinary techniques actually develop and work; the former is evident in description of the "deployment" of a theoretical sexuality. Both inversions presuppose Foucault's historicist vision of truth, knowledge, and rationality as the contingent results of unrelated practical events. This means that consideration of *Discipline and Punish* and *The History of Sexuality* requires special care. The need is to counter hasty dismissal of what those books contain on the basis of an initial impression that historicizing truth, knowledge, and rationality is academic madness. Taking care begins with making a methodological point that is illustrated in "Nietzsche, Genealogy, History." Contrary to expectations, Foucault does not support what he says in the article with arguments. He presents a picture that he expects to be compelling. Foucault does not argue against traditional history's claims. His is a holistic impeachment of traditional history's attempts to assimilate individual events into progressions and to count as significant only those events that can be so assimilated. The indictment of traditional, synthesizing history is achieved by providing an alternative to it. In this way "Nietzsche, Genealogy, History" typifies Foucault's general strategy. His strategy of providing alternatives is also illustrated in "Two Lectures," a piece he seems to have intended as a brief introduction to his work.[49] There he focuses on the unearthing of "popular knowledges" that traditional history has "disqualified" and placed "beneath the required level of cognition or scientificity."[50] Disqualified or suppressed knowledges constitute alternatives to what is accepted as "properly" intellectual and "truly" scientific. These knowledges or lores constitute alternatives and challenge dominant theories simply by being presented and noted. In calling attention to suppressed knowledges Foucault also demonstrates that synthesizing history continually obscures lores and practices to maintain and enhance the continuity it imposes on past events.

Posing a philosophical challenge by providing an alternative construal of something is what Rorty calls redescription in a new vocabulary. Rorty contrasts redescriptions with the provision of new theories that compete on issues of truth with theories they are intended to supplant. The point of the contrast is that offering a competing theoretical account forces one to share the language of the theory one is trying to supplant. Redescriptions are not counter-arguments in a common language. Redescriptions highlight difficulties in what they challenge and invite uptake as more productive construals. Foucault's account of genealogy is redescription of traditional history and renders it problematic by highlighting discontinuities that traditional history glosses over.[51] There are two aspects to Foucault's redescription of history. One is the offering of genealogy or "effective history" as an alternative construal of doing history. The other is offering detailed alternatives to particular historical accounts. Cases in point are the new construal of madness as invented, the new construal of the penal system's evolvement as the growth of disciplinary control, and the new construal of human sexuality. Traditional history claims *correctness*. That means that the very existence of an alternative either to its self-conception or its accounts of the past poses a challenge. The catch is that a Foucauldian alternative, or a Rortyan redescription, has to be *plausible*. It has to look like what it is claimed to be, namely, a more productive construal of whatever is at issue.

The plausibility requirement is hard for Foucault to meet in some quarters. Whatever the merits of his particular redescriptions of madness, penality, and sexuality, analytic philosophers dismiss Foucault's redescription as *at best* implausible. This is because his redescriptions presuppose Foucault's historicist conception of truth, knowledge, and rationality themselves. (It is an important question whether Foucault's redescriptions of penality and sexuality *entail* historicism. A good deal of what he says in *Discipline and Punish* and *The History of Sexuality* seems compatible with ahistoric rationality, though not with essentialist history. However, subtracting historicism would diminish the *philosophical* content of those works.) This conception is perceived as an attempt to historicize reason itself and so as irrational. Therefore, as suggested above, the particular redescriptions Foucault offers are ignored because they are taken as based on unacceptable premises. Speaking as a *de facto* spokesperson for analytic philosophers and others, Hilary Putnam argues that historical standards "cannot define what reason is." His contention is that historical standards "presuppose reason . . . for their interpretation."[52] Rationality is considered to be "a regulative idea" that governs all inquiry and enables us "to criticize the conduct of all activities and institutions."[53] In short, truth, knowledge, and rationality are taken as prior to and necessary for inquiry, assessment, and debate. Foucault is well aware of this view of his thought and work and charges those who take Putnam's side with "blackmail." He claims they react to "every critique of reason or every critical inquiry into the history of rationality" with imposition of a falsely exclusive dichotomy. Foucault claims they do so by arguing that "either you accept rationality or you fall prey to the irrational."[54] Unfortunately, this response does nothing to resolve the issue. Instead it contributes to making it an impasse.

Rorty sees the impasse as a matter of language or vocabularies. In connection with his own critical work, he notes that holistic critics of traditional philosophy face a difficult task. They "face a dilemma: if their language is too unphilosophical, too 'literary,' they will be accused of changing the subject." But if their language "is too philosophical it will embody Platonic assumptions." The result is that they must try "to find ways of making antiphilosophical points in nonphilosophical language."[55] However, Rorty's response itself presupposes historicism. That is, since he is not willing to allow that truth, knowledge, and rationality are ahistorical, Rorty sees only a clash of idioms where Putnam and the like-minded see irrationality—or possibly disingenuousness. But surely Putnam must be right that we cannot make truth, knowledge, and rationality historical. (This is not the place to pursue the point, but we could reject the strong claim that there are no ahistorical standards and be agnostic about them, maintaining that conventional standards suffice. The bulk of learned debate is conducted without reference to the ultimate ground of governing standards.) What does Foucault see that makes him think he can offer historicist but cogent critiques of truth, knowledge, and rationality? How can his inescapably reflexive analysis of reasoning itself lead to the conclusion that reasoning's regulative principles are historical products, and still present that conclusion as intellectually compelling?

Rorty, like Habermas and Hoy, doubts that Foucault manages to keep his analytics wholly historicist. We saw that Rorty regards Foucault's archaeology, conceived of as an essence-unearthing activity, as a proffered replacement for epistemology. Rorty sees genealogy, along with all postmodernist critiques, as vitiated by an inability to expose false appearances while disavowing commitment to hidden realities.[56] Unlike Putnam and others, Rorty does not think Foucault goes far enough and sees him as likely preserving a little of the ahistoricism Foucault claims to reject. It does seem impossible to conform to the historicist conception of genealogy without demoting its analyses to just so many more historically contingent accounts on a par with those they oppose. If so, then Foucault's historicist redescriptions of truth, knowledge, and rationality, and his accounts of penality and sexuality, are just so many more proposed construals. We might put the point this way: If Foucault is right about the historical nature of truth, knowledge, rationality, and various disciplines, then his redescriptions are so many interpretive recommendations. That means that if he is right, what he offers is on a par with what he rejects. (Notice the force of Putnam's point. It is unclear in what sense Foucault would be *right* on his own premises.) It therefore is possible to say to Foucault: Yes, you may be right in some ultimate sense, but we are better off—or simply prefer—keeping our standards and construals in preference to yours. (Ironically, this would be a Rortyan ironist response to both Foucault *and* Rorty.)

It may be that the foregoing is too adversarial a way of putting things. Rorty, for one, does not argue that his redescriptions are necessarily preferable to traditional construals of standards or disciplines. Rorty's main aim is to defeat conception of traditional construals as inevitable and preclusive of alternatives. Rorty's primary goal is to gain acceptance of alternative contingent accounts as the norm. The main task, therefore, is to impugn the possibility of ahistoric theories rather than to press acceptance of particular historicist ones.[57] The case of Foucault is less clear. As we have seen, Foucault contends that all intellectual inquiry can do is to trace the descent and emergence of both what we theorize about and what we use to theorize. His alternative accounts do function to undermine the exclusivity of traditional essentialist ones. However, *Discipline and Punish* and *The History of Sexuality* certainly seem to be offered as getting things right. No amount of discussion will settle the point. In later chapters I offer quotes from Foucault in which he claims to be right about his views, as opposed to offering his accounts as productive alternatives. What we can say to make some progress is that Foucault cannot offer his genealogical analyses or redescriptions as competitive *theories*. To do so would be to illegitimately exempt himself from historicity in a way that needs to be made clear.

Rorty maintains that pragmatists do not offer a competing "'relativistic' or 'subjectivist' theory of Truth." According to him what pragmatists do is try "to change the subject."[58] Foucault's genealogical analyses minimally are changes of subjects from theoretical proposals about allegedly underlying continuities to descriptions of putatively exhaustive surface discontinuities. His redescriptions are—again minimally—intended to reveal the pointlessness of ahistoric theorizing. Foucault cannot offer competing theories. The new perspective he offers claims to show that theories cannot achieve the objectivity that is their main reason for being because theories are historical products. If we take holistic critics like Foucault as offering competing theories about truth, knowledge, rationality, and disciplinary structure, "we shall get them wrong." This is because doing so will "ignore their criticisms of the assumption that there ought to be theories about such matters."[59]

We now can say something about how Foucault thinks himself able to historicize truth, knowledge, and rationality and still offer cogent redescriptions. Once we recognize that Foucault does not offer competing theories, we can understand how he thinks "a rational critique of rationality" and a "contingent history of reason" are possible.[60] What enables Foucault to historicize what is most basic to intellectual inquiry is his appreciation of something that was "glimpsed at the end of the eighteenth century." That was the realization "that anything could be made to look good or bad, important or unimportant, useful or useless, by being redescribed."[61] The point here is that we learned how to change and manipulate the lan-

guage we use to articulate even the most fundamental ideas. By adopting
new idioms, coining more inclusive/exclusive neologisms, shifting emphases, and altering nuances, we can enhance or impugn ideas without raising issues of truth. In other words, the glimpsed potency of redescription
developed until it "became possible, toward the end of the nineteenth century, to . . . juggle several descriptions . . . without asking which one was
right." It became possible "to see redescription as a tool rather than a claim
to have discovered essence."[62]

Rorty thinks redescriptions ceased to be mutually exclusive competing
accounts and came to be mutually inclusive alternative ones. Redescriptions began to be assessed relative to particular purposes instead of as either correct or incorrect. In this way redescription of everything from individual disciplines to the fundamental principles of reasoned inquiry escaped
the boundaries set by the bivalent logic that governs traditionally conceived
inquiry. Encountering alternative redescriptions stopped being a matter of
having to choose between established descriptions and challenging redescriptions. However, none of this happened without reason (*pace* Foucault). Kant's abandonment of a fundamental Platonic idea enabled redescriptions to cease being mutually exclusive competitors. The idea Kant
abandoned was that expert or disciplinary description is always of something autonomous that remains unaffected by how it is described. Rorty
contends that "nothing is left save utility" once we relinquish realist conception of description as accurate representation of objective things and
events.[63]

What is crucial is that once we switched our philosophical loyalties from
Plato to Kant, once objective representation became problematic, two
things occurred. First, we began to emphasize purposes and usefulness in
assessing descriptions, and to de-emphasize strict representative accuracy.
Second, doubts inevitably arose about the objectivity of reason and rationality. It then became possible to speculate about how reason and rationality might be described differently, perhaps more usefully, with respect to
different interests and purposes. It was these changes that made Foucault's
historicist vision possible. However, while the changes may explain the basis of Foucault's historicist views of truth, knowledge, and rationality, reference to them does not make those views any more plausible to philosophers
who agree with Putnam. On the contrary, those philosophers see the
changes as mistakes. They consider attempts to historicize reason as irrational and the juggling of redescriptions as a relativism entailing irrealist[64]
denial of an objective world.[65]

Even if redescription clarifies how Foucault thinks it possible to historicize reason, Putnam's point is persuasive. The pressing question is what
Foucault can hope to achieve in writing *Discipline and Punish*, *The History
of Sexuality*, and other works. It seems that if he historicizes reason he can

only expect acceptance or dismissal that is every bit as historical as he claims are the established accounts of the development of penality and of the nature of human sexuality. This is to say that it is open to us, as readers of Foucault's works, to say: These are our standards, our values, our history; we prefer them to yours. But *Discipline and Punish*, *The History of Sexuality*, and Foucault's other books do not seem to be offered as only construals we might adopt. It remains unclear how Foucault can intend his genealogical analyses to be compelling and how we are to assess them if they impugn our assessment-standards. These questions are not easily answered. However, we can make some progress by considering what Foucault is up to in broader terms.

Foucault aspires to be what Harold Bloom calls a "strong poet." That is, he wants to be a thinker who reinvents himself or herself, who invents new metaphors, and who thereby provides new vocabularies for the rest of us. This is his Heideggerian ambition to think the "unthought," mentioned in Chapter 1. Strong poets are the creators of new logical spaces wherein fresh thoughts can be thought and familiar things redescribed.[66] They are innovators who enable us to accomplish things we could not imagine in our old vocabularies.[67] In science strong poets produce what Kuhn calls new paradigms. Isaac Newton, Albert Einstein, and Sigmund Freud were strong poets. Each provided the ideas and idioms that enabled whole new fields of study. Karl Marx was also a strong poet, though his new vocabulary proved surprisingly short-lived. Ironically, Plato and Descartes, philosophers whose visions Foucault opposes, were themselves strong poets. Both of them invented the vocabularies that made possible traditional metaphysics and epistemology.

Philosophical argumentation can proceed according to normal standards and practices within an established vocabulary or paradigm. When philosophizing is a matter of offering a new vision, normal standards and practices must be circumvented or even flouted. Wilfrid Sellars characterizes philosophizing as saying, in the most general way, how things hang together, in the most general way. Trying to say how things hang together in a *new* way not only requires different methods, it requires disruption of the familiar. What is crucially important is that a novel vocabulary, or a new scientific paradigm, is not assessable by the standards of the vocabulary or paradigm it replaces. Overcoming resistance to a novel proposal cannot be a matter of marshaling arguments that meet established standards. Instead, "rebutting objections to one's redescriptions . . . will be largely a matter of redescribing other things." The strategy must be "to try to make the vocabulary in which these objections are phrased look bad . . . rather than granting the objector his choice of weapons and terrain by meeting his criticisms head on."[68] The basic idea is that if we accept "that there is no standpoint outside [a] particular historically conditioned and temporary vocabulary . . . from which to judge this vocabulary," we have to give up "the idea that intellectual . . . progress is rational, in any sense of 'rational' which is neutral between vocabularies."[69]

All of this will look hopelessly untenable to my intended audience and others. It will look like reduction of intellectual disputation to no more than a swapping of impressionistic constructions or what John Caputo disdainfully calls "just talk."[70] However, disdain and dismissal are inappropriate responses to a challenging idea. Many serious philosophers think that Kant failed to reestablish apodictic certainty in philosophy after critiquing "the realist conception of objects waiting around to be accurately represented."[71] For them, philosophy lacks independent correctness-criteria to justify its own standards in response to redescriptions of itself. This is why Foucault claims that there is now "something ludicrous" about philosophy trying "to dictate to others, to tell them where their truth is and how to find it."[72] Rorty agrees, saying "philosophy makes itself ridiculous" when fundamental interpretive issues arise and "it steps forward . . . to adjudicate."[73]

There has been no "demise of modernity," even assuming there is a holistic way of thinking describable as "modern."[74] Those who portray "postmodernism" as a radically new way of thinking are victims of a baseless intellectual exuberance. Nonetheless, we can no longer do philosophy on the assumption that its standards are ahistorical and untouched by social and political influences, academic fashion, and vested interests. Foucault saw this decades ago, and he saw his only viable option to be genealogical analysis and redescription of disciplines, institutions, methodologies, and even reasoned inquiry's most sacrosanct principles. "Nietzsche, Genealogy, History" poses a challenge. Taking up that challenge requires that we turn now to *Discipline and Punish* and *The History of Sexuality* in the right frame of mind. They have to be considered as radical works. As for how we are to assess them, we must follow Sellars and see if they "hang together" as accounts of their topics.

Notes

1. Bouchard 1977:139n.
2. Foucault 1971:78.
3. Foucault 1971:77.
4. Matson 1987:200.
5. Foucault 1971:81.
6. Foucault 1971:78; allusion is to Nietzsche's *Dawn*, #123.
7. Baynes, Bohman, and McCarthy 1987:104.
8. Foucault 1971:76.
9. Rorty 1982:xlii.
10. Foucault 1971:78; allusions are to *Dawn*, #123, and *Human, All Too Human*, #34.

11. Foucault 1971:78.

12. Foucault 1971:79.

13. Foucault 1971:79, quoting *Dawn*, #49.

14. Foucault 1971:81.

15. Foucault 1971:81.

16. Foucault 1971:82; allusion is to *Gay Science*, #348–49.

17. Foucault 1971:83.

18. Foucault 1971:83.

19. Foucault 1971:83.

20. Foucault 1971:83.

21. Foucault 1971:85; allusions are to *Beyond Good and Evil*, #260, and *Wanderer*, #9.

22. Foucault 1971:86.

23. Foucault 1977:76.

24. Rorty 1991b:193.

25. Bernstein 1983.

26. Rorty 1989:73.

27. Rorty 1989:73.

28. Rorty 1989:80.

29. Foucault 1971:77, 80.

30. Foucault 1971:76–77.

31. Foucault 1971:86; allusions are to *Genealogy*, preface, sec. 7, and chap. 1, sec. 2, and *Beyond Good and Evil*, #224.

32. Foucault 1971:76.

33. Foucault 1971:87.

34. Foucault 1971:87–88.

35. Foucault 1971:88.

36. Foucault 1971:88.

37. Foucault 1971:89.

38. Foucault 1971:90.

39. Foucault 1971:91.

40. Foucault 1977:93.

41. Foucault 1971:93; allusion is to *Beyond Good and Evil*, #223.

42. Foucault 1971:79.

43. Foucault 1971:94; allusion is to *Human, All Too Human*, #274.

44. Foucault 1977:95–96.

45. Foucault 1971:96–97.

46. Foucault 1971:93.

47. Foucault 1988b:262.

48. Foucault 1971:79.

49. Foucault 1976. Ironically, and perhaps typically, "Two Lectures" is of little help to anyone not already familiar with Foucault's work.

50. Foucault 1980b:82.

51. There are some who argue that history has become widely genealogical in practice, if not in name. See Szeman 1993.

52. Putnam 1987:227.

53. Putnam 1987:228.

54. Foucault 1988b:27.

55. Rorty 1982:xiv.

56. Rorty 1986; 1991c.

57. It is Foucault's pressing of his construals of history, madness, penality, sexuality, and so on that makes Rorty suspect Foucault's historicism.

58. Rorty 1982:xliii.

59. Rorty 1982:161.

60. See Foucault 1988b:27.

61. Rorty 1989:7.

62. Rorty 1989:39. Perhaps the clearest examples of the potency of redescription are found in courtrooms. Prosecutors and defense attorneys vie with one another to describe an act to the jury in ways that will best serve their respective aims, even when there is agreement on what actually took place.

63. Rorty 1984.

64. I use "irrealist" and "irrealism" in preference to the more familiar "idealist" and "idealism" because the latter entail positive metaphysical claims.

65. I pursue this issue in Chapter 7.

66. Rorty 1991c.

67. Bloom 1973:80.

68. Rorty 1989:44.

69. Rorty 1989:48.

70. Caputo 1983. Caputo was referring to Rorty's characterization of philosophy as an ongoing conversation. I realize that I could be making things worse by using Rorty to clarify Foucault's ideas. Some of my readers likely are more negatively disposed to Rorty's well-known views than to Foucault's less familiar ones. However, my concern is not to win advocates for Foucault; it is to present his views as clearly as possible.

71. Rorty 1984.

72. Foucault 1986:8–9.

73. Rorty 1989:51.

74. Latour 1993.

Chapter Four

Making Subjects

Discipline and Punish basically is about how people who were subjects of a sovereign became subjects of a new kind. The book is about how people originally controlled by overt monarchical authority came to be controlled by being changed as persons. The focus in *Discipline and Punish* is on law-breakers, malefactors, and criminals—people apprehended and punished for contravening a sovereign's or society's laws. Later, in *The History of Sexuality*, Foucault generalizes his claims to cover everyone. But as suggested earlier, in *Discipline and Punish* application of genealogical analysis and the concept of power is to individuals whose actions are controlled in initially obvious ways. The subjects in question, then, are persons under the control of lawful authority, whether that authority is a monarch's sheriff or a contemporary penal system.

Discipline and Punish is ostensibly about how the treatment of lawbreak-ers changed from apprehension and punishment being the brutal exacting of monarchical vengeance, to being carceral isolation enabling the protection of society, deterrence, and rehabilitation. What the book is really about is the production of compliant subjects through the imposition of disciplines. It is about how constant observation, assessment, and regimentation manu-facture new subjects. It is about how persons are reshaped and reoriented with management techniques that intrude into and govern every aspect of their lives. *Discipline and Punish*, however, is not just a study of penality. Its portrayal of the techniques of control employed in carceral institutions is of-fered as a case study, a micro-cosmos illustrating the production of contem-porary norm-governed social individuals. In this way, *Discipline and Punish* grounds and presages *The History of Sexuality*. In the latter, the arena for subject-determining control is not the prison but the whole of society, and what is imposed is not an institutional regimen but a sexual nature.

As stressed earlier, Foucault's point of departure in rethinking a subject matter is to impugn the commonplace, to query accepted knowledge. Fou-cault addresses penality by questioning the commonplace view that the present penitentiary-centered penal system is the result of progressive humanization of earlier ruthless methods of retributive punishment. He challenges the accepted view that changes effected in the treatment of criminals were due to an increasingly humane attitude toward them. Foucault offers an alternative account of how and why treatment of criminals ceased to be public and brutal. He also offers an alternative account of how and why the penitentiary emerged as the favored institutional device for dealing with lawbreakers.

At the heart of Foucault's alternative accounts is characterization of what he calls "disciplines" or what can be glossed as techniques for managing people. His point is that disciplinary or managerial techniques were initiated and developed into a technology for the control of individuals. The new techniques continued to operate on the body. But unlike monarchical torture, the new techniques did not inflict pain on the body or maim it. Instead they managed the body by imposing on it schedules, restrictions, obligatory comportment, and constant diagnostic and evaluatory examinations. In contrast to their brutal predecessors, the new techniques did not do violence to the body. What they did was instill controlling habits and value-sustaining self-images. This is a central notion in *Discipline and Punish*. The idea is not new; it has been around at least since Aristotle and may be found articulated both in highly abstract psychological and educational theories and popular clichés. Basically the idea is that imposition of behavioral habits on an individual shapes that individual's perspectives, attitudes, values, desires, and all other affective or broadly "emotional" aspects. Foucault takes this further in a way I consider below, but in essence the idea is that modification of physical behavior modifies every aspect of personality.

The new management techniques developed in the penitentiary. However, it is one of Foucault's main contentions that the intent behind their development and application was less redressing wrongs and rehabilitating wrongdoers than increasing efficient subjugation and control. This is why the disciplinary techniques proliferated in all institutions involving the management of large numbers of people: the convent, the school, the barracks, the hospital, and the factory.[1] The techniques proved far too useful to remain unique to the penal system. However, even more important than their usefulness is that the techniques marked a sea change in conception both of how people might be dealt with and so of people themselves. The heart of the new conception was that individuals are not only susceptible to being physically constrained but are *internally malleable*. Foucault sees the penitentiary as a crucible in which a new vision of human beings was forged.

The Development of Political Technology

In *Madness and Civilization* Foucault considers the exclusionary institutional treatment of the newly defined insane. In *The Birth of the Clinic* he considers the exclusionary institutional treatment of those with various afflictions.[2] In *Discipline and Punish* his real focus in considering exclusionary institutionalization of people emerges most clearly. That focus is putative knowledge of the body not limited to "the science of its functioning." The knowledge in question goes beyond investigation and control of an organism to "what might be called the political technology of the body."[3] In Foucault's view, the aim of this technology is not mere control, which is achievable through imposition of restrictions and prohibitions, but pervasive management. What is new in Foucault's consideration of pervasive management is description of how it is achieved not just through restrictions, but through enabling conceptions, definitions, and descriptions that generate and support behavior-governing norms. What is also new, and intellectually jarring, is description of this degree of management as requiring the complicity of those managed. Complicity is required because what need to be achieved are not only obedience to law, but also what is more clearly thematized in *The History of Sexuality*. That is the deep internalization of a carefully orchestrated value-laden understanding of the self.

Discipline and Punish begins with a horrendous account of the drawing-and-quartering of a regicide. It is an account made even more ghastly by the fact that the victim was fully conscious and had to have sinews and tendons partially severed before the horses could tear his body apart. Foucault spares no detail; he recounts the execution in a detached academic manner that makes the description all the more gruesome. The point of the account is to highlight how at the time individuals were juridical subjects on whom monarchical power could be exercised in hideous but legal rituals of restitution and reestablishment of authority.

Public punishment consisting of torture and maiming (mutilation, branding) and public execution (hanging, drawing-and-quartering) were routine and integral to the exercise of monarchical power. They served both to punish those who broke the sovereign's laws and to "reconstitute" the defied sovereign's power. Public retributive punishment of transgressors was reassertion of total domination. Transgressors were literally broken (and often killed) as property of the sovereign. The display served both to punish the guilty and to warn others that they were vulnerable to the same retributive treatment because they too were subjects. But what Foucault is after is a bit subtler. Monarchical subjects were susceptible to sanctioned violence; their bodies were the targets of possible torture and execution. What was still to come was susceptibility to sanctioned and expert violence to subjects' very selves as persons.

Sometime during the mid-to-late seventeenth century the practice of public torture and execution began to decline. The common view is that the change was due to increasingly enlightened and humane attitudes toward lawbreakers. Foucault claims that the change had nothing to do with enlightenment or humanization, but rather with a new perception of lawbreakers. This perception was a readily visible aspect of a new management-oriented conception of human beings. This was a reconception that enabled control of people through reconfiguration of them as subjects. Rather than continuing to use violence and the threat of violence to force conformity, a way was seen to make individuals *want* to conform, even *need* to conform.

The new conception of the subject has two separate aspects. The first is that an individual is a subject in the sense of *being subject to* regulation by other individuals, institutions, and the state.[4] The second aspect is that an individual is a subject in the sense of *experiencing subjectivity*, of being aware. But being a subject in this second sense is not merely being aware or conscious. It includes having aims, desires, and—most important in the present context—a self-image or sense of who and what one is.[5] Throughout Foucault's discussions of subjects and subjectivity, particularly in his genealogical works, the notion of "the subject" includes both of these aspects. "Subject" and "subjectivity" are used in ways that are deliberately ambiguous between the subject as a member of a governed society and as a self-aware identity.

Foucault provides a welter of factual material in tracing the change from harshly retributive to subject-defining punishment. This material is the substance of the genealogical account of the development of the prison and the reconception of its inmates. Unfortunately, the material tends to limit productive interpretation of *Discipline and Punish*. The reason is that its detailed nature makes the book appear to be only a kind of contrary sociohistorical account of the development of the contemporary penal system. Foucault can be plausibly read as offering no more than an account that challenges the established one. He can be read as simply denying that the development of the penitentiary-based penal system was due to reform arising from a change in perception of criminals as individuals owed a measure of humane consideration rather than as the disposable property of the sovereign. If read in this way, Foucault is taken as arguing that penality changed not because of a genuine humane regard for the criminals it processes, but because of vested interests operating covertly behind a mask of humaneness. This possible but limited interpretation distorts Foucault's notion of power by attributing the changes in penality to concealed or conspiratorial agency. This distortion is the beginning of the common but erroneous view that Foucauldian power is covert domination. This easy but mistaken understanding of power is attractive because it forestalls the need to master Foucault's difficult conception of power as impersonal. The misreading of *Discipline and Punish*, then, precludes successful understanding of *The History of Sexuality* as well as degrades the genealogical analysis of the growth of the prison.

The mass of material presented in *Discipline and Punish* supports Foucault's contention that the idea of a "soul" was introduced into legal and penal thinking and practices as an integral part of the reconception of sub-jectivity.[6] What he means is that a whole new dimension of personhood was invented that made possible kinds of control not previously envisaged. The invented soul is not a basic humanity newly recognized in criminals. Nor is it new ontological notion or revitalized religious one. It is something "born . . . out of methods of punishment, supervision and constraint."[7] The production of the soul in the context of the development of penality is nothing less than a shift from a premodern to a modern conception of the self.

The manufacture of the soul constitutes a conceptual shift from a self de-fined by familial, social, and political roles and having the identity-deter-mining immortal soul of religion, to a self defined by Cartesian autonomy and inwardness. The latter is a self that is wholly self-determining. The modern self is one that has the capacity for intentional consciousness as an inherent property. It is a self that is "selfconstituting" in being itself "the source or agent of all meaning."[8] The modern self is an irreducible node to which beliefs and affective states are ascribed, so it may hold different be-liefs and have different affective states. The modern self is the ultimate source of action, so is capable of different kinds of behavior. Nothing is set or predetermined by nature or context. Given this conception, it is possible and necessary to shape the self through discipline so that it will act cor-rectly. The best way to achieve this end is to imbue the self with the right sorts of beliefs and affective states. *Discipline and Punish* is all about how disciplines developed to imbue selves with the right beliefs and affective states.

Foucault focuses on the introduction of the soul to show that the self is not a singularity, a self-sufficient Cartesian ego overlaid with beliefs and in-tentions and the sole source of deliberate action. Foucault wants to show that the self is a construct. He wants to show that the self is *produced* by precisely those techniques that supposedly only shape it. In *The Archaeol-ogy of Knowledge* Foucault speaks of wanting to "cleanse" history of "transcendental narcissism."[9] In *Power/Knowledge*, he maintains that "the individual is not a pre-given entity" and that "we must rid ourselves of the constituting subject, rid ourselves of the subject itself." He contends that we must produce "an analysis which can account for the subject itself within an historical account."[10] For Foucault, the subject is something to be understood as an historical product, as emergent. Therefore, there could not be discernment or acknowledgment of the soul in the process of hu-manizing penality. Instead, the process of changing penality contributed to the manufacture of the modern self.

Foucault's point is that "the subject" is a product of discourse rather than being prior to discourse. Discourse generates the subject rather than being "the majestically unfolding manifestation of a thinking, knowing, speaking subject." Once this is understood, discourse is seen as "a totality, in which the dispersion of the subject and his discontinuity from himself may be determined."[11] When we attend to the discontinuities genealogy uncovers we come to understand what it is we actually do in speaking about people. Then we appreciate that "the subject" is what we say it is. This is clearly a philosophical view of the self; it is not a socio-historical account of how basic humanity came to be recognized in criminals. The bulk of detail in *Discipline and Punish* lays out how prisoners came to be talked about and treated, and in doing so it lays out how a subject was manufactured.

It is crucial for readers with an analytic background, and hence certain philosophical expectations, to appreciate that Foucault is not doing metaphysics or philosophy of mind in saying discourse generates the subject. He precisely wants to block ontological theorizing and deal with questions about the self in genealogical terms. His interest in the historicity of the subject is not an interest in ontological issues about the self or self-identity. The decentralizing of the subject and dissipation of its apparent unity and totality has to do with the locus of power. It has to do with denying traditional philosophy's monolithic subject as the bearer of cognitive and affective attributes and as the initiator of action. For Foucault, subjectivity is not a "given" as it is for Descartes and Kant. It is not the condition of everything cognitive, affective, and behavioral. That is why Foucault insists that it is the body that bears subjectivity. It is the body that is the "locus of a dissociated self," a self has "the illusion of [being] a substantial unity."[12] The body bears the emergent subjectivity that is the multifaceted effect of regulating discourse. It bears that subjectivity in its habits and gestures, in its postures, in its speech, in how it is dealt with. The disciplined body is logically prior to subjectivity. Foucault's task is not to establish the nature of the self and to articulate that nature in a philosophical theory. His task is "to expose a body totally imprinted by history."[13]

Foucault's admittedly revisionary retrospectives of his own work are articulated largely in explanatory asides and self-commentary in interviews. In many of these he claims that his goal over two decades was not to "analyze the phenomena of power," but rather to "create a history of the different modes by which, in our culture, human beings are made subjects."[14] Foucault strongly tended to present his work as more homogeneous, coherent, and focused than it was. However, the subject or subjectivity is unquestionably the focal point of the main genealogical texts. But it must be kept in mind as we proceed that "the subject" here is not the entity figuring in debates in the philosophy of mind or ontology. It is something that is at once produced in and borne by a disciplined body. And it is the focus of institutionalized authority. We now need to look more closely at *Discipline and Punish*.

The Book

Unlike "Nietzsche, Genealogy, History" and *The History of Sexuality*, *Discipline and Punish* does not lend itself to systematic exposition because of the amount of detail it contains. Such exposition would be only repetition of parts of the material presented. Miller says of *Madness and Civilization* that "the author's own convictions are insinuated more than argued . . . leaving an impression that outweighs page after page of detailed, often intricate historical documentation."[15] This is even more true of *Discipline and Punish*. In both books Foucault's philosophical points are embedded in often tedious historical commentary. *Discipline and Punish* is full of wearisome discussion of legal procedures, the efforts of particular penal reformers, the French, English, and American penal systems, and even of architectural plans for the construction of schools, prisons, and other institutions. Foucault even provides illustrations of discipline-enhancing features of schools and prisons and of disciplinary devices such as spanking machines.[16] My strategy here will be to discuss the text in general terms, stressing what is of greatest relevance to understanding Foucault's project. I shall then devote a full section to consideration of what permeates *Discipline and Punish*: Foucauldian power.

Discipline and Punish is in three parts. The first two discuss torture and punishment. The third part discusses discipline. As noted, a wealth of detail is provided. An example of how philosophical points are buried in the detail is a passage that looks like a prelude to a socio-historical treatise. In it Foucault claims that "a general process has led judges to judge something other than crimes" while the penal system established "by the great codes of the eighteenth and nineteenth centuries" has been in operation.[17] At first glance this passage looks like an observation that judges have increasingly considered social factors in their rulings. But the point being made is considerably more important than that and is central to everything that follows. What is referred to is one of the changes in penality that led to "a whole new system of truth." It has little to do with greater social awareness on the part of judges and all to do with the construction of the subjects that judges convicted.

In describing the development of a new system of truth, *Discipline and Punish* is a "history of the modern soul and of a new power to judge."[18] The claim about the changed nature of judgment is that the focus of judgments came to be souls rather than acts. Foucault describes his notion of a soul as "the correlative of a technique of power."[19] The soul is a manipulable representation that facilitates control that surpasses physical domination. The soul is the mind reconceived "as a surface of inscription for power." The notion of the soul facilitates "the submission of bodies through the control of ideas."[20] Judges came to assess not particular crimes but the perpetrators of those crimes. This meant that souls were judged not just by the severity of their crimes, but with a view to how they were to be managed, manipulated, and controlled. The aim is to contain and eradicate desires and unacceptable behavior. And the supremely important correlative of this perception of the transgressor is tacit recognition of the "normal" person. The normal individual is a sort of substantive shadow of the lawbreaker. The discourse that established and refined "the criminal" correlatively established and refined the criminal's counterpart.[21]

The changes in penality basically recast the lawbreaker as someone who defies the authority of society rather than the authority of a sovereign. Punishment accordingly underwent reconception from "the vengeance of the sovereign" to "the defence of society."[22] Therefore punishment came to be less a retributive practice than "a procedure for requalifying individuals as subjects." Disciplinary punishment is "essentially *corrective*."[23] Modern punishment "*normalizes*."[24] If the lawbreaker is perceived as threatening society, rather than defying a sovereign, correction and deterrence are seen as rehabilitating the lawbreaker and thereby better serving society. It is no longer a matter of inflicting compensatory and authority-reconstituting suffering. One result is that normalizing judgment is not limited to court-presiding judicial agents of society. The "judges of normality are present everywhere." Our society includes "the teacher-judge, the doctor-judge, the educator-judge, the 'social worker'-judge." The "universal reign of the normative" is based on all of these agents of society.[25]

Implicit in talk of normalization is the privileged paradigm of the normal person. Foucault stresses the contrast of criminal and normal individuals to illustrate the role of exclusionary "binary division" in the changes that concern him. He contends that "all the authorities exercising individual control function according to . . . binary division and branding."[26] This contention is characteristic of Foucault's analyses. In *Madness and Civilization* he considers the exclusionary division and consequent labeling or "branding" of the sane and insane; of the healthy and unhealthy in *The Birth of the Clinic*; of offenders and conformers in *Discipline and Punish*; of the deviant and the normal in *The History of Sexuality*. Once the division and branding are initiated, the "universal reign of the normative" is implemented in diverse ways. The implementation discussed in *Discipline and Punish* is constant surveillance. It is here that Foucault makes brilliant new use of the familiar. He uses the penal system's widespread reliance on Jeremy Bentham's architectural plan for the ideal prison to articulate the conceptual model of constant surveillance.

The idea embodied in Bentham's "Panopticon" is that "the fact of being constantly seen, of being able always to be seen . . . maintains the disciplined individual in his subjugation."[27] In Bentham's ideal prison, cells are arranged around a central observation tower. Inmates are always observable to watchers in the tower, but the watchers are not visible to the inmates. Because inmates do not know when they are in fact being observed, they must behave as if constantly observed. Even though inmates know that they cannot be individually constantly watched, they know they may be being watched at any given time. The practical effect is the same as constant surveillance.

Foucault takes Bentham's idea further, suggesting that surveillance can turn submission to directives into conformity with norms. This idea is not only central to *Discipline and Punish* but to *The History of Sexuality*. The thought has two parts. The first is that panopticism can convert deliberate obedience of regulations into habitual compliance with norms. The second part was suggested above, namely, that habitual compliance itself converts to adoption or "internalization" of those norms. Foucault's enhancement of the panopticon concept is basic to his efforts "to discover and describe the confinements that imprison human life and thought."[28] This is the attempt to show how physical, regulatory, and judicial control of the body becomes control of "the soul" through the imposition of values, beliefs, and self-identity.

The larger point about enforced compliance morphing into adoption of norms is that the disciplinary techniques described in *Discipline and Punish* are now applied well beyond penitentiary walls. But widespread use of these techniques is not merely an expansion of their use. It is not just that procedures found to work well in the penitentiary were applied in other contexts. Use of the techniques is of a piece with invention of the modern soul. It is reconception of the subject that makes the disciplinary techniques Foucault describes work in the school, the hospital, the factory, and society at large. To understand this, one must see that the disciplined penitentiary inmate is not only made and kept obedient. The overseen inmate is made into a specific sort of person through imposition of habits that define a new subjectivity. Penal confinement and regulation would be inefficient and short-term if they only exacted obedience. Invention of the soul gave confinement and regulation of the body the capacity to change people by remanufacturing their identities. That is the whole point, and it is why the disciplinary techniques work outside the prison. If individuals are made to believe that they are malleable souls, the constraint and regulation of their bodies can have lasting effects.

Recall the dual-aspect nature and deliberate ambiguity of Foucault's notion of the subject. To be a subject is to be subjugated. It is to be "subject to someone else by control and dependence." To be a subject is also to have one's identity defined "by a conscience or self-knowledge."[29] The subject, in being subjugated, is made to adopt a certain construal or understanding of his or her own thoughts and actions and so of his or her very self. The subject's "conscience or self-knowledge" is an imposed one, but the individual experiences it as what he or she is. Adoption of the imposed construal is redefinition of one's subjectivity. In the case of penality, inmates who have been judged, sentenced, and incarcerated are made to believe themselves the objects of legitimate categorization, study, and assessment. The inmates then become persons on who there are dossiers and about whom experts know more than they do about themselves. They become persons who are classified as particular sorts of felons for particular sorts of reasons. They become persons who are abnormal and who require retributive and rehabilatory treatment. And if the disciplinary techniques work as they should, the inmates conspire in their own redefinition by adopting their classification and wanting to be made "normal." This is how the judged and disciplined soul is something new and "unlike the soul represented by Christian theology." The modern soul is "not born in sin and subject to punishment, but is born rather out of methods of punishment, supervision and constraint."[30] Disciplinary techniques create a soul that can then be managed beyond the mere imposition of physical constraints on the body. In managing souls "discipline produces subjected and practiced bodies, 'docile' bodies."[31]

Foucault describes significant developments in the managing of souls that occurred during the early evolution of the modern penitentiary-centered penal system. He begins by discussing how spectacular public punishment and executions constituted the standard way of dealing with lawbreakers to roughly the mid-eighteenth century in Europe's monarchical order. Foucault then focuses on how public torture and execution began to decline. He considers two notable changes that took place. The first was that punishment and execution came to be conducted within official enclosures. Public punishment could be a risky occasion. Spectacles like the one detailed in the opening to *Discipline and Punish* could precipitate a conflict of wills between the sovereign and the people. The person being punished might be popular or represent what was perceived as merited opposition to the sovereign.[32] The use of official enclosures proved safer, and it had an unanticipated but largely productive result. Concealing punitive measures behind the walls of official buildings made those buildings into foreboding symbols of what they sheltered and so gave them deterrence value. The second change was that incarceration in penitentiaries, a practice without strong precedents at the time, emerged as the chief means of punishment and deterrence. Both changes involved genuine efforts made by humanitarian reformers. It is not Foucault's intent to deny that these occurred. His concern is to show what these efforts actually achieved, regardless of the intentions that drove them. There were also economic reasons for the development of the penitentiary, such as the increasing reliance on prisons for cheap labor. And there were changes of administrative and procedural sorts. Most notable were changes in the nature and importance of evidence, the manner of eliciting and treating confessions, and creation of the police as a force separate from the sovereign's armed retinue. According to Foucault, the latter change marked a critical shift of focus from enforcement of laws to surveillance.

Foucault offers a list of five devices that were used during the development of the prison and other institutions that dealt with sizable populations. These are (1) hierarchical observation, (2) normalizing judgment, (3) the examination, (4) panopticism, and (5) surveillance. These devices can only function in an institutional context such as a school, an industrial plant, a prison, or an asylum. To be effective, discipline "requires *enclosure*." Disciplinary techniques require "a place . . . closed in upon itself."[33] Observation and disciplining of large groups require that they be gathered in given places for significant periods of time. Group members must also be constantly aware of a localized seat of authority—the warden's office, the administration wing, and the executive suite.

(1) Hierarchical observation involves physically structuring institutions to maximize visual and/or auditory access by those with greater authority and responsibility over those with less authority. An example is a tiered work-area, where increased height affords oversight from a given level over echelons below.[34] (2) Normalizing judgment is negative assessment of individuals or groups. What makes it unique is that it is not outright criticism or condemnation. It is invidious comparison with a favored paradigm, whether real or imagined. An example is the glorification of a team or other cohort as a model of high productivity. (3) The examination is the requirement and application of all manner of tests. These are presented as ways of enabling those tested to achieve their full potential and of enabling the managing authorities to treat those tested in the most appropriate and supposedly beneficial manner. (4) Panopticism, as sketched above, is application of the idea embodied in Bentham's ideally efficient prison. The Panopticon is a hollow cylinder with an observation tower at its center. The cells are located in stories in the hollow cylinder. In the original plan, the bars make up the inside and outside walls of each cell. The walls between cells, the cell floors, and the ceilings are concrete. In this way prisoners are isolated from each other while their every move is visible to guards in the central tower. The central tower has narrow observation slits that do not allow prisoners in their cells to know when they are being observed. The Panopticon allows a few guards to maintain *de facto* surveillance over many prisoners. (5) Surveillance is actual observation, but Foucault extends the notion. He includes the compiling of detailed dossiers and reports that track patterns of inmate behavior and incorporate expert assessments. Observation thus is augmented by material enabling prediction of future behavior and preemptive action.

Central to the foregoing devices is the idea that "being able always to be seen" keeps the disciplined individual subjugated.[35] Initially, subjugating surveillance is thought of as observation by authorized agents. But once it is appreciated that the ever-present possibility of observation works as well as actual surveillance, it is a small step to realize that the subjects of surveillance can be made complicitous in their own subjugation. If what the subjects are made to believe works as well as actually watching them, instilling certain additional beliefs can make control complete. In other words, subjects might be made to watch *themselves.* And that can be achieved by inculcating norms. What follows is a shift in emphasis from the enforcement of rules and regulations to the inculcation of norms through disciplinary techniques. The avowed objective is to normalize individuals, to rehabilitate wrongdoers, to train productive members of society. What actually occurs is that new subjects are manufactured who carry within them the norms that constitute self-surveillance.

Foucault maintains that the development and use of disciplinary techniques caused the penal system to become more concerned with "administering illegalities" than attempting to eliminate them.[36] This was not a matter of the authorities despairing of stopping crime, or being overcome by cynicism, or serving their own purposes. All of these were to some extent true, but more decisive was the fact that as penality developed into the employment of increasingly elaborate management techniques, the techniques acquired a self-sustaining importance. They came to be perceived as the best way to deal with an ineliminable subclass of individuals whose offending actions required control and containment. The complexity of disciplinary techniques was seen as necessitated by the existence of "a criminal class" rather than as problematic. The issue then became not how to eliminate crime but how best to control it.

In Part Three of *Discipline and Punish* Foucault considers models of disciplinary institutions. His aim is to show how then new managerial practices contributed to producing the contemporary prison. The Flemish model allowed the length of incarceration to be determined by administrators in light of inmate conduct. It also involved obligatory but remunerated labor and relied on continual supervision and strict timetables to instill good habits to aid rehabilitation. The English model also involved remunerated labor, supervision, and scheduling, but it added isolation to provide opportunity for reflection. Like the Flemish, the Philadelphian model allowed administrative moderation of sentences. And like the others, it involved supervision, scheduling, and compulsory labor. However, it used isolation for punishment and added a measure of confidentiality in that only the administration and the prisoner knew the judicial penalty. All of these models were products of reform prompted by efforts to control recidivism and effect transformation of the criminal. In their application there was great emphasis on development of good habits and remunerated labor. Punishment was not to be retributive but forward-looking and responsive to individual variables, such as inmate conduct. The avowed objective was to transform criminals into normal citizens by rewarding advancement. But Foucault stresses that while penal reformers thought mainly in terms of abstractions, corrective penality acted directly on the bodies of criminals. The model policies and methods were implemented as directives bearing on incarcerated bodies. His point is that penality is thoroughly corporeal. It uses rigorous physical repetition of disciplinary routines to modify conduct. Penality's objective is the production of docile bodies. The transformation of minds is only a means to that end.[37]

The implementation of the model policies Foucault reviews produced a huge carceral system that used confinement to exclude individuals from society and to manage them. However, the system's effects are very different from the intended effects that prompted its development. Most notable is that judging the conduct of persons, as opposed to judging only particular acts, did not lead to wiser assessment and treatment of lawbreakers. Instead it led to extensive and intrusive control of lawbreakers. The implementation of supposedly enlightened policies and methods did not produce more socially responsible and productive inmates and parolees. It produced only docile bodies. Instead of the penal system correcting a societal problem, it provided the techniques for pervasive social control.

Foucault contrasts the earlier "juridical" and later "carceral" systems by cataloging elements central to each. The juridical system centered on the law, the courts, indicted subjects, specific offenses, and sentences specifying duration and penalties. Key to the juridical system is the specificity of its elements. Its law is a series of prohibitions of carefully delineated acts; its courts have strictly defined procedures; offenders are charged with specified acts or responsibilities; offenses are articulated as unequivocal charges; sentences impose specific punishment for specified periods of time. Once an individual is sentenced and imprisoned, serving the sentence is a matter of meeting rather minimal requirements. The individual is jailed for the assigned term and punishment is administered. There is little concern with how the inmate responds to the process so long as he or she conforms adequately to prison and parole regulations.

The prison is a necessity for the juridical system; for the modern carceral system the penitentiary is an instrument. The carceral system has a far greater impact on the inmate. Rather than simply confining lawbreakers, the system processes them. First, it employs devices of politico-moral isolation. Inmates are housed in regularly surveyed cells. They are strictly supervised in all activities. They are subjected to "corrective" counseling. All their activities are not only supervised but take place in rigidly delineated areas: the cellblock, the workshop, the exercise yard, the infirmary, and the refectory. Second, the system relies heavily on a theoretical basis for treatment of inmates. Essentially this is the "disciplinary rationality" that transforms the premodern juridical prisoner into the modern psychological subject. The juridical subject guilty of specific offenses and serving his or her time becomes a delinquent characterized by an abnormal case history and needing reeducation. Third, the carceral system uses organizational devices. Inmate populations are divided into different classes of offenders (e.g., juvenile, felony, and capital) and are grouped or segregated. Parolees are also classed and grouped by degree of supervision and reporting schedules. Fourth, the carceral system employs reform movements that operate both within the prison and outside it. Finally, it relies on reconception of the police as less concerned with enforcement than with surveillance. All of this goes toward reshaping behavior and literally reforming subjects rather than simply restricting their movements for a specified time.

The disciplinary mechanisms Foucault reviews in *Discipline and Punish* changed institutionalized incarceration. It ceased to be confinement for the purpose of exacting retribution on monarchical subjects for specific offenses. Incarceration became confinement for the "requalification" of abnormal members of society. Crude punitive methods turned into political strategies.[38] But however important the change, Foucault's deeper point does not have to do with the development of the penal system as such. The point has to do with reconceiving power in understanding how disciplinary techniques manufacture subjects. The crucial first step is "ceas[ing] once and for all to describe . . . power in negative terms," that is, as always prohibitive, repressive, and coercive.[39] *Discipline and Punish* tells the story of the development of highly effective techniques for controlling people. But it is not a story about force and compulsion. It is a story about the manufacture and control of souls. *Discipline and Punish* is more than an account of institutionalized management and regulation because the techniques it details do not work only by compelling and forbidding. They work by enabling as much as by inhibiting, and what they enable is the production of truth and knowledge. The knowledge and truth produced are far more efficient tools of control than compulsion because they produce a soul that they then constrain.

Power is enabling in that "it produces reality; it produces domains of objects and rituals of truth."[40] A reality is produced in which normal society is pitted against a subclass of its members: the criminally abnormal. In structuring this adversarial situation, power also produces the means for society to conduct its struggle against criminality. It produces "domains of objects" by classification and exclusion. Not only is a subset of society identified as "the criminal class," finer distinctions are made. "Delinquents" are differentiated from "sex-offenders" and "recidivists" from those who merit counseling. Felons are graded by the seriousness of their offenses, running from capital crimes to armed robbery to assault to theft. "First offenders" and "white-collar" criminals are determined as types requiring monitoring though seldom imprisonment. Delineation of criminals generates the institutions that apply and house the required scientific and administrative procedures: the courts, prisons, halfway houses, academies, and laboratories. And correlative to the criminals are the judges, lawyers, coroners, police, parole boards, prison guards, forensic psychologists, forensic pathologists, counselors, reformers, and support groups. Dealing with lawbreakers produces "rituals of truth." These include indictment, the trial, the parole hearing, expert-witness testimony, compilation of dossiers on defendants and convicted felons, and statistics-based generalizations about crimes and motives. These are rituals of truth in that each determines that something is the case; that something establishes something else; that someone is of a certain type; that something is or is not relevant to a judgment; that something does or does not merit consideration in charging, sentencing, or paroling; that something done is or is not likely to be done again.

What Foucault calls the "penal ritual" begins with "the preliminary investigation" and carries through "to the sentence and the final effects of the penalty." A subject is created and sustained in this ritual. An individual is made a subject in being subjugated to penal authority, and classification and treatment conceptually and descriptively define that individual's subjectivity. The penal system creates and sustains subjects "by solemnly inscribing offenses" on bodies it makes docile. What legitimates the process is that the individuals are deemed "susceptible of scientific knowledge." They are taken as proper objects of study and as manageable and changeable by resultant theory-generated disciplinary techniques.[41] In this way, the penal system imbues "the mechanisms of legal punishment with a justifiable hold not only on offenses, but on individuals; not only on what they do, but also on what they are, will be, may be."[42] The modern soul, then, is "the present correlative of a certain technology of power over the body" because disciplinary control of the body both subjugates individuals and shapes their subjectivity. However, the soul is not "an illusion or an ideological effect," a mere device used to effect greater control. On the contrary, the soul "exists, it has a reality, it is produced permanently around, on, within the body by the functioning of a power that is exercised on those punished." Outside the penal system souls are produced in "those one supervises, trains and corrects."[43] The soul is not a preexistent essence; it is produced wherever there is normalizing supervision and constraint.

Production of the soul through management or disciplinary techniques means that individuals are not enslaved by our social institutions, as is often lamented. The view that free spirits are hamstrung by the institutional and social strictures is a romantic fantasy. Part of Foucault's point is that there are no preexistent individuals to be enslaved. Instead "the individual is carefully fabricated" by our social institutions.[44] What there are, initially, are not free spirits but bodies. The subject-fabricating techniques enslave

nothing. They act always on the body: "It is always the body that is at issue—the body and its forces, their utility and their docility, their distribution and their submission." The body is all that is available to power because the soul is itself a product of power. It is the body that "power
relations have an immediate hold on . . . they invest it, mark it, train it, torture it, force it to carry out tasks, to perform ceremonies, to emit signs."[45]

This brings us to the nub of the matter: power, or power relations. All of
the foregoing could be—and often is—read as being about a huge conspiracy. The development and application of disciplinary techniques and the
production of subjects could be—and often is—understood as an extensive,
covert program managed and implemented by a few to control the many.[46]
However, to interpret *Discipline and Punish* in this way is a mistake. The
hard part is that Foucauldian power is impersonal, does not act on individuals, and is purely relational and blind.[47] It is not anything anyone has or
controls and it serves no ends or goals.

Power

Foucauldian power is neither force nor capacity nor domination nor authority. The key point is that Foucauldian power is not *attributable* to anyone or anything. It is not possessed or exerted by anyone or anything.
Power is impersonal because it is neither possessed nor exerted by individuals, groups, or institutions. What Foucault rather unfortunately termed
"power" is a *complex set of relations*. One might think of it as an environment in which particular acts of domination or coercion occur. Power is the
sum total of influences that actions have on other actions, or what Foucault
calls "comportments."[48] As such, power serves no end, serves no purposes,
and has no objectives.[49] Power has direction only in the sense that its component actions are cumulative. Unlike its purposive and directed component actions, power is blind and purposeless.

Foucauldian power is hard to describe and to grasp, both because of the
concept's inherent difficulty and because of the tendency to understand the
term in its ordinary sense. When we talk about disciplining and regulating,
we think in terms of constraining, intimidating, and coercing. We think in
terms of compulsion exerted on a person or group by another person or
group. This certainly happens; there could be no disciplining or regulating
without individuals compelling other individuals. But to understand power
we need to get beneath these events to how doing something affects the doing (or not doing) of something else. We also have to get past intentions because the effects of things done or not done have little to do with what individuals or groups intend. A remark quoted earlier captures this point,
saying that while people know what they do and may know why they do
what they do, they do not know what what they do does.[50] Acting to

achieve a given objective may have unexpected results because what is done is modified by other actions. And whatever is done in turn modifies still other actions.

The common conception is that power is attributable to and exercised by agents and is exercised on agents. Agents possessed of power coerce agents who lack power.[51] Against this, Foucault insists on "the strictly relational character of power relationships."[52] He insists that we must be "nominalistic" about power because "power is not an institution, and not a structure; neither is it a certain strength."[53] Power is a "set of actions upon other actions," not actions on individuals like persuading and coercing.[54] Foucauldian power "is a way in which certain actions modify others." Power "is a mode of action which does not act directly and immediately on others. Instead it acts upon their actions." Power is "a total structure of actions brought to bear upon possible actions" in the sense that power enables or enhances some actions and inhibits or precludes others.[55] And because power is actions upon other actions, it is impersonal or, as Foucault puts it, "nonsubjective."[56]

Unfortunately, the negative things Foucault says about power—that it is not domination, that it is not anyone's power—seem inconsistent with power's subject-defining role. The inclination then is to think that power must be something more than relations among actions if it can manufacture subjects. Power must be a determinant of some sort, and most likely it is hidden coercive persuasion, indoctrination, or domination. Foucault is aware of this inclination and remarks that just as it is wrong to believe history is "the ruse of reason," it is equally wrong to believe that "power is the ruse of history."[57] What this rather obscure comment amounts to is that those who conceive history as discerning ahistoric determinants of events, like class struggle, see power as conspiratorial manipulation that serves those determinants.

Misinterpretation of Foucauldian power is worth pursuing because doing so facilitates better understanding. Construing power as conspiratorial determinants of behavior, as covert domination, goes like this: Power or power relations are reified as Capital-P Power; that is, power is taken as force or "a certain strength." Application of Capital-P Power—whether knowing or otherwise—is seen as serving historical inevitability or class struggle or The Divine Plan, or so on, and so as what makes people think and behave as they do. Usually another and particularly un-Foucauldian idea is grafted onto this misinterpretation. That is the idea that if we get clear enough on the role of Capital-P Power and how it is exerted on us, we can liberate ourselves from it.[58] Unfortunately, distortion of Foucauldian power as covert domination is supported by his own method. Foucault explicates power by cataloging behavior-conditioning and subjectivity-defining techniques. That is what *Discipline and Punish* and *The History of Sex-*

uality are all about. Behavior is conditioned and subjectivity defined in the prison by imposition of disciplines, and in society at large by "deployment" of a theory-generated sexuality. It then looks as if *Discipline and Punish* and *The History of Sexuality* are exposés that reveal conspiratorial determination of behavior. Additionally, Foucault portrays power as "masked." He presents his treatments of penality and sexuality as showing what actually happened under the appearance of reform and repression. He is careful to maintain that power is impersonal, but that is overlooked in interpreting power as conspiratorial. Even Rorty seems to overlook the impersonal nature of power. He describes "the most valuable part" of Foucault's work as showing "how the patterns of acculturation characteristic of liberal societies have imposed on their members . . . constraints of which older, premodern societies had not dreamed."[59]

Foucault does not merely inventory covert manipulative devices. His notion of power would be superfluous if he did only that. If the devices he reveals were conspiratorial in nature, they would be explicable in terms of the traditional conception of power as the ability to coerce, to prohibit, and to dominate. What Foucault does is provide a new way of saying something about how the vastly complex totality of human actions regulates behavior *without that totality having regulation as its objective.* He then enables us to understand how blind regulation of behavior shapes subjectivity, again without that being anyone's or anything's objective. Covert or overt instances of domination, and conspiracies, are elements of the hugely manifold web of interrelated constraints that constitutes power. To see particular instances of intimidation, coercion, prohibition, and domination as power is to mistake components for the whole.

A related misinterpretation of Foucauldian power is equation of power and knowledge.[60] This error occurs in spite of Foucault often describing knowledge as a product of power and insisting that the two are reciprocally related, and so distinct. Speaking of power and knowledge he tells us that "the very fact that I pose the question of their relation proves clearly that I do not *identify* them."[61] Foucault's use of the term "power/knowledge" does not imply the identity of the two. His point is that it is "not possible for power to be exercised without knowledge [and] it is impossible for knowledge not to engender power."[62] When behavior is constrained, as in the implementation of disciplinary techniques in the prison, expert knowledge is what grounds and authorizes the constraining. But the constraining of behavior also generates or adds to knowledge. It may do so by "confirming" what is supposedly known when the results of constraint are as expected. And it may do so by prompting further theorizing and research when unexpected results occur. Power is not knowledge nor is knowledge power. Power and knowledge are dual aspects of the comportment-conditioning environment within which individuals act, and so within which subjects are formed and have their being.

The strategical situation or the web of relations that is Foucauldian power "must be understood . . . as the multiplicity of force relations imma-nent in the sphere in which they operate and which constitute their own or-ganization."[63] Power is the totality of relations as well as "the process which, through ceaseless struggles and confrontations, transforms, strengthens, or reverses" the relations it comprises.[64] Power is a dynamic whole; its component "force relations" are constantly being modified by one another as well as changing internally. For example, an instance of A coercing B may alter because of B's resistance or compliance. The change in that force relation may affect a related instance of C coercing D. This con-tinuous, mutually influencing interaction is how power is a totality of rela-tions that includes "the support which these . . . relations find in one an-other" as well as "the disjunctions and contradictions which isolate [relations] from one another."[65]

Once we appreciate the identity of power with the totality of action-con-straining relations, we see that our traditional paradigm of power—the state—cannot be the paradigm of Foucauldian power. Power is only "em-bodied in the state apparatus, in the formulation of the law." The state's acts of domination are components of power as are individuals' acts of co-ercion or resistance. In like manner, ruling elite, the wealthy, and other so-cial groups possessing the capacity to intimidate and coerce cannot be par-adigms of power. Power is embodied "in the various social hegemonies" such as caste systems and economic classes, but their acts are so many more component force relations. What we normally take as paradigms of power are only instances of power's "institutional crystallization." They are not power itself.[66]

Understanding how power is the dynamic sum of force relations helps clarify how power constrains actions rather than individuals. Consider Foucault's initially surprising contention that power can be "exercised only over free subjects, and only insofar as they are free."[67] The point is that when an individual has no options, when his or her actions are wholly dic-tated by another or others, there is only domination. Foucauldian power requires for each individual "a field of possibilities in which several ways of behaving, several reactions and diverse comportments may be realized."[68] In total enslavement it is precisely the agent who is constrained, not ac-tions, because the agent's every act is coerced. Enslavement dictates specific behavior excluding everything else.[69] "Where the determining factors satu-rate the whole there is no relationship of power; slavery is not a power re-lationship"; in slavery there is only "a physical relationship of con-straint."[70] What emerges here is that power constrains actions by providing a "field of possibilities" regarding behavior. Power enables a range of op-tions, of electable courses of action. Conversely, power inhibits other op-tions. Differently put, the complex web of past and current actions incline individuals to do some things and disincline them to do other things. A

simple example is how someone in an institutional context acts in certain
ways because of how others act.[71] This is how actions constrain actions
rather than individuals.

It should not be thought that power provides preexistent subjects with
free choices. Power's enabling and inhibiting of behavior is the enabling
and inhibiting of acts that constitute subjects. This is the point about modification of behavior shaping and defining subjectivity. The totality of past
and current actions enables and inhibits things an individual might do and
does. By doing some things and not doing others an individual—an inscribed, docile body—shapes and defines his or her subjectivity. Doing or
not doing something always involves beliefs and usually values because
they both are the bases for action and are generated, enhanced or diminished by action. And the process is cumulative. An individual's previous
acts and omissions, and resultant beliefs and values, prioritize the behavioral options open to her or him.

Foucault's conception of power as impersonal is not as implausible as it
first appears. He contends that if Machiavelli "conceived the power of the
Prince in terms of force relationships, perhaps we need to go one step further." That further step is doing "without the persona of the Prince."[72] This
is to understand power as a "strategy that is immanent in force relationships." It is to go beyond conceiving of power as always present in the will
of an agent or the collective will of a group or the state.[73] We can amplify
the foregoing account of power as actions on actions with a simple model.
Imagine a number of small magnets spread out on a surface just far enough
from each other not to clump together. We understand that magnetic force-
vectors will be established among the magnets. Iron filings scattered over
the surface will trace those vectors by aligning themselves in various ways
relative to the closer magnets. Now imagine shifting the magnets around.
Movement of the magnets alters the force-vectors and so the alignment of
the filings changes. In this model or analogy, the magnets are agents, the filings are behavioral options, and the force-vectors are power. Every time a
magnet moves, that is, every time an agent acts, the "strategical situation"
in its vicinity changes and in turn affects the whole. Each magnet contributes to the totality of force-vectors by being where it is or by moving. In
like manner, agents' actions contribute to the relational totality that is
power. However, that totality is not any one agent's nor any group's power
any more than the totality of force-vectors is any one magnet's magnetic
field.

If we stretch the model, we can say that the dispersion of filings in a
given magnet's vicinity is the range of actions or comportments open to an
individual. The point, then, is that the dispersion of filings around a particular magnet is constantly changing as other magnets move. The dispersion
is also changed, of course, by the particular magnet's own movement.

The magnet model presents a graphic picture of power as relational. It illustrates how power is impersonal, it is not *anyone's* power, because it is a web of relations among actions rather than among agents. The model also illustrates how power is pervasive, how there is "no escaping from power." Power "is always already present, constituting that very thing which one attempts to counter it with."[74] To act in defiance is to act within power, not against it. To escape from power one would have to be utterly alone and free of all the enculturation that makes us social beings. The opposite and equally unachievable case is complete enslavement or being only the extension of another's will. We cannot escape power without achieving complete solitude or total enslavement. Resistance is, in fact, integral to power relations. We remain defined by and immersed in power even when we resist coercion or domination. "Where there is power, there is resistance, and yet . . . this resistance is never in a position of exteriority in relation to power."[75]

Even wholly passive persons in power relations offer resistance because they partly define those power relations. Passive individuals inescapably constrain the behavior of even the most intimidating or coercive relation-partner. Acts of compliance constrain intimidating or coercive acts as much as acts of defiance. This is why power "depends on a multiplicity of points of resistance."[76] The point is that in the relevant sense, resistance is never to Foucauldian power as such. Resistance is always to particular constraints that enable or compel some acts and inhibit or prohibit others. But resistance, in balancing constraint, completes relations of power so is internal to power. Additionally, the internality of resistance to power in turn shows how power is pervasive. Foucault contends that it is wrongheaded even to assert that we cannot escape power. That would be "to misunderstand the strictly relational character" of power, to fail to see that power has no contrast.[77] Power is not something that we can or cannot escape. It is the intricate web of constraining interrelationships that exists the moment there is more than one agent. The point is that there cannot be interaction among individuals outside power. There can be no state of affairs in which we are both agents among other agents and do not constrain each other's actions. Being an individual and interacting with other individuals involves imposing constraints on actions, so all interactions occur within the environment of power. Power relations "permeate . . . and constitute the social body."[78] Power "is not something that is acquired, seized, or shared," because it is the ever-present environment in which we are subjects and agents.[79]

Power looks dubiously coherent as a philosophical concept if it is relational, impersonal, and constrains actions rather than agents. The relational nature of power, as depicted in the magnet model, clarifies how power is impersonal and constrains actions rather than agents. However, these remain the most problematic aspects of Foucault's notion of power.

They are the aspects that both make power a novel and productive philosophical idea and prompt philosophers like Taylor to argue that Foucauldian power is incoherent. Can the notion be made out more clearly?

Foucault's description of power is as "a complex strategical situation in a particular society."[80] The "strategical situation" is how myriad relations of constraint on actions stand at any given time in a given society. It is only in the context of those relations that something is an instance of coercion or resistance. But power is not something *other* than the myriad relations of constraint. "Relations of power are not in a position of exteriority with respect to other types of relationships."[81] We are all variously juxtaposed to each other and to groups and institutions in relations that affect what we do and can do. Foucault wants to talk about the totality of these juxtapositions. He then wants to say that what we do and what we *become* results in large part from the totality of juxtapositions and not just from the particular things others do to us. The reason he wants to say this is that the particular things we do and have done to us all happen in this totality and—according to him—are modified by the totality.

Consider this example: Prison reformers succeed in psychological testing being adopted as part of the routine processing of new inmates. The intention is to offer inmates effective counseling. First of all, the intention is theory-based; it is prompted—and its realization is justified—by psychological theorizing about criminal behavior. That means that certain ideas about normality and abnormality are operant in what motivates the reformers, in the design and administration of the testing, and in the conclusions drawn about results. Second, incoming inmates will have positive or negative attitudes toward psychological testing. For instance, some may see the testing simply as an opportunity to appear disturbed in the hope of getting preferential treatment. Third, those entrusted to assess and apply the results of the tests will be more or less competent and/or effective in assessing and applying those results. There are many other aspects but these should suffice to make the twofold point. The testing produces problematic items that are included in inmates' dossiers and that administrators can use to apply various regulations and regimens. For their part, many inmates will believe that administrators know something about them that they do not know themselves and accept regulation and regimens more readily than they might have done. The upshot is that what was intended to benefit inmates instead enhances their control and benefits the penal institution.

As far as it goes, this example might be seen as only illustrating a kind of systematic irony in how institutions work. If seen in that way, the example does no more than hint at how power works. What must be appreciated is that all of the factors mentioned in the example occur in the web of interacting power relations. Psychological theory, views of normality, design and administration of a technique, assessment of a test instrument, and implementation of conclusions drawn are all modified by the actions among which they occur. A simple example is a newly hired prison psychometrist whose assessment of inmates' test results is affected by the practices of new coworkers. When we multiply this instance by a thousand, we begin to see what Foucault tries to gather up in his talk of power and actions constraining actions.[82]

One issue raised by Foucault's desire to capture something with his idea of power is whether what he tries to capture has its own history. Certainly much of what he says in *Discipline and Punish* and *The History of Sexuality* sounds as if power is something fairly new. It seems that power either had a relatively late historical beginning or an escalation in degree tantamount to a beginning. In one sense power must be as old as we are, since it is the dynamic totality of interactive human action. But it could be a misinterpretation of Foucault to understand power as coextensive with human history. *Discipline and Punish* has to do with the historically circumscribed displacement of juridico-discursive rule of law by disciplinary techniques and regulatory norms. Foucault is ambiguous on the point. He tells us that "from the seventeenth and eighteenth centuries onward, there was a veritable technological take-off in the productivity of power." He also points out that not only did "the monarchies of the classical period develop great state apparatuses (the army, police and fiscal administration)," but that "there was established at this period . . . a new 'economy' of power."[83] It could be that power was new sometime in the seventeenth century; it could be that at that time there was a significant increase or change. Again, it could be that there was a new economy of power or that power itself was new.

Construing the apparent historical emergence of power as only a matter of degree initially may look at odds with what seem to have enabled Foucauldian power relations. These are such things as increases in population, greater complexity of social interaction, more complicated societal structuring, increasingly sophisticated manipulative techniques, and refinements in enculturation. It might seem more plausible to think that power is relatively new in human history and has a history of its own. If so, it seems that at some point the number of people interacting, and the complexity of their interactions, reached a "critical mass" resulting in new constraints on action. However, on reflection it seems fruitless, if not impossible, to distinguish this sort of novelty from a change of degree. Power's apparent historical beginning is best construed as how actions constraining actions became significant only when management techniques became useful to deal effectively with substantial populations. The deployment of penality requires large numbers of lawbreakers who pose a considerable collective problem for authorities and society at large. More important, the number of lawbreakers must be large enough to enable and call for categorization of individuals as "delinquents," "recidivists," and so forth, and the production of

experts to deal with the various types. The notion of power has little content until the action-constraining relations among a goodly number of
agents become complex and extensive. It is only then that the totality of action-constraining acts coalesces into an environment in which individuals'
subjectivity is defined in significant and discernible ways.

The crucial point is that it is to wrongly reify power to ask about its history if that history is thought separable from the history of the interactive
human actions. However, the *idea* of power has a history. The idea of
power is an invented or fashioned instrument for dealing with history; it is
a tool that facilitates conceptual objectification and treatment of the web of
interrelated actions that power comprises. The notion of power enables us
to think and talk productively about the environment within which we are
agents and patients. Power helps us map that environment or the relations
among the actions that occur in that environment. The apparent historical
novelty of power, then, should be understood as the way numerous strategies, development of discourses, and establishment of institutions became
visible and amenable to investigation at a point in time. That point was
when there was enough history to provide contrastive raw material and
enough people behaving in ways that established discernable patterns. It is
not power that is new, not as something in itself, but rather use of the idea
to trace discourses and institutions of a new order of complexity.

The question of power's history, then, is not one about the history of a
particular phenomenon. It is a question about the utility of Foucault's instrument for investigating institutional development, measures of control,
and ways of averring and assessing truth and knowledge. If Foucault had
lived in the twelfth century, he could have written a genealogy of the pa-
pacy, contrasting it with previously localized religious seats of authority.
The notion of power would have been an effective enough instrument in
that exercise. But the wealth of complexity, and the vast increase in population added by another eight centuries to genealogy's raw material, makes
the twentieth-century notion of power a hugely more effective instrument.
The complexity and larger population also make it much more likely that
the notion of power would be fashioned in the twentieth century rather
than the twelfth. We must bear in mind the paramount importance of history in considering Foucault's genealogical analytics. We must also bear in
mind that the notion of power is not the name of a mysterious force but a
device[84] to deal with history, a way of producing accounts that are interpretations without being teleological "grand narratives."

To further clarify power's emergence and the notion of power itself, it is
important to note that Foucault uses the term "government" to designate
the disciplinary management of people. He tells us that power is basically
"a question of government." However, he adds that the word "government" must be given "the very broad meaning which it had in the Sixteenth

Century."[85] This archaic sense was considerably more inclusive than the current, largely political sense. The archaic sense was not used to refer only or even primarily to "political structures or the management of states." Instead the term "designated the way in which the conduct of individuals or states might be directed."[86] This further illuminates how power emerges as a viable tool in genealogical analysis. Power relations become an analytic concern only when there is appreciable government—in Foucault's sense—of the "modes of action" that in various ways structure and constrain "the possible field of actions of others."[87]

The most important way in which power is government has to do with the production of knowledge and disciplines. As "knowledges"[88] and disciplines develop they produce the experts who determine not only how we should act but also what we are. Traditionally, topics of intellectual inquiry are taken merely as so many given problematics that invite study for purposes of control or for their own sake. But for Foucault, topics of disciplinary study do not antedate disciplines; they are artifacts or products of those disciplines. Intellectual and empirical inquiry traditionally has been seen as reasoned effort to discern the nature of objective topics of study. For Foucault inquiry itself both constitutes what is studied and bestows on what is studied whatever objectivity it is thought to have. This is how "power perpetually creates knowledge."[89] However, knowledge is not only a product; it reciprocally enables and sustains power relations. Power-produced knowledge enables penologists to impose regimens on inmates, thus constraining their actions. In turn, inmates' modified behavior is interpreted as confirming and perhaps expanding what penologists are deemed to know. This is why Foucault often speaks of "power/ knowledge" and insists that "there is no exteriority" between "techniques of knowledge and strategies of power."[90]

Development of the penal system, as laid out in *Discipline and Punish*, illustrates the reciprocity between techniques of knowledge and strategies of power. It shows how juridical subjects were remade into psychological subjects when the soul was manufactured and punishment was reconceived from retribution to normalization. Once the modern soul was manufactured, numerous fields of study developed to deal with it. Prison psychometrists and counselors were needed to handle a manufactured aspect of the inmate. In turn, their reports, assessments, and recommendations bulked up the content of their disciplines. In *The History of Sexuality* the reciprocity is shown by how the creation of a new field of study generated new sexual subjects. Foucault maintains that "sexuality was constituted as an area of investigation" because "relations of power had established it as a possible object." And "conversely, if power was able to take [sexuality] as a target, this was because techniques of knowledge and procedures of discourse were capable of investing it."[91] Power enabled certain behavior and relationships to constitute a structured whole of interest to experts: human sexuality. Foucault contends that the term itself "did not appear until the beginning of the nineteenth century."[92] What some three hundred years earlier had been disparate urges, inclinations, and activities were delineated as a set of traits and drives that define an essential aspect of being human. Power produced a nature and Freud and Alfred Kinsey became possible[93] and proceeded to determine and to teach us what we are, to define us as sexual subjects.[94]

The power/knowledge reciprocity raises another point that merits mention. Our paradigm of legitimate constraint is the state. But Foucauldian power's relational nature means that its constraints are "not ensured by right but by technique, not by law but by normalization, not by punishment but by control."[95] It is knowledge that authorizes the exercise of constraint, and authorized constraint enhances power relations. Power normalizes and controls when techniques are implemented "on all levels and in forms that go beyond the state and its apparatus."[96] Implementation of those techniques then produces more knowledge that in turn authorizes new constraints.

What we have, then, is that power is a "multiplicity of force relations" that "constitute their own organization." Power is "the process" that "transforms" these force relations. Power is also "the support which these force relations find in one another [and/or] the disjunctions and contradictions which isolate them from one another." Finally, power is "the strategies in which [force relations] take effect."[97] However, none of this should be read as deterministic. Power is inherently dynamic and fluid. The changes that occur in the totality of power or force relations are not consequences of the characteristics of individual acts or relations but of their interaction, and that interaction is unpredictable. Even if it were possible to map the dynamic whole of force relations at a given moment, its consequent state would not be predictable as a successor state to the mapped state. Recall Hacking's remark about the "tiny local events where battles are unwittingly enacted by players who don't know what they are doing."[98] The effects of particular actions and relations occurring in the web of force relations are quite unforeseeable.[99]

We can conclude this section by saying that power is *the dynamic totality of previous and concurrent actions blindly modifying presently ensuing actions*. However, what remains unclear is how power manufactures subjects by modifying, enabling, or inhibiting actions. Foucault insists that "it is . . . one of the prime effects of power that certain bodies, certain gestures, certain discourses, certain desires, come to be identified and constituted as individuals."[100]

It now should be clearer how agents act in a web of other agents' actions. The disposition of that web determines that a given agent's act is, say, an act of domination or compliance. An apparent act of compliance need not be that. Compliance with a particular order may be defiance in the right circumstances—that is, in a certain disposition of the web of force relations. For example, deliberately complying with a petty order may demean the person issuing it more than the person obeying. Another example is how brutally coercing someone to do something may mark not continuing dominance over that person, but the end of dominance. It is in this way that power determines what counts as someone dominating or defying another. But while it may be clear enough how power determines the nature of an individual's act, what is less clear is how power determines the *individual*. How is the individual a product of power and not "a sort of elementary nucleus, a primitive atom . . . on which power comes to fasten or against which it happens to strike"?[101] To close this chapter we need to look more carefully at the determination of the subject.

Defining Subjectivity

Difficult as the idea of power as actions acting on actions may be, Foucault's claim that our subjectivity is historical, that it is a result of discourse and practices, is more difficult. However, the ideas are tightly connected. Power is an explanatory concept; it explains how subjectivity is produced and shaped. Foucault's historicist conception of the subject both enables and requires his relational conception of power. Without power we could not understand the production of subjectivity. But while we can imagine not having certain beliefs and attitudes, or having different beliefs and attitudes, it is more difficult to imagine ourselves as fundamentally *other* than we are because power produced us differently. And Foucault goes even further. Because of the constitutive role of discourse and the possibilities thus afforded, he maintains that "the subject . . . is obviously only one of the . . . possibilities of organizing a consciousness of self."[102] He asks whether "the subject is the only form of existence possible," and whether there might not be "experiences in which the subject . . . is not given any more,"[103] which might not be subject-centered. He thinks that the subject is "obviously only one of the . . . possibilities of organizing a consciousness of self."[104] For instance, we might have been multiple "personalities" and conscious from different perspectives in a way that we presently think is pathological. Nonetheless, however difficult to imagine, Foucault conceives of the subject as historical, as a particular, and as a kind.[105]

Here again we need to mention a likely misinterpretation, and it is again one that clarifies the point. Foucault is not a constructivist in the familiar sense. As touched on earlier, Mead characterized our experience of self as a product of cognition rather than a unity preceding cognition. Mead offered his constructivist account of self as an ontological alternative to the Cartesian and Kantian conceptions of the self as conditional or logically prior to experience. Susan Hekman remarks that though Foucault sees the subject as "constituted within discursive formations," he does not merely "replace the constituting subject with the constituted subject." Instead he offers "a conception of the subject that explodes the polarity between constituted and constituting by displacing the opposition."[106] Unlike Mead, Foucault does not offer a competing ontological conception of the self.[107] In a sense that must be handled carefully, Foucault is not concerned with the self or ego, as are Descartes, Kant, and Mead. Foucault's constructed subject is not intended as an alternative to the Cartesian ego or the Kantian "I think" or Mead's "combination" of remembered selves and internal responses to actions.[108] Foucault is equally opposed to essentialist conceptions of the self, like Descartes's and Kant's, and to constructivist ones, like Mead's.

For Foucault, the construction of the subject means the investing of a body with a pattern of subjectivity-determining habits. That body is then assigned certain attributes and a certain status. Recall the deliberate ambiguity in Foucault's concept of the subject. The habit-invested body is both a subject in being subject to institutional and state authority, and in being a subject of experience. The former is clear enough; the latter is more elusive. The point is that habits determine subjectivity in that conditioned behavior alters attitudes and instills new ones. This is precisely the avowed aim of disciplinary techniques: to change people by making them behave differently. What it is to be a power-constructed subject, in the subject-of-experience sense, is for a habit-invested body to adopt a certain perspective on itself and its surroundings. The individual comes to experience the world in a certain way as a result of behaving in certain ways, being categorized in certain ways, and being dealt with in certain ways. *A constructed subject then is an experiencing self of a particular sort in that an individual internalizes power-assigned attributes and comes to intend power-imposed actions.*

Foucault's objective is to displace the duality of preexistent/constructed subjects by providing a genealogical account of what it is to become and to be a subject through disciplining of the body. Ontological theorizing about the ultimate nature of the self thus is undercut by showing how the subject is the result of "a process of self-knowledge." For Foucault the subject is a product of an "obligation to seek and state the truth about oneself."[109] This is a matter of subjectivity being defined in the process of "learning" what one is by internalizing power-produced truths and "acting as one should" to conform to what is learned about oneself. Constructed subjectivity is not a metaphysical emergence but a cognitive result.[110] Becoming a subject is coming to hold certain things as true about oneself, saying certain things about oneself, and intentionally acting in certain ways. This is the sense in which the subject "is not a pre-given entity. The individual, with his identity and characteristics, is the product of . . . power exercised over bodies."[111]

Notes

1. Foucault 1979:135–228.
2. Foucault 1965, 1975.
3. Foucault 1979:26.
4. Foucault 1983a:212.
5. Foucault 1983a:212.
6. Foucault 1979:29.
7. Foucault 1979:29.
8. Marshall 1992:82.
9. Foucault 1972:203.
10. Foucault 1980b:73,117.
11. Foucault 1972:55.
12. Foucault 1971:82.
13. Foucault 1971:83.
14. Foucault 1983a:208–9.
15. Miller 1993:98.
16. Foucault 1979: ten "figures" inserted between pages 169–70.
17. Foucault 1979:22.
18. Foucault 1979:23.
19. Foucault 1979:101.
20. Foucault 1979:102.
21. In *The History of Sexuality* the interplay is between the normal individual and the deviant one. Deviancy is not just transgression, even repeated transgression. It is manifestation of a perverted nature.
22. Foucault 1979:90.
23. Foucault 1979:130,179.
24. Foucault 1979:183.
25. Foucault 1979:304.
26. Foucault 1979:199.
27. Foucault 1979:187.
28. Bernauer, J. W. 1993:6.
29. Foucault 1983a:212.
30. Foucault 1979:29.
31. Foucault 1979:138.
32. Foucault 1979:73.
33. Foucault 1979:141.
34. Electronic audio-visual surveillance has made redundant most of the mechanisms Foucault discusses. It may be some time before we understand the disciplinary effect of such pervasive surveillance.
35. Foucault 1979:187.
36. Foucault 1979:89.
37. Foucault 1979:138.

38. Foucault 1979:23.

39. Foucault 1979:194.

40. Foucault 1979:194.

41. My aim here is expository rather than critical, but one objection needs to be noted because it helps to clarify the foregoing discussion. It may be argued that the carceral system deals with ongoing realities rather than producing anything, and that the only novelty is better recognition and description of those realities. It may be claimed that the shift from the juridical to the carceral system was a progressive move to more effective treatment of what was already there, not a shift to greater control enabled by the creation of new subjects and categories. This objection captures what is at issue between totalizing and effective history. The objection turns on postulating certain givens or "essences" that the penal system now deals with more effectively in virtue of accumulated experience and better theories. The objection articulates the fundamental difference between genealogy and what it opposes and its real force has to do with the cogency of genealogical claims and why we should deem them superior to what they oppose.

42. Foucault 1979:18.

43. Foucault 1979:29.

44. Foucault 1979:217.

45. Foucault 1979:25.

46. The most common contemporary interpretation is that power serves patriarchal control.

47. This is also what makes *Discipline and Punish* a philosophical rather than an historical or sociological work.

48. Foucault 1983a:221.

49. This is the most fundamental reason why it is so wrong to interpret Foucauldian power as covert domination.

50. Dreyfus and Rabinow 1983:187.

51. "Agent" must be understood here to include individuals, groups, institutions, and the state.

52. Foucault 1980a:95.

53. Foucault 1980a:93.

54. Foucault 1983a:219–20.

55. Foucault 1983a:219–20.

56. Foucault 1980a:94. What Foucault means by "nonsubjective" is that power has no point of view, as does power in the ordinary sense when it is used by an individual or group.

57. Foucault 1980a:95.

58. If the interpretation is more sophisticated, it will include reference to Foucault's own intellectual history and how he was to develop the idea of Capital-P Power through adoption of Nietzsche's "will to power" and reinterpretation of Marxism. If the interpretation is still more sophisticated, Foucault's Capital-P Power-producing reinterpretation is taken to be not of Marxian but of structuralist underlying determinants.

59. Rorty 1989:63.

60. Nola 1994:21–24.

61. Foucault 1988b:43.

62. Foucault 1980b:52. Reference to power being "exercised" does not contradict what was said earlier. The reference is a bit of shorthand for application of disciplinary techniques and their concomitant effects.

63. Foucault 1980a:92. The phrase "force relations" should be read as referring to particular acts in which an individual or group coerces, intimidates, or dominates another individual or group. In other words, particular applications of force or power in the ordinary sense are the components or elements of Foucauldian power.

64. Foucault 1980a:92.

65. Foucault 1980a:92.

66. Foucault 1980a:92–93.

67. Foucault 1983a:221.

68. Foucault 1983a:221.

69. It is notable that as the state fails to be a proper paradigm of Foucauldian power, enslavement, another paradigm of power, fails to be even an instance of Foucauldian power.

70. Foucault 1983a:221.

71. The usually vague notion of "peer-pressure" is a concrete case in point. People in institutional settings conform in behavior and dress without being specifically told how to behave or dress. The actions of others determine what they do and what they wear.

72. Foucault 1980a:97.

73. Foucault 1980a:97.

74. Foucault 1980a:82.

75. Foucault 1980a:94–95.

76. Foucault 1980a:95.

77. Foucault 1980a:95.

78. Foucault 1980b:93.

79. Foucault 1980a:94, 93.

80. Foucault 1980a:93.

81. Foucault 1980a:94.

82. This is the point at which Rorty's reservations apply, because it is just here that we most expect power to be offered as some sort of successor to epistemology.

83. Foucault 1980b:119.

84. The notion of power is an instrument, an analytic tool; it is not a theory. Foucault rejects the idea that his conception of power is a theoretical one. Foucault 1980a:92–93, 97. He tells us: "I am no theoretician of power." Foucault 1989:254.

85. Foucault 1983a:221.

86. Foucault 1983a:221.

87. Foucault 1983a:221.

88. Recall that Foucault usually pluralizes "knowledge" to stress its historicity.

89. Foucault 1980b:51–52.

90. Foucault 1980a:98.

91. Foucault 1980a:98.

92. Foucault 1986:3.

93. I am here paraphrasing Foucault's remark about Hume.

94. Kinsey 1948:53.

95. Foucault 1980a:89.

96. Foucault 1980a:89.

97. Foucault 1980a:92–93.

98. Hacking 1981:29.

99. Foucault often speaks of "random" events and "accidents" when discussing the development of techniques of knowledge and strategies of power. He even claims that reasoned inquiry itself "was born . . . from chance." Foucault 1971:78. But what sort of randomness and chance is this? Force relations interact in contributing to the dynamic whole of power. Changes in the totality of force relations are due in part to some constituent force relations reinforcing one another and in part to some constituent force relations diminishing the effects of others. The effect of any given constituent act or force relation on the whole is not a function of something intrinsic to the act or force relation itself. It is a function of how that particular act or force relation relates to other acts and force relations. Changes in the whole therefore are unpredictable. It is not that some individual acts or force relations are uncaused or without histories; it is that their specific contributions to the multiplicity of force relations cannot be anticipated. Foucauldian randomness contrasts, not with causal determination, but with what genealogy opposes: totalizing history. The mechanics of power cannot be predicted; they can only be retrospectively traced through the "gray, meticulous, and patiently documentary" detailing of developments in the asylum, in the clinic, in the prison.

100. Foucault 1980b:98.

101. Foucault 1980b:98.

102. Dreyfus and Rabinow 1983:175.

103. Foucault 1991a:49.

104. Dreyfus and Rabinow 1983:175.

105. Descartes made clear that there is a difference between conception and imagination. We can conceive a thousand-sided figure even though we cannot imagine it.

106. Hekman 1990:47. Hekman refers to "postmoderns" rather than Foucault in particular, but the point applies to Foucault if it applies to anyone.

107. Brenda Marshall points out rather than being a move in a familiar polemic, the postmodern critique "is most consistently an impulse to look at the historical, philosophical, and cultural construction of the subject." Marshall 1992:82.

108. Thayer 1982:355.

109. Foucault 1988b:240.

110. None of this is to suggest that Foucault would accept a metaphysical account of the subject. For him, any such account would be a product of power and so historical. Historicity precludes metaphysics by disallowing reference to anything outside of discourse.

111. Foucault 1980b:73–74. If the philosophical question is asked about what there is *ab initio* if subjects are constructs, the short answer is: bodies. In Chapter 7 I consider Foucault's implicit views on "what there is."

Chapter Five

The Manufacture of Knowledge

In *The History of Sexuality*, Volume 1, Foucault describes the production or "deployment" of human sexuality. By "deployment" he means two things: first, the discursive and disciplinary implanting or engendering of the idea that human beings have an objective sexual nature. Second, the discursive and disciplinary construction and dissemination of a particular account of that sexual nature. Foucault's main concern is that deployment of sexuality generates norms that condition much of human thought and behavior.

The History of Sexuality lays out how a norm-based sexuality was developed and made into the truth about sex. The book is short and lacks the welter of detail given in *Discipline and Punish*. The difference is due in part to a change in Foucault's method, and in part to his planning the history of sexuality as a six-volume work.[1] It is in the first volume that we find the genealogical treatment of sexuality. The second and third (published) volumes, *The Use of Pleasure* and *The Care of the Self*, are ethical works in Foucault's rather proprietary sense. In Volume 1, he paints a picture of the workings of power relations that is more compressed and explicit than that offered in *Discipline and Punish*. He shows how power manufactures a particular subjectivity by producing norms and self-images that people internalize and take as the truth about themselves as sexual beings.

The easy way to understand *The History of Sexuality* is to take the book as only about beliefs and perceptions. To do so is to read Foucault as if he is concerned that we misconstrue our objective sexual nature and attempting to correct that misconstrual. This is a serious misinterpretation. Unfortunately, it is also a very common misinterpretation. It is the most common misinterpretation on the part of those who first encounter Foucault's work in *The History of Sexuality*. Foucault explicitly challenges the idea of an objective sexual nature: "It is precisely this idea of sex in *itself* that we cannot accept without examination."[2] Nonetheless, the book too often is read as only about how culture organizes and regulates perception and valuation of an objective sexual nature. The irony is that this misinterpretation is attributable to how successfully sexuality has been deployed. Many readers are simply unprepared to take seriously that Foucault's investigation could reach all the way down to what they see as natural and unquestionable.

The History of Sexuality is not about the culturally determined construal of a biological given. What is hard to grasp, and harder to accept, is that for Foucault the very idea of an objective sexual nature is a historical product and open to genealogical analysis. *The History of Sexuality* lays out how our sexual nature and cultural interpretations of it result from the discourses that define sexuality and the disciplinary techniques that regulate sexual behavior. Foucault asks whether our putative objective sexual nature is "really the anchorage point that supports the manifestations of sexuality, or is . . . rather a complex idea that was formed inside the deployment of sexuality." His answer is that "the deployment of sexuality . . . was what established this notion [of objective] 'sex.'"[3]

It is prudent to prevent possible confusion at this point. Foucault is claiming that an "objective" sexual nature is a product of the deployment of sexuality. He is not claiming that obvious physiological and anatomical differences between men and women are products of the deployment of sexuality. The product of deployment is a particular conception of those physiological and anatomical features as integrated elements that constitute natural kinds or types: "the masculine," "the feminine." However, this clarificatory point is tricky. On the one hand we need to distinguish between the mistaken view that Foucault is dealing only with how we construe objective sexuality, and correct understanding that Foucault is not denying that male and female bodies differ in the strictly biological sense. On the other hand, extra-discursive reference to male and female bodies is not consistent with Foucault's views. He will not allow us to step outside of language to acknowledge certain given differences. We cannot refer to brute reality outside of discourse. The trouble is that not making the distinction invites hasty rejection of Foucault's historicist claim about objective sexual nature. The reality of the human body easily may preclude Foucault's claim being taken seriously. For the time being, we will allow reference to the reality of human bodies as a heuristic device. I hope to justify this move when I consider the question of realism in Chapter 7. What matters here is to head off hasty dismissal of the central claim made in *The History of Sexuality*.

Even if it is understood that *The History of Sexuality* is not about the cultural face of sex as opposed to its natural reality, a subtler interpretive mistake may be made. In an important sense, the book is not inevitably about the history of sexuality any more than it is about a misconstrued objective sexuality. The book is an Aesop's tale about sexuality. *The History of Sexuality* is about how a particular institutionalized ideational construct came to be "the truth" and to constitute knowledge. It is about how we came to take that construct as *our nature*. The book is about sex or sexuality only because of the importance of the deployed sexuality in our lives. It could have been about religion or even etiquette.[4] In *Discipline and Punish* the focus is on how disciplinary techniques produce subjects in bodies made docile. In *The History of Sexuality* the focus is on how classification and regulation of various activities[5] came to be control of *sexual* behavior. This is Foucault's key point.[6] Categorization of some activities as sexual, and consequent control of those activities, initiated and sustained the production of a sexual nature, of sexual subjects, and of knowledge about sexuality.

Part of the produced knowledge is the view that sexuality was repressed from the Victorian period onward. This point is central because the alleged repression of sexuality is Foucault's stalking-horse. He argues that the alleged repression was crucial to the deployment of sexuality. Briefly, the supposed repression fostered learned discourse about sex.

Unfortunately, this is another point that invites misinterpretation. *The History of Sexuality* may look to some readers like an historical exposé. Even if it is appreciated that Foucault is not concerned only with the cultural face of an objective nature, it is also a mistake to see Foucault as concerned about misrepresentation of objective *events*. *The History of Sexuality* competes with the established history of sexuality as a genealogical analysis of it. It does not compete with the established history as an exposé of that history. The book attempts to establish how the chronicled disciplinary discernment of human sexual nature in fact was the manufacture of that nature. The book does not attempt to correct a distorted account of the discernment of sexuality because it argues that the "discernment" really was the production of knowledge about sex.

The character of Foucault's own intellectual and political background tends to bolster the wrongheaded view that *The History of Sexuality* is an exposé of manipulation of sexuality. Some see Marxist ideas at work. They read Foucault as arguing that power disguises what actually happens with a deceptive facade of its own making, a facade designed to foster the ends of those with power. As he himself puts it, they take him as thinking that history is "the ruse of reason" and that "power is the ruse of history."[7] Foucault does refer to capitalism and the bourgeoisie in *The History of Sexuality*, but this is an erroneous interpretation of *The History of Sexuality* in particular and of Foucault in general. It is an interpretation that requires understanding power as covert domination. Foucault is aware that too many take him to be arguing that knowledge is "no more than a thin mask thrown over the structures of domination." He scorns this view, remarking that those "who say that for me knowledge is the mask of power seem to me quite incapable of understanding."[8] It is worth reiterating that it is wrong to think that power is only covert domination. This misconception casts power as conspiratorial or, worse still, as a dark force shaping events. As we saw in Chapter 4, Foucauldian power is neither anyone's power nor any kind of force. Our present sexuality is not a product of power in the sense of being the consequence of a successful conspiracy or the effect of an irresistible mysterious force. To understand just how sexuality is a product of power, we have to look at *The History of Sexuality* in detail.

The Will to Knowledge

To begin, we must recall what is detailed in *Discipline and Punish*, namely, how power forms subjects by disciplining individuals. The main difference between *Discipline and Punish* and *The History of Sexuality* is that penal disciplinary techniques fall short of forming subjects by imposing a *nature* on the bodies they make docile.[9] The deployment of sexuality does just that. It makes individuals believe themselves to have a particular inherent nature.

Successful formation of subjects requires that it seem to power-shaped subjects that they are what they are naturally,[10] and nothing is more fundamental than sexuality in what power-shaped subjects are disciplined to take as natural. "Since Christianity, Western civilization has not stopped saying, 'To know who you are, know what your sexuality is about.'"[11] As Hekman remarks, "Foucault is maintaining that the essence of . . . the subject is to be found in sexuality because, in the west, subjects fin[d] their 'truth' in their sexuality."[12] This is why Foucault's treatment of sexuality is the cardinal application of his genealogical analytics and of his views on the constitutive and enabling aspects of power relations.[13]

The History of Sexuality begins by describing us as inheritors of the Victorian Age. The point is to highlight and characterize the dominant view of sexuality as repressed. It is this view that Foucault questions, rejects and redescribes as a device operant in the deployment of sexuality. In contrasting his own view with the dominant one, Foucault draws a crucial distinction: On one side is a regime of sexuality in which questions about sex and sexual behavior have to do with what is licit and illicit. On the other side is a regime in which questions about sex and sexual behavior have to do with what is normal and abnormal. The crucial difference is that in the first regime prohibitive laws regulate sexual activity and in the second social beings become self-regulating sexual agents. They do so by adopting norms that become continuous with their own values and desires. In the law regime adherence to rules or conventions is imposed from without. In the norm regime adherence is from within. When behavior is governed by internalized norms, individuals need not be coerced to adhere to rules and conventions. They behave according to norm because they *want* to.

Foucault describes the law regime as involving a "deployment of alliances."[14] Law-based regulation of sexual activity includes alliances or compacts that legitimize and enforce standards of conduct and redress delinquent behavior falling short of outright illegality. The alliances are relations among families. In the law regime, socially recognized sexual union—marriage—is not a matter of mutual attraction, sexual bonding, and cohabitation of two individuals. It is a procreative partnership and the contractual bonding of two families. Alliances of this kind involve complex rules about sexual behavior. For instance, brides must be virginal and wives monogamous to insure that offspring are genetically as well as legally "legitimate." Sanctions include disinheritance and disownment. In the law regime legal prohibitions supervene on various regulatory affiliations and associations that develop to govern individuals' behavior through the enforcement of standards. The law is construed as articulating and institutionalizing aspects of broader standards for desirable conduct. The law is considered necessary because the standards it embodies are taken as essentially running counter to "natural" inclinations. The first line of defense against "immoral" or unacceptable conduct is the alliances. The law is secondary in that it institutionalizes the central prohibitions.

In contrast to the law regime and its deployment of alliances, Foucault describes the norm regime as the "deployment of sexuality." What is deployed is a particular conception that determines what is sexual and regulates every sexual aspect of thought, discourse, and behavior. The deployment of sexuality manufactures sexuality as a particular nature, thereby making individuals into sexual subjects having specific needs and desires. Regulation of sexual behavior then does not have to be conducted through coercive prohibitions. It is achieved by shaping perception of one's own and others' needs, desires, and behavior. Individuals' acceptance of the deployed nature as their own makes them accept the norms that nature generates. Seeing oneself or another as having a sexual nature is also seeing sexual behavior as either in conformity with that nature or as deviating from it. The key point is that the idea of conforming to one's own nature has a built-in normative imperative. Everyone wants to be "normal." No one *wants* to be deviant, so everyone strives for normalcy—though with greater or lesser success. The deployment of sexuality makes sexual subjects self-regulating just as successful penal disciplinary techniques make docile bodies watch and control themselves.

The deployments of alliances and of sexuality differ with respect to the range of what is regulated. In the alliances-deployment case sexual activity is taken as a diverse given and only acts judged "unnatural" are legally proscribed. Acceptable sexual activity is delineated more or less by default.

Heterosexual intercourse is taken as natural and in effect sanctioned by the legal proscription of "unnatural" homosexual sodomy. In the sexuality-deployment case, heterosexual intercourse becomes more than a natural, and so allowable, form of sexual activity. It becomes the defining expression of human sexual nature and, as such, the norm. Homosexual sodomy then becomes an abnormality: "The sodomite had been a temporary aberration; the homosexual was now a species."[15] Even occasional practice of or desire to engage in such acts ceases to be sporadic or anomalous and becomes a manifestation of something deeply amiss with the individual's nature. In the alliances-deployment case, a homosexually active individual is a criminal mainly concerned with not getting caught. In the sexuality-deployment case, a homosexually active individual is a pervert mainly concerned with having a shameful affliction. Another aspect of the difference between heterosexual intercourse as an accepted act and as an act definitive of human sexuality is that *not* wanting to engage in it also becomes abnormal. Celibacy in healthy adults becomes suspect even if religiously motivated.

Foucault contends that there was a major shift in attitudes about sex in the seventeenth century. The change was one from candor and relative openness to a view of sex as properly restricted in its conduct and discussion to certain individuals in certain places. Sex was restricted to the heterosexual married couple in the couple's home. "A single locus of sexuality was acknowledged . . . the parents' bedroom."[16] As important as the restriction of normal sex was the localization of deviancy. "The brothel and the mental hospital would be . . . places of tolerance." The localization of deviancy involved classification of individuals into types: "the prostitute, the client, and the pimp, together with the psychiatrist and his hysteric." Each type is assigned a proper location, whether it be an institution or a district in which deviancy is tolerated for the sake of containment. Through localization and classification the deployment of sexuality "surreptitiously transferred the pleasures that are unspoken into the order of things that are counted."[17]

This last remark is another of Foucault's occasional compact but complex observations. What he means is that prior to the seventeenth century, sexual behavior was a manifold collection of pleasurable acts that were sexual only in being sensually satisfying[18] and, to a lesser degree, conducted in privacy. Sometime during the seventeenth century sexual behavior began to be classified qualitatively and normatively. Socially sanctioned heterosexual intercourse done for procreation came to define acceptable sexual behavior. Oral sex, same-sex relations, and other acts came to be problematic or censurable. Once these distinctions were imposed, it became possible to study sexual behavior because there then was such a thing as sexual behavior. Once diverse acts were collected into normal and abnormal patterns of behavior, those patterns were amenable to study. The study of those patterns of sexual behavior resulted in learned pronouncements about their causes and effects and thereby reinforced the original classifications.

Foucault's contention about the quantification of "pleasures that are unspoken" can be read as revealing a normative dimension of his claims and raises a point that needs to be briefly noted.[19] Some see Foucault's claims about sexuality as in part rationalizations of his own sexual orientation. Certainly there are problematic passages in his works, such as the insensitive portrayal of child molestation in *The History of Sexuality*.[20] The passage is intended to illustrate innocent pleasure but reads as tendentious and self-serving. There is also ongoing discussion about how Foucault's sexual orientation and his questionable interest in sadomasochism and necrophilia may have colored his work.[21] We need to try to keep Foucault's own predilections separate from his attempts to rethink the accepted and familiar. Happily, this is easier to do with *The History of Sexuality* than with *The Use of Pleasure* and *Care of the Self*.

Foucault states that the deployment of sexuality defines "the regime of power-knowledge-pleasure that sustains the discourse on human sexuality."[22] His genealogical aim is to trace the interrelated strategies and devices operant in the deployment. He wants to describe the means by which variegated sexual activity is integrated and objectified into something that then is perceived as requiring both rigorous control and specialized investigation. Foucault raises three questions: (1) Has sexuality actually been repressed? (2) Do "the workings of power . . . really belong primarily to the category of repression?" (3) Did "the critical discourse that addresses itself to repression . . . act as a roadblock to a power mechanism . . . or is it . . . part of [what] it denounces"?[23]

Foucault's first question challenges the familiar view that sexuality has been repressed since the Victorian period. This is a typical Foucauldian question: Does the accepted or obvious conceal its opposite?[24] Foucault answers this first question by arguing that repression of sexuality was only apparent. He claims that the appearance of repression hid an explosive increase of interest in sex. Much of the text is concerned with sorting out how that heightened interest was disguised. In the process, what is thought to be late-twentieth-century liberation from sexual repression is redescribed as the effects of subject-defining disciplinary techniques.

The second question provides Foucault with the opportunity to expand the conception of power he presents in *Discipline and Punish*. Foucault's answer to the second question is the most philosophically intriguing of the three. He claims that conception of power as domination and prohibition—and in the case of sexuality as coercive repression—fails to recognize the productive nature of power relations. What Foucault is saying is that the concept of power we have relied on for a very long time is seriously deficient. A concept we have thought adequate to a fundamental aspect of human life in fact is inadequate. This amounts to saying that we do not really

understand much of what we do when we interact with others. We have focused on only one aspect of power or power relations. We understand only
part of how we deal with one another. What we have focused on is domination and prohibition. Understandably, we have paid close attention to how
we are made to do some things and are prevented from doing others. What
we have missed is that everything anyone does affects what others may or
may not do in highly complex and interwoven ways. Worse still, we have
missed that having our behavioral options constrained in ways that are not
obviously coercive or preventive *changes* us.

Foucault's third question raises the possibility that talk about repression
of sexuality does not serve to introduce candor and counter repression.
Talk about repression may advance, extend, and consolidate the deployment of sexuality. Foucault's point is that learned discourse about the repression of sexuality is not liberating; it is the principal instrument used in
the deployment of a sexuality we have come to take as our very nature.

These questions make clear that the focus of *The History of Sexuality* is
not sexuality as such. To focus on sexuality would be to contribute to its
deployment. The focus must be on sexuality's emergence and descent. Foucault sets out "to account for the fact that [sex] is spoken about, to discover
who does the speaking." He says that the issue to address is "the way in
which sex is 'put into discourse.'"[25] Foucault is not concerned "to formulate the truth about sex" or to expose the "falsehoods designed to conceal
that truth."[26] His aim is to understand the will to knowledge that shapes
and supports what are taken as truths and falsehoods about sex. The aim is
to understand how learned discourse and disciplined inquiry produce a certain conception of sexuality that is presented and hailed as the discovery of
truth. This is a difficult idea for those who think that if there is a question
about sexuality, the correct procedure must be to look more carefully at
sexuality. It is hard to accept as an initial premise that sexuality is the product of discourse. As noted earlier, this premise will be seen as relativistic
and irrealist in nature, but it must be tentatively accepted if we are to proceed. The premise can be clarified and its force demonstrated only by working through *The History of Sexuality*.

The French title of *The History of Sexuality*, Volume 1, is "the will to
know." The phrase underscores the importance of the premise that sexuality is a product of discourse. The point is that sexuality is not discovered
but produced by the will to know. The irony in Foucault's title is that there
is no timeless, objective truth to be discerned and the discernment of which
constitutes knowledge. The will to know is an imperative to learn how
things are in themselves. It is a futile imperative to learn what cannot be
known.[27] The imperative can be satisfied only by disciplined inquiry and
learned discourse producing the knowledge they claim to acquire. The will
to know in effect is a drive to manufacture knowledge. As a result, experts

manufacture knowledge about sexuality and we—and they—appropriate it as knowledge about us.

Before turning to the text, it is crucial to keep in mind that power is impersonal. As noted, *The History of Sexuality* is not an exposé. Power is "nonsubjective."[28] The deployment of sexuality is the work of power, but it is not the work of a class or group or gender.[29] The change from a law-regime to a norm-regime was not part of a conspiracy. *The History of Sexuality* is a study of how impersonal power, not scheming individuals, deployed sexuality so successfully that it is taken as manifest truth by billions of people.

The History of Sexuality

Part One, "We 'Other Victorians,'" sets out the questions or "doubts" Foucault addresses. As listed above, these are whether sexuality actually was repressed, whether "the workings of power" are primarily repressive, and whether talk of repression was not itself an integral part of the deployment of sexuality.

The two chapters that make up Part Two, "The Incitement to Discourse" and "The Perverse Implantation," outline what Foucault calls "the repressive hypothesis." This is the view that sexuality has been repressed since Victorian times. Foucault does not simply deny the repressive hypothesis; he acknowledges the reality of selective suppression of sex.[30] Foucault admits that there was, roughly from the latter half of the seventeenth century onward, a new and increasingly extensive policing of sexual activity. There was an increase in censorship. What he tries to show is that the policing of sexuality was not primarily repressive. In particular he wants to show that along with tighter policing of sexual activity there was "a veritable discursive explosion" about sex.[31] Social, political, medical, and religious policing of sexual activity is shown not to be repression because "the opposite phenomenon occurred . . . There was a steady proliferation of discourses concerned with sex." Even more significant was "the multiplication of discourses concerning sex in the field of exercise of power itself."[32] Every aspect of the policing of sexual activity produced more learned discourse about sex, more studies, more surveys. These in turn tightened the control over sex by detailing and justifying more effective regulative procedures.

Foucault sees the institution of confession—whether to one's priest, doctor, or friend—as central to how discourse about sex grew and how individuals were made participants in their own control. Confession enhanced the objectification, quantification, and codification of sexuality. It required disclosure and specification of violations against sexual norms and codes and induced detailed examination of motivation. Disclosure and examination were justified as necessary for understanding one's sexual nature. That understanding was depicted as prerequisite to achieving mental health and normalcy. In this way, people were "drawn for three centuries to the task of telling everything concerning . . . sex." The inducement to tell all involved an "optimization and an increasing valorization of the discourse on sex." The effect of telling all was "displacement, intensification, reorientation, and modification of desire itself."[33] The process of disclosure, specification, and motivational investigation reshaped and redirected individuals' sexual desires. Individuals' perception of themselves as embodying the newly discerned (read "manufactured") sexuality changed what they could allow themselves to want—and eventually what they actually did want.

Foucault describes sexual behavior as coming under increasingly extensive control. However, what came under control was not previously uncontrolled or differently controlled sexual behavior. It was something new. Foucault argues that deployment of sexuality assimilated formerly diverse acts into a unitary kind of activity. Disciplinary techniques projected and objectified a sexuality that integrated diverse acts into a certain sort of behavior, and that behavior automatically came under their jurisdiction. People accepted the discursively manufactured sexuality as *their* sexuality, and as the cause of their desires and actions. In accepting sexuality they also accepted the norms that sexuality generated and so collaborated in their own control. One consequence was that the extent and level of control meant that sexual activity under the deployed sexuality no longer could be "something one simply judged." Sexuality became "a thing one administered."[34] Sexuality had to be *managed*. Control of sexuality ceased to be a matter of regulating what people actually did. Regulation involved inculcating attitudes, imbuing values, shaping desires, orienting inclinations, enabling sexual identities, and classifying all sorts of interests, appetites, and acts. Implementing this kind of control involved medical, educational, political, civil, and religious institutions. It was no longer possible for the family, the police, or the priesthood simply to forbid particular acts.

Prohibition ceased to suffice as control when sexuality was made a matter of truth and knowledge about a nature. Proscribing particular acts came to be insufficient when there was ongoing discernment of new complexities in motivation and behavior. By making sexuality a proper object of scientific study, discursive treatment made sexuality susceptible to theoretical development. The control of sexuality had to be continuously adjusted in light of new "discoveries" about its nature. Accepted standards could be overturned by new findings. Control could not be simple prohibition of statically conceived and defined actions. Control had to be administrative in the sense of being responsive application of a growing body of knowledge about sexuality.

Part Two of *The History of Sexuality* characterizes contemporary sexuality as a product manufactured and promulgated by learned discourse and disciplinary techniques. The parallel is to the account in *Discipline and*

Punish of the production of the modern soul. Foucault's principle aim is to show that something taken as natural, human sexuality, is actually an artifact. He wants to show that sexuality is at once a product of control and enables an unprecedented measure of control. Foucault's point is that deployed sexuality is the product of the imposition of a new kind of control on certain activities. He maintains that those activities previously were diverse and connected only by being pleasurable. These diverse activities came to be seen as issuing from a unitary nature—human sexuality—when they ceased to be controlled by prohibitions and started to be controlled by disciplinary techniques. In a sense, the control preceded what it controlled. The idea is that the unified conception of sexuality resulted from many different pleasurable actions being regulated as actions of a kind. Pleasurable actions were brought together as actions prompted by the needs and wants of a single nature. It then became necessary to regulate not only the actions but also the needs and wants, just as in the penal context it became necessary to regulate the modern soul. The key device in controlling the soul was surveillance; the key device in controlling desire was confession. Panopticism enabled self-regulation. Confession enabled the quest for normalcy.

Part Three of *The History* of *Sexuality* deals with how sexuality became the subject of scientific inquiry. Foucault's focus is how "sex was constituted as a problem of truth." Sexuality became "not only a matter of sensation and pleasure, of law and taboo, but also of truth and falsehood."[35] The title of the section, "Scientia Sexualis," is intended to indicate that our culture largely lacks an *ars erotica* or a tradition of artful treatment of sexuality. In our culture erotica is at best a dubious commodity, always in danger of sliding into pornography. Erotic art's aim is usually taken to be titillation rather than insight into sexual reality and possibility. Little credit is given to the idea that erotic art might enhance practical understanding of sexuality. In our culture sexuality is the proper subject matter of scientific investigation, not of artistic exploration. Artistic or clinical portrayal of the sexual should not be for its own sake, as in some books and films, but should serve investigative and educational ends.

One result of sexuality's becoming "a problem of truth" is that new power-relations developed that turned on greater or lesser knowledge about sexuality. Some became expert on sexuality. Sexual behavior came to be discussed and explained in terms not recognizable to most people, regardless of how sexually active and practically knowledgeable they might be. Inexpert individuals accepted half-understood theoretical accounts as accurate descriptions of their own most intimate needs and wants. Like penitentiary inmates who accepted experts' assessments of their proclivities, laypeople accepted that others knew more about their sexual desires than they did themselves. It was central to the process that experiences that once were merely gratifying were rethought as not gratifying in themselves. The gratification was seen as arising from satisfaction of various drives and other introspectively inaccessible determinants. Sexually active individuals came to feel a need for theoretical explanation to understand their own pleasure. The pleasure of sex became suspect because it might arise from displaced or masked abnormality.[36]

For Foucault, the most important consequence of sexuality becoming a problem of truth was that expertise about sexuality enabled establishment of "the normal" and "the abnormal." Suddenly individuals became vulnerable to classification based on conformity with or deviance from norms generated by a supposedly objective sexual nature. However, conformity with or deviance from norms is not just a matter of what individuals do or do not do. Classification as "normal" or "abnormal" is not mere cataloging of normal or abnormal actions. It is categorization of individuals as certain sorts of sexual beings.[37] This is why even faultless compliance with relevant prohibitions is insufficient for normality. Such compliance may only mask abnormal desire. The law regime's focus on acts changed to the sexuality regime's focus on nature.[38] Particular acts came to be manifestations of a normal or abnormal sexual nature. Regulation centered on *changing desires*. Perhaps nature could not be changed, but subjectivities could be reshaped enough to displace and inhibit abnormal desires.

Discipline and Punish shows how prisoners are regulated with implementation of theory-based techniques that control every aspect of their lives. The disciplinary techniques produce docile bodies. They also impose a new self-perception on the subjects or "souls" those bodies support. The effect of regulation and this imposition is to make inmates complicitous in their own surveillance. *The History of Sexuality* shows how members of a society are made to perceive themselves as having a certain sexual nature by application of theories that define that nature and determine normality and abnormality. Here too there is imposition of a new self-perception, and here too individuals are made complicitous in their own control. The self-surveillance gained in the case of sexuality is individuals' becoming vigilant regarding the normalcy of their desires. The other side of the coin is that some members of society are empowered by special knowledge to exercise control over sexuality to prevent and correct deviancy.[39]

Interestingly, Foucault points out that the consequences of deployment might have been less constraining had sexuality become the object of scientific study in the usual way. That is, learned discourse about sexuality might have remained arcane and had little impact on most people. But in the nineteenth century disciplinary interest in sexuality went beyond the study of biological and physiological topics. Standard scientific procedures and the boundaries they normally impose were repeatedly exceeded. There developed a "medicine of sex" supported only by a "distant and quite fictitious guarantee" of scientific legitimacy.[40] The line dividing science and the "medicine of sex" was blurred. The literature of the time shows how otherwise scientifically meticulous biologists and physiologists issued highly problematic tendentious and sexist pronouncements on sex, gender, and sexual traits. Feminists have written a good deal on how science, particularly medical science, is bent to generate, maintain, and enhance sexual stereotypes.[41]

Foucault again displays his ability to rethink the familiar in connection with development of the "medicine of sex." He claims that, properly understood, Freud's work threatened rather than expedited the deployment of sexuality. Freud's psychoanalytic work "rediscovered the law of alliance, the involved workings of marriage and kinship."[42] This meant that Freud offered the "guarantee that one would find the parents-children relationship at the root of everyone's sexuality." Freud's rediscovery "made it possible . . . to keep the deployment of sexuality coupled to the system of alliance." That would have forced recognition that sexuality was "constituted only through the law" and was not an objective nature.[43] The deployment of sexuality would have been seen for what it was: imposition of a sexual nature by learned discourse. Despite his ambivalence about Freud's work, Foucault contends that Freud threatened the conception of sexuality as defined by heterosexual procreative intercourse and the reconception of other sexual activities as perversions of that paradigm. Freud showed sexuality to be diffuse. He showed sexual actions to have discernible causes. And he showed the regulation of sexual behavior to be about what society is willing to tolerate.

The developments Foucault describes in Part 3 of *The History of Sexuality* brought together previously separate interests in human beings as a species and in the workings of the human body.[44] Prior to these developments, human nature was thought problematic only in a holistic way with regard to whether it was God-created or had evolved. In *The History of Sexuality, Madness and Civilization,* and *The Birth of the Clinic* Foucault describes how human nature became an object of detailed scientific study that enabled and supported regulative disciplinary techniques. These techniques were first employed in institutional contexts like the prison and asylum. In these contexts the techniques were used to manage well-defined group of individuals excluded from society for socially unacceptable traits and behavior. The deployment of sexuality extended disciplinary control globally. Theory-based disciplinary techniques were expanded to cover everyone. The suppositions that enabled and justified the expansion were that sexuality is an essential part of human nature and that it requires regulation to function properly as part of human nature.

An Interim Recapitulation

A certain amount of repetition is required to provide the clearest exposition of Foucault's views. It is useful here to reiterate major points in slightly different terms.

Foucault maintains that beginning in the seventeenth century human beings came under scientific scrutiny in a new way. They came to be scrutinized as possessing a nature that determined their needs and desires and
conditioned their behavior. The most central part of that nature was
thought to be sexual. Recall the remarks quoted above: Foucault claims
that our culture tells us: "To know who you are, know what your sexuality
is about."[45] Hekman says, "the essence of . . . the subject is to be found in
sexuality."[46] The new scrutiny aimed to discern whether individuals properly conformed to their nature. Individuals were measured against theoretical standards to see whether they were "normal" or "abnormal." In practice the new scrutiny focused almost entirely on conformity to sexual
nature. Previously people had been scrutinized juridically, politically, and
socially. They had been scrutinized to see if they obeyed or broke the law,
observed or violated secular and ecclesiastical prohibitions, kept or broke
marital and other contracts, paid or failed to pay their taxes, were good or
bad neighbors, and so on. When individuals came to be scrutinized to assess their normalcy, they came to be governed less by laws and prohibitions
than by norms. Much of human behavior was reconceived. It stopped being the diverse actions of individuals and became the proper or perverted
expression of natural drives and needs. Learned discourse about human
nature and its manifestations produced disciplinary techniques that integrated previously distinct juridical, political, civil, and social regulatory
practices. Piecemeal prescription and proscription of particular acts
melded and morphed into far-reaching regulatory techniques that managed
natural inclinations.

Discipline and Punish details how monarchical repressive measures were
displaced by consolidated regulatory techniques. Lawbreakers came to be
considered—and to consider themselves—as inclined to behave abnormally
and therefore in need of constraint. *The History of Sexuality* tells how men
and women came to be seen—and to see themselves—as having natural
traits that carry the potential for perverted expression and therefore are in
need of control. Implementation of penality's disciplinary techniques made
inmates participants in their own regulation. The deployment of sexuality
also transferred the main burden of regulation to the individual. It did so
by making individuals *want to be normal*. Getting inmates to watch themselves is efficient penality. However, penal disciplinary techniques are always grounded on the threat of force, isolation, and punishment. Compliance must be coerced until imbued habits alter subjectivity. The deployment
of sexuality is far more efficient. It makes people want to attain and maintain sexual normalcy by acting in specified ways and not acting in ways
judged aberrant.

What Foucault means by saying power must be masked becomes clear
when we appreciate how people come to participate in their own sexual

regulation. Individuals whose sexual behavior and desires are regulated must believe that it is something about *them* that requires control. People must believe that their own nature calls for regulation. This happens when learned discourse promulgates a picture of sexual nature as prone to aberrant expression. Control then appears necessary to achieve normalcy rather than arising from a particular historical conglomeration of theories, practices, and vested interests. One of the most important devices in the deployment of sexuality is institutionalized confession. In confession individuals objectify their desires, pleasures, and fears. Once objectified, desires, pleasures, and fears are amenable to theoretical analysis and assessment and to being reshaped by implementation of disciplinary techniques. Confession also establishes specific subject-defining power relations. The confessing individual enters into a relationship with one or more other individuals with authority deriving from special expertise. Confession "unfolds within a power relationship, for one does not confess without . . . a partner who is not simply the interlocutor but the authority who requires the confession."[47] Regulation of sexual behavior proceeds, not as imposed control as in the deployment of alliances, but as cooperative efforts to prevent and curtail deviancy.

The Mechanics of the Will to Power

Foucault lists five devices used to produce self-regulating subjects who "fin[d] their 'truth' in their sexuality."[48] The devices are the "clinical codification of the inducement to speak," the "postulate of a general and diffuse causality," the "principle of a latency intrinsic to sexuality," the "method of interpretation," and the "medicalization of the effects of confession."[49]

The first device, clinical codification of the inducement to speak, is the integration of confession into diagnostic examination. This accomplishes two things. It enhances individuals' participation in their own regulation. It also orders and classifies what individuals confess. Admission of a desire becomes evidence of suppressed aberration; disclosure of a forbidden act establishes deviancy. Everything from general questionnaires to focused one-on-one questioning contributes to eroding the difference between third-party records of individuals' conditions and individuals' own perceptions. People's most intimate thoughts are made relevant to medical and psychological records. Subjects are persuaded that total disclosure is necessary to achieve normality and to value that goal more than their individuality. Everything told by an individual is assimilated into a record: his or her "file." That record then acquires a greater authority about the individual's states of mind than any introspective conviction she or he may have.

Much of the force behind the inducement to speak derives from the second device, postulation of a diffuse causality. This is the view that sexuality can be the cause of almost any affliction. For instance, even blindness or crippling pain may be diagnosed as due to hysteria. Categorization of hysteria as a sexual disorder means there are no antecedent criteria to determine what maladies are related or unrelated to sexual problems. A notorious and deplorably common case in point is persistent diagnosis of various women's complaints as due to the psychological effects of menopause. Perception of sex as the possible cause of almost any sort of distress reinforces the view that the most intimate and private desire or act may be relevant to diagnosis. Confessors tell all and answer any question put to them, persuaded that candor facilitates effective diagnosis and normalizing treatment.

The third device, the principle of a latency "essential to sexuality," further augments the inducement to speak.[50] Simply put, the intrinsic or essential latency is similar to the diffuse causality of the sexual. It is the idea that the causes of aberrant sexual behavior are very diverse and deeply buried.[51] Therefore, the most apparently trivial or irrelevant thing may be a clue to those causes. The principle makes virtually anything an individual says potentially crucial to diagnosis and therapeutic regulation. The individual being diagnosed again is compelled to tell everything and the diagnostician must consider every utterance as possibly significant. As a consequence, a huge amount of data is produced that admits of varying interpretations that can satisfy practically any theoretical expectations. However, this interpretive excess is not seen as a problem with the principle being applied. It is seen as evidence of the elusiveness of sexual motivation and as corroborating the special latency principle.

The method of interpretation, the fourth device, has to do with how confessions are used. The key point is that what a given individual confesses is not limited to his or her particular diagnosis. The material is interpreted as fitting one or another theoretical category because of conforming to one or another pattern of behavior. Confessions thus serve to authenticate the deployed sexuality by demonstrating anew that human beings have a common sexual nature. The appearance is that confessional revelations collectively reveal the nature of sexuality and the range of sexual motivation. What actually goes on is that confessional revelations are interpreted in ways that confirm the theories that are applied in eliciting those revelations.

The fifth device, the medicalization of the effects of confession, is related to the fourth. It has to do with reconceiving the purpose of confession as primarily comparative and only secondarily cathartic. Confession no longer serves as healing admission of wrongful thought or action. Rather than being purgative in the traditional way, confession becomes comparative. Confessions provide intimately detailed portraits of the confessing individuals that may be compared to the accepted norm: the model heterosexual individual concerned first with procreation and only then with gratification.

The detailed portraits produced by individuals' confessions are also used to produce composite "profiles" of varying types of deviants. These comparative uses mean that what is said in confession no longer is strictly confidential. At one time those confessing were protected by the moral accountability of those who heard their confessions. After the deployment of sexuality, the restrictions on the use of confessional revelations ceased to be moral and became professional. Revelations may be used in various ways deemed beneficial to the person being diagnosed and treated and to others in similar situations. This requires that those revelations be accessible to all professionals involved in diagnoses or treatment. The only protection afforded to those who confess is anonymity outside the immediate context of diagnosis and treatment.

Foucault sees the cumulative effect of the five devices as making sexuality something that needs to be dealt with scientifically. Other cultures cast sexuality as a multifarious aspect of life that defies comprehensive understanding and is best dealt with artistically. Our culture made sexuality an object of intense and extensive disciplinary research and study. Our culture imposed on itself and pursues the task of "producing true discourses" about sexuality. According to Foucault, what emerged "in the nineteenth century" was not the "refusal of recognition" of sex, as is commonly thought. Instead what emerged was extensive "machinery for producing true discourses concerning [sex]."[52] Those discourses determined what we think it is to be sexed creatures.

A problem posed by Foucault's five devices is that they look to many like parts of a deliberate deception. This raises anew the problem about *The History of Sexuality* being read as a liberating exposé. This is a reading Foucault is anxious to defeat for two different reasons. First, he is not exposing five manipulative or conspiratorial devices. He describes the devices to show how power relations operate in the deployment of sexuality. As we have seen, power is blind and "nonsubjective." The devices function impersonally and without direction.[53] Describing them is not showing how some group or class conspired to make sex an object of scientific study. The deployment of sexuality was the work of power, not a conspiracy. Second, Foucault rejects the idea that "truth is intrinsically opposed to power and therefore inevitably plays a liberating role."[54] Description of the five devices may be enlightening, but it is not liberating. Foucault denies the traditional conception of truth as objective and its discernment as the means to liberation from ideological distortions and deception. Power admits only the possibility of change from one set of subjectivity-shaping practices to another, not liberation. There is no discourse-independent truth that will make us free.[55]

In Part Four of *The History of Sexuality*, "The Deployment of Sexuality," we find Foucault's most focused discussion of power. He provides a detailed account of how power relations enable and produce truth and knowledge in describing the manufacture of a norm-generating conception of sexuality. However, two things must be kept in mind as we proceed. The first is that Foucault is primarily interested in how power produces subjects. This may be obscured by the emphasis on the production of truth and knowledge in *The History of Sexuality*. Similarly, the emphasis on disciplinary techniques and regulation in *Discipline and Punish* may obscure that the book's main concern is the production of subjects. Foucault is quite clear on the point: "It is not power, but the subject, which is the general theme of my research."[56]

The second thing to remember is that Foucault does not offer a theory of power in Part Four or anywhere else. If one "tries to erect a theory of power one will always be obligated to . . . reconstruct its genesis."[57] That would be to search for essences. It would be to seek power's Capital-O Origins and thereby to make power into a force or set of objective determinants. To offer a theory of power would be to cease being nominalistic about power,[58] which is why "Foucault's account of power is not intended as a theory."[59] What Foucault offers is a certain kind of depiction—renderings or mappings—that he calls "analytics" of power relations.[60] Power "is in reality an open, more-or-less coordinated . . . cluster of relations." We do not need a theory to understand power, even if one were possible; we need "a grid of analysis which makes possible an analytic of relations of power."[61] That is, we need a method to map the complex, dynamic web of interactions among human agents. Genealogy is the method, and the "analytics" produced are depictions or mappings of moments in the always-fluid disposition of power relations. An "analytic" of power relations is wholly historical. It can be neither theoretical nor "a context-free, ahistorical, objective description."[62]

The first chapter of Part Four, "Objective," describes both what Foucault intends to establish in the first volume of *The History of Sexuality* and the thrust of the six projected volumes.[63] The aim is to trace and investigate the production of our sexual subjectivity. The discussion of power is not conducted for its own sake. As in *Discipline and Punish*, power is discussed in Part Four of *The History of Sexuality* to illuminate the mechanics of subject formation.

To contrast it with his own, Foucault calls the traditional conception of power, that is, as coercive and prohibitive, the "juridico-discursive" conception.[64] The traditional conception of power as proscriptive is exemplified in the state's promulgation and enforcement of laws. The point of the contrast is that unlike Foucauldian power, juridico-discursive power is not enabling. Even when it is productive, in the limited sense of forcing something to be done, it functions by forbidding the lack of compliance with promulgated prescriptive rules and laws. That is, juridico-discursive power does not enhance possible actions; it coerces specific ones.

Foucault attributes four defining characteristics to juridico-discursive power. First is its prohibitive character. With respect to "sex and pleasure," juridico-discursive power "can 'do' nothing but say no to them."[65] Interdictions, exclusions, refusals, and taboos exhaust juridico-discursive power over sexuality. What is not prohibited is ignored or tolerated by default rather than being explicitly condoned. It is Foucault's contention that in the premodern era sexual behavior was not unified as a kind in the realm of law. It was not an object of coercive and prohibitive regulation as a whole. Sexual behavior was defined piecemeal by proscriptive description in the prohibiting of specific acts. This is clear in the second and closely related characteristic, the "insistence of the rule." The second characteristic is conception of juridico-discursive power as regulatory in nature and as operating by classifying particular acts as illicit. The sundry prohibited acts are not grouped as aberrant expressions of a unified nature, as in the deployment of sexuality. What juridico-discursive power prohibits is specific things people might do. Therefore, juridico-discursive power cannot regulate unspecified acts that are judged manifestations of aberrance when done.

The third characteristic of juridico-discursive power is the "logic of censorship." What Foucault has in mind is the complement to the prohibition of certain sexual acts and material that might provoke those acts. The complement is denial of their existence. Foucault observes that "the logic of power exerted on sex is the paradoxical . . . injunction of nonexistence, nonmanifestation, and silence."[66] It is not enough to prohibit certain acts and anything that might elicit them. Their existence must be denied. When these unthinkable acts are done and cannot be denied in the particular instance, previous denial makes the acts appear more monstrous. This in turn makes punishment, prevention, and continued denial more compelling. Part of the point here is that the most effective prohibition of an act is preclusion of its possibility.

Preclusion of possibility is what the fourth characteristic of juridico-discursive power is all about. "Uniformity of the apparatus" has to do with censorship and prohibition of specific sexual acts cutting across class and other social distinctions. At least in theory, no one is exempt from preventative and proscriptive regulation of sexual behavior. Prohibition and censorial denial must be universal. Otherwise they serve not to prevent but to incite commission. The reality is that privileged position confers some impunity regarding access to censored material and even to commission of forbidden acts.

Juridico-discursive power's four characteristics are "centered on nothing more than the statement of the law and the operation of taboos."[67] Chapter 1 of Part Four makes the same point made in *Discipline and Punish*: the dominant conception of power is as constraining force best exemplified in prohibitive law. Juridico-discursive power is thou-shalt-not coercion backed up by incarceration, punishment, or execution. Juridico-discursive power's proscriptive nature means that unlike Foucauldian power, it allows for liberation. Liberation can be achieved through damaging exposure of prohibitive laws' false or inadequate grounding, illegitimate procedures, or unwarranted application.[68] Against this, it is fundamental to Foucault's conception of power that while we may be liberated from particular instances of domination, we can only escape from one set of power relations to another set of power relations. The only alternatives to immersion in power relations are total enslavement, where our will becomes another's will, or death.

In the second chapter of Part Four, "Method," we find the most positive and extended description of Foucauldian power given in *The History* of *Sexuality*. In particular, we find the definitional passage I quote from in Chapter 4's section on power.[69] Given what was said in that section, it suffices here to reiterate the central point about the relational nature of power. In an interview Foucault stresses that he "hardly ever" speaks of power. He claims that when he speaks of power "it is always a short cut," a gloss on power relations or relationships of power.[70] His aim is to underscore that power is wholly relational, that power is nothing over and above the "multiplicity of force relations." Force relations are the interactive juxtapositions of agents' actions to one another. They are not anything imposed from without. Force relations are "immanent in the sphere in which they operate and . . . constitute their own organization."[71] Force relations are interrelated past and present actions or "comportments" that facilitate or inhibit ensuing actions or comportments. "[T]he process which . . . transforms, strengthens, or reverses" force relations is not anything external. As the magnet analogy used in Chapter 4 illustrates, what changes or cancels force relations is nothing outside them; it is alterations in the very actions that are their component elements. The past and present actions of two individuals in an interactive situation, together with the past and present actions of others, constitute a force relation between those two individuals. A new action by either individual or by others changes that force relation. This is how force relations are identical with "the strategies in which they take effect." The multiplicity of force relations is not a structure imposed on the actions of agents; it is the interactive totality of those actions. Nor are force relations independent of one another or related only in a mutually exclusive way. Some force relations sustain or enhance others. Power is also "the support which these force relations find in one another."[72]

Chapter 3 of Part Four is titled "Domain" and focuses on four elements that Foucault describes as pivotal to the deployment of sexuality. The first is the "hysterization of women's bodies," or conception of women as "saturated with sexuality" and prone to a multitude of related infirmities. The second is the "pedagogization of children's sex," or conception of children as embryonic sexual beings requiring strict control to prevent the development of abnormality. The third is the "socialization of procreative behavior," or the setting up of the heterosexual couple as the fundamental societal unit. The fourth is the "psychiatrization of perverse pleasure," or categorization of abnormal sexual behavior.[73] These elements amount to "the very production of sexuality."[74] They contribute constitutively to the establishment of what then is perceived and disseminated as a definitive aspect of being human. Chapter 3 of Part Four also contains the gist of the socio-historical thesis of *The History of Sexuality*. That is the claim that these elements were produced by discourses initiated in the late seventeenth century. This is where we find explicit statement of the constructivist claim that contemporary sexuality is a product of learned discourse. The claim is articulated in negative terms as denial that there was repression of sexuality. It is articulated in positive terms as description of how the illusion of repression masked the development of the discourses that deployed our present sexuality.

Chapter 4 of Part Four, "Periodization," describes the historical progression of the development of late and post-seventeenth-century sexuality. It emphasizes the role of social classes in that development. In this chapter Foucault argues against mainstream Marxism, contrary to the French ideological climate at the time *The History of Sexuality* was written. He maintains that the deployment of sexuality was primarily "self-affirmation" by the bourgeoisie rather than repression and exploitation of the working class.[75] Marxists see bourgeois sexual values and practices as designed to restrict sex to labor-serving procreation and to diminish its counterproductive effects. Foucault contends that the deployment of sexuality served to institutionalize the bourgeoisie's status rather than to manipulate the working class. The deployment of sexuality provided the bourgeoisie "with a body to be cared for," a body defined and catered to by "a technology of sex."[76]

Part Five of *The History of Sexuality* echoes the message of *Discipline and Punish*. It stresses that the deployment of sexuality reflected a crucial change in how people are managed and their behavior regulated. The change was from "dealing simply with legal subjects over whom the ultimate dominion was death" to a "taking charge of life." Government of people, in Foucault's broad sense, changed from prohibiting specific acts to subject-shaping management of action.[77] The development of modern penality and sexuality turned on a shift from managing populations with proscriptive rules to managing populations by inculcating values and perspectives. Rather than trying to stop people from doing unacceptable things, modern disciplinary techniques make them into subjects who have "normal" desires and aversions and so regulate themselves.

Favored Perspective or Correct Account?

At the end of *The History of Sexuality* we are left with three main issues. The first is about the correctness of Foucault's historical claim that sexuality mushroomed into a topic of discussion and study instead of being repressed. The second is about the devices described in the deployment of sexuality and whether they must be understood as the workings of "power," that is, as working blindly and impersonally. The third issue is about how to understand and assess Foucault's claim that truth, knowledge, rationality, and subjectivity are historical. All three issues are important, difficult, and intriguing, but the claim that truth is historical, a product of power, is the most philosophically fundamental and demands the most immediate attention. However, before turning to Foucault's conception of truth in the next chapter, a little must be said about how one might approach the other issues. It also must be made clear that *The History of Sexuality* raises a question about its own cogency as a didactic text.

Foucault's contention about the repressive hypothesis is well supported in his own work and elsewhere. Sex and talk about sex were certainly suppressed in social contexts from the Victorian era until as late as the permissive 1960s, but there was great proliferation of learned discussion of sex. Whatever its source, the social suppression of sex and talk about sex was supported and extended by learned pronouncements about deleterious effects on children, incitement to prohibited sexual behavior, and the like. Foucault's contention is highly plausible, but in being so it poses a philosophical question. The question is what we are to make of the likely *correctness* of a genealogical account. This is the question about cogency and about the consistency of Foucault's historicism. If Foucault's historical claim is persuasive we have two options open regarding its cogency. We can consider it persuasive because it is true. Or we can consider it persuasive because it is an account we find compelling due to our present power-determined circumstances.

The same question arises about Foucault's contention that knowledge is historical. To see this we have to restate the contention in minimal form. When Foucault speaks of knowledge or "knowledges" he means disciplinary knowledge and the lores of other eras. On this minimal interpretation it is not very mysterious how knowledge is historical. To clarify we have to recall the main premise of archaeology. Archaeology is critical investigation of disciplinary systems and the discursive practices that produce those systems. However, archaeological investigation is conducted without asking whether what its targets "say is true, or even . . . make[s] sense." Archaeology "must remain neutral as to the truth."[78] Once we put truth aside, we see how "knowledges" are historical. Consider an example: At one time part of our knowledge about the physical universe was that orbital motion is perfectly circular and that planets remain in orbit because there is no reason for them to deviate from their paths. Later, part of our knowledge about the physical universe came to be that planetary motion is elliptical and that planets remain in orbit because of gravity and velocity. We can see how knowledge is historical if we refrain from judging that Tycho Brahe's "knowledge" was false belief and that Johannes Kepler's "knowledge" was real knowledge because true. In short, in one historical era what Brahe believed was taken as knowledge. In another historical era what Kepler believed was taken as knowledge. We believe that what Kepler believed *is* knowledge because it is true. But Foucault claims that no knowledge is ahistorically true, that all knowledge is historical. He does not want us to merely suspend judgments about truth; he wants us to abandon those judgments as misconceived. The question is whether he is proposing adoption of a perspective or making an illegitimate truth-claim about knowledge.

Foucault's contention about the historicity of rationality also raises the same question. Here again we have to pare things down to clarify. "Rationality" is a vague term and Foucault tends to use it rather loosely. We can restate his contention as follows. Whatever else he may be saying, Foucault minimally is saying that *means-to-ends* rationality is temporally and culturally contextual. He maintains that every society has "procedures accorded value in the acquisition of truth."[79] These procedures are paradigmatic of what is deemed rational, and it is precisely enthronement of these procedures as privileged that is challenged by Foucauldian genealogical redescription. To say rationality is historical is at least to say that the criteria for what count as rational procedures vary from era to era. For instance, at one time invoking Aristotle's authority was a valid and effective argumentative move—a rational move—in philosophical or scientific debate. At another time invoking Aristotle's or anyone else's authority became an argumentative fallacy.[80] The point here is that at least part of what Foucault means by "rationality" is "sanctioned thought-processes." These are what are taught in critical-thinking courses: how to determine relevance, how to formulate premises, how to arrange them into valid arguments, how to avoid fallacies. Foucault's point is that a sanctioned process may be changed or abandoned. Even fundamental elements like, say, the law of excluded middle might be altered or discarded.[81] We can understand Foucault's contention about the historical nature of rationality as being that criteria for acceptable means-to-ends thinking vary from era to era depending on operant presuppositions.[82] Here we are brought back to the same question as above: Are we to take this as a proposed construal that best fits power relations' present distribution, or is it an illegitimate truth-claim?

Foucault's contention about the historical nature of the subject is more difficult. Others have challenged the entrenched Cartesian conception of subjectivity as what Hekman calls "the constituting subject" or the unitary self that is the source of all meaning.[83] Hume, Nietzsche, Freud, and Mead provided seminal critiques. More recently, Daniel Dennett, Davidson, Derek Parfit, and Ricoeur have contributed to the debate.[84] However, as mentioned earlier, Foucault is not advancing an ontological thesis about the self. He is not concerned to replace the substantive Cartesian ego with an ephemeral subject woven from language. What he is concerned to do is to show that the subject is fluid and shaped by how it acts, how it is acted on and treated, how it speaks, how it is spoken to, and how it sees itself. Once more, though, the question arises as to whether what Foucault says about the historicity of the subject is offered as a proposal about subjectivity that accords with contemporary power relations or as an ahistorical claim about the nature of subjectivity.

Certainly Foucault often *sounds* as if he is making truth-claims. He appears to make ahistorical or objective truth-claims about the workings of power while making truth a function of power. Readers of Foucault who unreflectively take philosophical inquiry as truth-establishing polemics[85] assume that he writes to establish his views as correct. They see nothing odd about his apparently ahistoricist claims. What puzzles them is why he should claim that truth is a product of power. After all, what could be the point of polemics if it is not discernment and establishment of objective truth? How could intellectual inquiry be historical without losing its import and any possibility of claiming cogency for arguments? These readers then conclude that Foucault simply is inconsistent. But this is too quick. What is missed is that the alternative, that Foucault's claims are historicist, is not as vapid as it appears to those who value inquiry only as a means to discerning ahistorical truth. If we are wholly immersed in power, and our subjectivity is shaped by power, persuasive historicist accounts have all the force and cogency of putative ahistorical ones. This realization brings us to a most important and usually overlooked aspect of Foucault's thought, namely, what Foucault thinks it is to be a productive intellectual. This is not just a personal or biographical point. Foucault's conception of intellectual productivity is central to his position.

Foucault provides genealogies of the assumptions and methods of established disciplinary systems. He wants to show how the elements of such systems, like the notion of objective biological sex, develop and come to constitute knowledge. In "Two Lectures" Foucault maintains that genealogies are "anti-sciences." However, in being so they do not merely "vindicate a lyrical right to ignorance." What they do is oppose "the institution and functioning of an organized scientific discourse within a society."[86] It is always "against the power of a discourse that is considered to be scientific that . . . genealogy must wage its struggle."[87] Genealogy is always oppositional and cannot aspire to being the new orthodoxy. It functions by constant problematization of established discourses. In an interview given not long before his death, Foucault reiterates the point, saying that what is "common to the work I've done since *Madness and Civilization* is the notion of problematization."[88] Why problematize? Why must genealogy struggle against dominant discourses?[89]

The answer is that power makes genealogical opposition *necessary*. Foucauldian power's internal development is predisposed toward ever greater and more pervasive control. Power undergoes a kind of entropy. What is lost is not energy but difference. The disciplinary techniques of penality undergo refinement; the science of sex grows increasingly authoritative. Both continuously expand their ranges of application. New forms of delinquency are defined; new categories of deviance are discerned.[90] The result is that "normal" behavior grows increasingly specific and constrained. The actions or "comportments" open to individuals grow increasingly limited. But power cannot be escaped. The only way to resist total determination of subjectivity is perennial struggle against the progressively more restrictive control of maturing disciplinary techniques. That is why the intellectual's mandate is "[t]o change something in the minds of people." Foucault asks what intellectual activity can consist in "if not in the endeavor to know how and to what extent it might be possible to think differently."[91] The intellectual, the genealogist, is pitted against power's inclination to become more and more restrictive. Genealogy's struggle is necessary to prevent established disciplines from gaining total hegemony over subjectivity and eventually obliterating differences among subjects.

It is a fair question why Foucault thinks change is intrinsically desirable. He sometimes seems bent on change for its own sake, particularly as he is portrayed in Miller's biography.[92] A partial answer to Foucault's fascination with change will emerge when we consider "limit experiences" in Chapter 6. The basic reason, though, is that novelty of thought is the only effective resistance to power, and without resistance subjectivity would grow increasingly inhibited. Our behavioral options would narrow and we would become too much like one another.[93] Genealogy affords the opportunity for novel thought by striving always to "emancipate historical knowledges from . . . subjection, to render them . . . capable of opposition" to dominant discourses. This emancipation is not for the sake of those lores or knowledges themselves. The point is to pit those lores or knowledges "against the coercion of a theoretical, unitary, formal and scientific discourse."[94] Genealogical accounts challenge the established discourses and histories by providing alternatives to them and thereby problematizing those discourses and histories. However, recall that resistance through problematization "doesn't mean the representation of a pre-existent object, nor the creation through discourse of an object that doesn't exist." Problematization is the development of a discourse that "makes something enter into the play of the true and false, and constitutes it as an object of thought."[95] In a word, problematization introduces new factors into disciplinary equations.

Alternity is all that intellectuals have to oppose the growing rigidity of dominant systems of knowledge and their attendant subject-shaping disciplinary techniques. Alternity cannot liberate us from power, but it does two things: it enables actions not otherwise open to us,[96] and it forces reflection on what we take for granted about our world and ourselves. Dominant discourses grow increasingly restrictive, not "because power [is] omniscient, but because it [is] blind."[97] Power "nonsubjectively" establishes truths and knowledges. Madness was unwittingly invented by being wittingly treated as a determinate ailment in the asylum. Delinquency was manufactured in being made the object of surveillance-based disciplinary penality. Diverse sexual activities were collected and codified into a "natural" norm-generating sexuality by the exercise of control. The genealogical objective, then, is to problematize accepted knowledge and truth in order to enrich, enhance, embellish, amplify, augment, and empower by providing alternity. Foucault asks, "what is philosophy today . . . if it is not the critical work that thought brings to bear on itself?"[98] Genealogy's task is to "separate out, from the contingency that has made us what we are, the possibility of no longer being . . . what we are."[99]

Where does this leave us with respect to Foucault's historicism? Many will remain unconvinced and take Foucault to be either inconsistent or disingenuous because they take him to be making truth-claims. Foucault himself claims that if his books are to be of value they must assert what is true.[100] He unquestionably wants them to be taken seriously and what they present as cogent. On the other hand, there is no question that Foucault claims truth is a product of power and is "produced . . . by virtue of multiple forms of constraint."[101] Every society has "its regime of truth." Every society has discourses that "it accepts and makes function as true." Every society has "mechanisms and instances which enable one to distinguish true and false statements." Every society has "techniques and procedures accorded value in the acquisition of truth." And every society has its experts "who are charged with saying what counts as true."[102] We are "subjected to the production of truth through power."[103] There is no room here for correct accounts of anything. Yet *The History of Sexuality* says that sexuality is manufactured and not fundamental to our nature. Is this, in the end, merely another construal of sex?

From a traditional perspective, the contention that truth is produced is a fundamental claim and should take priority over every other philosophical issue, since it affects the standards and procedures that guide philosophizing in particular and intellectual inquiry in general. Thus one would expect Foucault to take great pains to clarify his position on the sense in which he takes his claims about the deployment of sexuality to be true and how his books state what is true. But Foucault does not give the question of truth priority (at least in the sense of providing a sustained treatment of it). The relative neglect of truth relates to Foucault's fundamental conception of subjectivity as not preexistent. Subjects are wholly historical; discourses and practices constitute them. For Foucault "the individual is not a pre-given entity." The individual "is the product of a relation of power exercised over bodies, multiplicities, movements, desires, forces."[104] The subject "is not to be conceived as a sort of elementary nucleus . . . on which power comes to fasten or against which it happens to strike." Instead, it is "one of the prime effects of power that certain bodies, certain gestures, certain discourses, certain desires, come to be identified and constituted as individuals."[105] The consequence is that truth cannot be anything but historical and perspectival for Foucauldian subjects. There can be no difference between what is true and what passes for true.[106] Even if Foucault allowed the conceivability of objective truth, it could be nothing to us; it could play no role in cognition. As suggested above, historical truth has all the force of putative ahistorical truth if it is the only truth we can attain. However, this is unsatisfactory as it stands. We must turn now to a more detailed consideration of Foucault's conception of truth.

Notes

1. Six volumes were projected. Three were published and apparently a fourth exists in manuscript or note form.

2. Foucault 1980a:152.

3. Foucault 1980a:152.

4. In my classes I have used the example of a book Foucault might have written: *The History of Eating*. Our practice of sharing meals might have been precluded by a deployed human nature that required that food be ingested in private, as now is the case with evacuative bodily functions.

5. Foucault usually describes these as "pleasurable" activities. He distinguishes between things people do that involve certain sort of satisfactions, and those same things as integral parts of behavior that manifests a natural aspect of being human.

6. It is also a somewhat suspect point and I will allude to it again. Foucault's insistence that gratifying acts are deemed sexual only because of the deployment of sexuality often looks self-serving. Below I mention his reference to homosexual sodomy. It is difficult to see how that act might have been deemed gratifying but not sexual prior to the deployment of sexuality. Foucault's attempt to portray the fondling of a child as innocent (pages 31 and 32 of *The History of Sexuality*) is another case in point. See below.

7. Foucault 1980a:95.

8. Foucault 1988b:265.

9. Some do maintain that criminality manifests something natural. However, aside from certain religious doctrines about our "fallen" nature, not many claim

that criminality is an inherent part of being human. That is exactly what is claimed about sexuality.

10. Effective disciplinary techniques insure that if individuals do reflect on their subjectivity, they only do so to discover something about their given nature, not to understand how they were produced as subjects.

11. Foucault 1989:138.

12. Hekman 1990:70.

13. However, there is no necessity in this. Some possible deployment might have made our status as, say, children of God the defining aspect of human nature.

14. Foucault's use of "deployment" is not quite the normal one in which the sense is "arrangement" or "positioning," as when we say that military commanders deploy their troops. Foucault's use has a prescriptive element; it carries more than a hint of enforcement. This is particularly so with respect to the deployment of alliances.

15. Foucault 1980a:43.

16. Foucault 1980a:3.

17. Foucault 1980a:4.

18. Note that many sensually satisfying acts need not involve intercourse or even genital contact.

19. See note 6, above.

20. Foucault 1980a:31–32.

21. Foucault 1989:212–31; Miller 1993.

22. Foucault 1980a:11.

23. Foucault 1980a:10.

24. This tactic is often confused with Derridean deconstruction.

25. Foucault 1980a:11.

26. Foucault 1980a:12. That would be to accept objective sexuality and to try to show how it has been distorted.

27. Foucault usually is read to mean that it is a futile imperative to learn what is not there to be known, but see Chapter 7.

28. Foucault 1980a:94.

29. Some feminists who identify power and patriarchy contest this point.

30. Foucault 1980a:17–18.

31. Foucault 1980a:17.

32. Foucault 1980a:18. Notice that here "power" does not mean Foucauldian power but the control exercised by institutions.

33. Foucault 1980a:23.

34. Foucault 1980a:24.

35. Foucault 1980a:56.

36. The most notorious instance of this is the idea that heterosexual pleasure hides or displaces homosexual desires.

37. Recall the remark about the sodomite becoming "a species."

38. A contemporary case in point is pedophilia. Pedophiles are publicly identified and often are detained in various ways after completing their sentences on preventive grounds.

39. Foucault's admiration for California's permissive subculture reveals indignation with the presumption to identify and control deviancy. This emerges clearly in

Miller's biography. Miller 1993. Its relevance here is that though we must separate Foucault's sexual orientation from his analysis of sexuality, we must acknowledge the feminist argument that it is the marginalized who see most clearly what is amiss in a given social order.

40. Foucault 1980a:55.

41. E.g., Ehrenreich and English 1973.

42. Foucault 1980a:113.

43. Foucault 1980a:113.

44. Dreyfus and Rabinow 1983:134–35.

45. Foucault 1989:138.

46. Hekman 1990:70.

47. Foucault 1980a:61.

48. Hekman 1990:70.

49. Foucault 1980a:65–67.

50. Foucault 1980a:66.

51. The causes of normal behavior supposedly are just as deep, but the focus is always on the abnormal.

52. Foucault 1980a:67–69.

53. Their lack of direction is difficult for some to grasp. What is missed is that direction is attributed retrospectively in light of effects.

54. Dreyfus and Rabinow 1983:127.

55. Allen 1993:182.

56. Foucault 1983a:209.

57. Foucault 1980b:199.

58. Recall that we must be "nominalistic" about power because "power is not an institution, and not a structure; neither is it a certain strength." Foucault 1980a:93. Power is no more—but no less—than a "set of actions upon other actions." Foucault 1983a:219–20.

59. Dreyfus and Rabinow 1983:184.

60. Foucault 1980a:82.

61. Foucault 1980b:199.

62. Dreyfus and Rabinow 1983:184.

63. As noted, only three volumes were published.

64. Foucault 1980a:82.

65. Foucault 1980a:83.

66. Foucault 1980a:84.

67. Foucault 1980a:85.

68. For instance, a law may be shown to be unconstitutional, to discriminate against one or another group, or to be excessively enforced.

69. The passage in its entirety is as follows.

> It seems to me that power must be understood in the first instance as the multiplicity of force relations immanent in the sphere in which they operate and which constitute their own organization; as the process which, through ceaseless struggles and confrontations, transforms, strengthens, or reverses them; as the support which these force relations find in one another, thus forming a chain or a system, or on the contrary, the disjunctions and contradictions which isolate them from one another; and lastly,

as the strategies in which they take effect, whose general design or institutional crystallization is embodied in the state apparatus, in the formulation of the law, in the various social hegemonies. Foucault 1980a:92–93.

70. Bernauer and Rasmussen 1988:11.

71. Foucault 1980a:92.

72. Foucault 1980a:92.

73. Foucault 1980a:104–5.

74. Foucault 1980a:105.

75. Foucault 1980a:122.

76. Foucault 1980a:122. Note that I put things neutrally. Foucault speaks of the bourgeoisie deploying sexuality. This makes it sound as if the deployment of sexuality was a deliberate exercise of power, in the ordinary sense, by one class on another. Foucault's point that the objective was not manipulation but self-affirmation then would be a matter of detail. However, he does not mean that the deployment of sexuality was a plot. He means that the learned discourses that deployed sexuality were bourgeois discourses. The power relations operant in the deployment were bourgeois relations.

77. Foucault 1980a:142–43.

78. Dreyfus and Rabinow 1983:xxiv. See the section on archaeology in Chapter 2.

79. Foucault 1980b: 131.

80. This is the fallacy of *argumentum ad verecundiam* or the appeal to authority.

81. Consider contemporary criticism of "binary thinking."

82. Consider just one example alluded to in *Discipline and Punish*. At one time confessions elicited with torture were taken as conclusive. Now we distrust anything elicited under duress. At one time it was rational to torture suspected criminals to establish their guilt or innocence. Now it is not rational to do so.

83. Hekman 1990:47.

84. Dennett 1991; Davidson, D. 1989; Parfit 1984; Ricoeur 1992.

85. Moulton 1983.

86. Foucault 1980b:83–84.

87. Foucault 1980b:84; compare Deleuze 1984:149.

88. Foucault 1989:295.

89. Genealogy opposes established discourses by problematizing their elements. This is why Foucault's work "is at root ad hoc." Gutting 1994a:2. Genealogical analysis is "non-centralized"; its targets provide its raw material, namely, their own histories and the lores they suppress. Genealogy does not offer competing theories, which is why the force of its analyses are "not dependent on the approval of the established regimes of thought." Foucault 1980b:81.

90. Just think of how many new afflictions have been "identified," such as "attention deficit disorder" and "general stress syndrome."

91. Martin, Gutman, and Hutton 1988:10; Foucault 1986:9.

92. Miller 1993.

93. Note that it could be argued that greater homogeneity in agency might be a fair price to pay for smoother social interaction. Conformity of thought and action, though, has long been abhorrent.

94. Foucault 1980b:85.

95. Foucault 1989:269.

96. Consider just one example: the gay and lesbian movement has enabled people who were deviants in the dominant heterosexual discourse to be normal in a new discourse. "Coming out" was an action enabled by alternity.

97. Foucault 1989:183.

98. Foucault 1986:9.

99. Foucault 1984a:46.

100. Foucault 1991a:36.

101. Foucault 1980b:131.

102. Foucault 1980b:131.

103. Foucault 1980b:93.

104. Foucault 1980b:73–4.

105. Foucault 1980b:98.

106. Allen 1993.

Chapter Six

The Faces of Truth

Foucault's views on truth initially look like facile modish postmodern relativism to readers with an analytic background. As mentioned in Chapter 1, this perception prompts dismissal of his work and precludes serious consideration of it. An introduction to Foucault's genealogy must dispel this perception to be effective. This means that while Foucault's reconceptions of subjectivity and power are the topics most central to his genealogical analytics, we must give priority to his views on truth. We must focus on the issue of truth rather than pursue questions about Foucauldian subjectivity or power. Truth is, in any case, a more fundamental philosophical issue because how truth is conceived underlies any assessment of Foucault's claims about subjectivity and power relations. My aim in this chapter is to clarify what Foucault says about truth and to show that his relativism is anything but facile. To do so, I winnow out the several different ways he uses truth and sketch how those uses are most productively interpreted.

Foucault says a lot about truth, despite the common impression that he dismisses the matter of truth out of hand, and the fact that he does not give truth the priority he should give it. He does so because countering the traditional objectivist conception of truth is basic to his project. Foucault also says a lot about truth because he is aware that many think he espouses some form of self-vitiating relativism. Foucault feels it necessary to avow his concern with truth and describes those who take him to be denying truth in some holistic way as "simple-minded."[1] He insists that someone claiming to be a philosopher could not be considered such if he or she "didn't ask . . . 'What is truth?'"[2]

The trouble is that Foucault says many *different* things about truth. This is because he explicitly contends that "there are different truths and different ways of saying [the truth]."[3] Unfortunately, some of the different things Foucault says or implies about truth look to many as mutually inconsistent. Most notably, as we have seen, Foucault describes truth as historical because it is relative to discourse and is the product of power, but at the same time he seems to make ahistorical truth-claims in his archaeological and genealogical works.

Demonstrating to newcomers that Foucault's uses of truth are not inconsistent is not easy. It is not simply a matter of listing those uses and then testing them for mutual consistency. Foucault does not offer a theory of truth, as I will continue to stress. His various claims about and uses of truth are not components of a unified theory the principles of which might be articulated and used as a standard to check problematic remarks. Moreover, the question of whether what Foucault says about truth is consistent is complicated by the fact that one of his objectives is to impugn the traditional philosophical conception of truth. We cannot assume that uses that may be at odds with one another on a traditional unitary understanding of truth are at odds in Foucault's revisionary and pluralistic conception of truth. Moreover, it is difficult to assess the mutual consistency of various uses of "true" and "truth" because it is often not clear which sense of truth Foucault is working with or discussing at any given time. Thus the best way to proceed is to separate out as clearly as possible the most significant ways Foucault treats truth. What follows, then, is an analytic list of Foucault's uses of truth.[4] Note that in what follows I will speak of Foucault's "uses," "senses," and "notions" of truth. Flexibility in terminology and a certain latitude in meaning are necessary. On the one hand, though the uses in question differ in important respects, they are interrelated, overlapping, and complementary. On the other hand, the uses are individually too robust to be only aspects of a unitary kind of truth.

The Criterial Notion of Truth

The first of Foucault's notions to consider, and which requires only brief treatment, is the criterial notion of truth.[5] This is the notion evident in explicit claims like those noted in Chapter 5, to the effect that each society "has its regime of truth." Each society has "types of discourse which it accepts . . . as true." Each society also has "mechanisms . . . which enable one to distinguish true and false statements" and "means by which each is sanctioned." Each society further has "procedures accorded value in the acquisition of truth" and "those who are charged with saying what counts as true."[6] This criterial notion of truth clearly is relativistic and, taken in isolation, is seen as a discursive version of familiar cultural relativism. This perception prompts analytic philosophers to lump Foucault with postmoderns like Derrida. It is the notion most philosophers focus on—if they even recognize there are others—when summarily dismissing Foucault's work on the grounds that it is vitiated by self-defeating relativism.

Those who reject Foucault's work out of hand construe his criterial relativism as assimilable to self-defeating relativism that they see as amounting to the hopeless claim that it is absolutely true that truth is relative. To reject Foucault's criterial notion of truth in this way is to miss that it is criterial in nature. The criterial use of truth has to do with what counts as true in a disciplined or learned discourse or, more broadly, in a given society. Criterial relativism having to do with the "mechanisms" that determine what counts as true in a given context is not self-defeating. It is, in fact, compatible with, say, an objectivist view of truth in the hard sciences.[7] It all depends on the scope of the application of the criterial relativism. This point initially looks incompatible with Foucault's claim that he is not concerned merely with ideologically distorted truth. That is, the point makes it appear that the criterial use only applies to circumscribed social or cultural perceptions and practices. But the incompatibility is only apparent. What Foucault rejects in ideological distortion of truth is the idea that there is ideologically conditioned truth and "real" underlying truth. The criterial notion, taken by itself, may be compatible with some sort of objectivism regarding truth other than social or cultural. Whether it is or not is a question that requires relating this first notion to the other four.

What is important here is that Foucault's views on truth do look inconsistent if the criterial character of this first notion is missed. This is because if it is missed, his criterial use looks to be his only notion of truth. If the criterial use were Foucault's only notion of truth, some things he says about truth would be contradictory. But this first notion is only one face of truth for Foucault; it must not be taken as either exhaustive or essential. At the same time, one must not go too far. The criterial character of Foucault's first use of truth does not imply that he is concerned only with how ideology shapes discourses and societies. As I have stressed, he does not believe that what counts as true is manipulated sets of ideas and beliefs that cloak deeper, suppressed truths.

The Constructivist Notion of Truth

The textually most prevalent use of truth is the constructivist one. This is the notion that power produces truth. Whereas critics err by focusing on the criterial notion to the exclusion of others, adherents make too much of the constructivist notion and avail themselves of it too readily and sometimes indiscriminately.[8] The relation between the criterial and constructivist uses is that Foucault's constructivist notion of truth is about how what is true in a social or learned discourse comes to be so. This becomes clear once the criterial nature of the first use of truth is appreciated. The constructivist notion has it that truth is relative to social and learned discourses because truth is produced by power relations. This is the sense in which we are constantly "subjected to the production of truth through power."[9] If each society has its own regime of truth, then truths must somehow be produced in a way that makes them specific to their respective regimes. If discourses vary because their truths differ, something must determine what is true in some and not others.

The constructivist notion of truth as a product of power baffles some, alienates others, and prompts even more misinterpretation than the criterial notion. One of the most important misinterpretations is, again, construal of power's production of truth as ideological distortion. Both critics and adherents hold this mistaken construal. As we have seen, this is perception of Foucault as supposedly concerned with the ideological nature of what passes for true or with the way ideology shapes and twists underlying truth. Foucault responds by saying that when he claims there is "a relation between truth and power," traditional philosophers and others say: "'Ah good! then it is not the truth.'"[10] Foucault's point is that many of his critics and some of his adherents are unwilling or unable to understand that his historicist claims about truth are about truth itself, not what passes for true. In other words, critics and adherents alike insist on distinguishing between what is true and what is taken as true in various contexts. They then understand genealogical analysis as dealing with something less than truth, namely, with what is taken as true or shared belief imposed by ideology.

Here we see the sort of problem that Foucault's different uses of truth raise for first-time readers, especially those with an analytic background. We also see how the different uses of truth qualify and limit one another. Foucault contends that it is wrong to interpret power-produced truth as only what passes for true in a discourse or society and contrast it with underlying truth.[11] Therefore, his constructivist notion of truth cannot allow a distinction to be drawn between truth and apparent truth. The criterial notion of truth has to do with what counts as true in a given discourse or society. Initially it seems compatible with some understanding of truth as objective, but the constructivist notion appears to eliminate that possibility. If power *produces* truth, rather than distorting or hiding it, the constructivist use should be exhaustive and not allow more to the concept of truth than what genealogy inventories. However, if truth is produced by power, then Foucault cannot avoid the dilemma Hoy poses. He must either be inconsistent in doing genealogy—or archaeology or ethics—or admit to offering only one more historicist story among others.

Understanding the criterial and constructivist notions of truth, and how they fit together, requires grasping how Foucault relativizes truth to discourse and discursive criterial standards. The first thing to appreciate is that a discourse, or what Rorty would call a "vocabulary," is not only verbal and written. A discourse is an integrated set of things we say and do. As Wittgenstein needed to remind us, the things we "say" include nonverbal but still communicative components like gestures and even silence. Discourses also include practices that, though integral to those discourses, are not themselves communicative. These practices include conventions that determine who may speak and when, and in what contexts expressions or actions constitute the establishment of something as true.[12] Truth is not relative only to the things we say and related communicative acts. Truth is also relative to the "mechanisms . . . which enable one to distinguish true and false statements," to the "techniques and procedures accorded value in the acquisition of truth," and to persons deemed expert and "charged with saying what counts as true."[13] These mechanisms, techniques, and procedures include considerably more than utterances, gestures, and strategic silences. In terms of scope, a discourse and its regime of truth are more like a Wittgensteinian form of life than a delineable language-game.

A tempting way of making sense of how truth is relative to discourse is to construe discourses as "conceptual schemes" and their truths as functions of how conceptual schemes organize noumenal, or directly unknowable, reality. This is a trap with respect to understanding Foucault's relativism.[14] It is a move similar to thinking that what he means by discourse-relative truth is ideological distortion of "real" truth. Foucauldian power does not produce truth by generating "categories" that organize our awareness of reality. Power does not produce truth in any systematic way; power produces truth blindly and nonsubjectively. It produces truth through actions that enable or inhibit other actions and themselves are unknowing with respect to consequences and occur "at the level of tiny local events."[15] However, power is not anything separate from what people say and do. Power is the interactive "strategies" that constrain discursive and nondiscursive acts. As such it is no more than individuals' employment of language and engagement in various practices.

The truth power produces is the correctness of certain discursive acts in a given discourse. "Correctness" is here to be understood in the same way that moving a pawn or a knight on a chessboard in accordance with the rules of chess is making a legal move. Speaking truth is making the right moves in a discourse, where what is right is what is dictated or allowed by a truth-regime's correctness criteria. That is, a discourse's truths are moves that are sanctioned by a discourse's mechanisms for distinguishing truth and falsity and that conform to its expert judgments. What makes some moves right and others wrong is the sum total of contributing actions that shape a discourse's content. It is also the codification of some right moves as disciplinary principles.

We come now to a crucial question raised by Foucault's constructivist contention that power produces truth: How do the truths of a discourse become what individual discourse-participants actually believe? How do discourse-participants come to hold power-produced truths instead of merely accepting them as one might adopt conventions for prudential reasons? How do penitentiary inmates and sexed social beings accept disciplinary truths as defining their own essences? This is, in effect, the large question of how subjects are manufactured. Foucault's answer is the whole of *Discipline and Punish* and *The History of Sexuality*, but something considerably more compact is required here.

What is important to the question about adoption of truths is that while discourses are obviously sustained by individuals' participation, discourses present themselves to subjects as environments very like the physical environment. Most individuals find themselves in discursive environments. Only a very few—the Darwins and the Freuds—play a role in the initial development of discourses. How is a discourse, while not anything in itself, still an environment? How are a discourse's truths presented to subjects as objective rather than as simply others' beliefs? This brings us to the next of Foucault's notions of truth.

The Perspectivist Notion of Truth

Foucault's most difficult notion of truth is the Nietzschean perspectivism that makes truth a function of interpretation and denies that there is anything *but* interpretations. This is a notion in which truth is not the linguistic capturing of facts because "facts [are] precisely what there is not." There are "*only interpretations.*"[16] The world, as what there is and as what true sentences mirror "is not a fact but a fable."[17] The idea of a single meaning that might be discerned with enough effort is a philosophical myth; there is no "meaning . . . but countless meanings."[18] These are strong claims and support reading Foucault as an irrealist as well as a relativist, a topic I pursue in the next chapter.

Understanding Foucault's perspectivist notion of truth first requires appreciating how perspectivism differs from the relativism usually attributed to him. To most analytic philosophers relativism is what Michael Krausz calls "extreme relativism," or the view most briefly articulated as holding that "all claims involving truth . . . are on a par."[19] Contrary to the common assimilation of perspectivism to extreme relativism, perspectivism is different in conception. It is not simple leveling of all truth-claims to the same status consequent on the abandonment of objectivity. Perspectivism is the denial of the possibility of descriptive completeness. Rather than denying that any truth-claim can be proven, and so making them all equal, perspectivism denies the possibility of a global and correct description of the world. The point is that there can be no holistic description within which diverse perspectives could be reconciled as so many true but incomplete points of view on "the same thing." Alexander Nehamas states that Nietzschean perspectivism denies that "there could ever be a complete theory or interpretation of anything, a view that accounts for 'all' the facts."[20] Traditional philosophy and science both desire such a complete theory or interpretation and assume one is possible. Both seek achievement of a description of the world so complete and objective that it rationalizes all interpretive differences.

Perspectivism undoubtedly is relativistic. Krausz describes it as the view that "cognitive, moral, or aesthetic claims involving such values as truth, meaningfulness, rightness, reasonableness, appropriateness, aptness, or the like are relative to the contexts in which they appear."[21] But it is important to distinguish Foucault's Nietzschean perspectivism from extreme relativism or the simple leveling of truth-claims. At the same time, we must take care to not distort perspectivism in the process. The likeliest distortion is an ontological version of the epistemic construal of relativism as holding truth relative to conceptual schemes. The distortion occurs when bafflement at how there can be only interpretations leads to introduction of a noumenal or "thing-in-itself" world as what interpretations are interpretations of. An example is found in Todd May's treatment of Foucault's genealogical analytics. Following Nehamas, and rightly describing perspectivism as not vulnerable to arguments against extreme relativism, May argues that perspectivism does not claim "that the world contains many meanings but, rather, that every view upon the world is an interpretation, a limited and revisable perspective."[22] He adds that it is "perspectives which are plural, not the world." May expands Nehamas's account by adding that in claiming that the world has countless meanings, Nietzsche meant that "the world is ontologically indeterminate." May's contention is that Nietzsche held that the world supports an unlimited number of interpretations.[23] He goes on to say that what "interpretations are interpreting cannot [itself] be rendered in any interesting sense."[24] By speaking of something that supports interpretations but cannot be "rendered" or described, May implies that a noumenal something—albeit an "indeterminate" something—underlies interpretations.

Nietzsche explicitly claimed that "[t]he antithesis 'thing-in-itself' and 'appearance' is untenable." His perspectivism is not one in which interpretations are phenomenal organizations of a noumenal world not knowable in itself.[25] Nietzsche is clear that there are only interpretations. However hard this claim may be to make out, it should not be made intelligible by supplying a noumenal world to bear interpretations. May fails to resist the linguistic and conceptual pressures to complete the idea of a perspective or interpretation by providing the seemingly required object that is interpreted. Certainly Foucault should not be read as qualifying Nietzsche's perspectivism in this manner. Positing a noumenal world to support perspectives or discourses is positing an unknowable absolute or precisely the sort of essence genealogy expressly opposes. Foucault is adamant in rejecting posited "conditional" transcendencies. He says of genealogy that it works "without . . . reference to a subject which is either transcendental in relation to the field of events or runs in its empty sameness throughout the course of history."[26]

It must be appreciated that perspectivism makes truth internal to interpretations and does not anchor interpretations in something that supports
interpretations while forever eluding them. Once that is appreciated, one
can better understand Foucault's agreement with Nietzsche that we should
press the question: "After all, why truth . . . Why are we concerned with
truth?"27 Most traditional philosophers would reject this question out of
hand, taking it as frivolous or perverse. However, the question arises as a
serious one when perspectivism denies any possibility of an interpretation-
rationalizing description of the world. The question then is why we have
"the will to truth," why we are concerned—even driven—to establish a
single perspective as the uniquely correct one. Foucault takes the question
of truth's value seriously. He says the question is the most important intellectual debt he owes Nietzsche.28 Foucault contends that "devotion to
truth . . . arose from the passion of scholars." He asks, "Why, in fact, are
we attached to the truth? Why the truth rather than lies? Why the truth
rather than myth? Why the truth rather than illusion?"29 He describes this
as "one of the fundamental problems of western philosophy." Foucault
adds that "instead of trying to find out what truth . . . is," we would be
better advised to try to answer Nietzsche's question of how it is that "'the
truth' has been given this value" and why we have placed ourselves "absolutely under its thrall."30

Foucault's Nietzschean question about the value of truth must not be interpreted superficially. He is not asking why we value the truth in cases
where an illusion or an evasion would prove more gratifying or useful. To
think that is what he is asking is to miss the point. We leave the deeper issue
untouched if we take the question "why truth?" and its variants in this
way. Doing so assumes that there is objective truth in contrast to illusions
and evasions. But objective truth is precisely what is at issue. Part of Nietzsche's question is why we think that things are just one way. The other part
is why, when we think that things are just one way, we give the highest priority and value to achieving the uniquely correct perspective on things. This
has been evident at least since Plato. Given acceptance of objective truth,
there can be no higher value than its attainment.31

The Nietzschean question Foucault poses about truth's value is about
why we take the world to be a certain way regardless of our perceptions.
When this is clear, it emerges that perspectivism denies that we can postulate that the world is a certain way independently of how we take it to be.
As implied in Nehamas's account, perspectivism is not a positive thesis
about the nature of truth. It is rejection of the need or possibility of positing
a determinate state of being beyond our perspectives. Perspectivism acknowledges a multiplicity of diverse interpretations and denies that we
might describe the way the world is in itself and thereby integrate and rationalize those diverse interpretations.

With a better understanding of Foucault's perspectivist notion of truth, we can return to the question of the appropriation of discourse-relative and power-produced truth by participants in discourses. We need to see how what is appropriated as truth is sustained in discourse and is presented to discourse-participants for appropriation. Writing about Nietzsche, William James, and Henry James, Deleuze says that for all of them "perspectivism amounts to a relativism." But Deleuze adds that theirs is not the familiar sort of relativism that some "take for granted" and others vigorously contest. Deleuze sees in the work of these perspectivist thinkers a form of relativism that is not "a variation of truth according to the subject." That is, it is not subjective relativism or relativization of truth to individuals' beliefs. He sees instead an understanding of "the condition in which the truth of a variation appears to the subject."[32] Deleuze goes on to say that perspectivism "is clearly a pluralism" but maintains that it is not a pluralism in virtue of what he calls "discontinuity"; it is not the fragmentation of truth into so many instances of holding something true.[33] The importance of this is that power-produced truth is sustained in discourse. It is not reducible to the beliefs held by individuals. Extreme or truth-claim leveling relativism attributes truth absolutely to the belief-bearers that hold things true. It thereby retains the idea of absolute truth that it supposedly repudiates, only fragmenting it or multiplying it by the number of believing subjects. If Foucault were this sort of relativist, a subjective relativist, his views would be vulnerable to a long series of traditional antirelativist arguments. Of greater immediate concern is that the problem of Foucault's historicism would be worsened. He could be charged with tacitly but inconsistently employing "principles . . . that have nothing to do with power relations."[34] That is, in presenting his genealogical accounts as preferable to what they counter, he would be illegitimately appealing to truth beyond the subjective "truth" of his own beliefs.

I take Deleuze's main point to be that when perspectives or interpretations held by two or more subjects agree or conform to one another, they do so by more than sheer coincidence. Similarity among interpretations is not just coincidental in the sense that two or more subjects happen to form the same interpretations. Deleuze is trying to say how perspectivist interpretations are intersubjective without positing a thing-in-itself world that underlies interpretations and explains their similarity. He wants to articulate how there may be objects of interpretation that are presented to different subjects for appropriation, without themselves being anything more than parts of discourse. If this can be done Foucault's genealogical analysis would be the mapping of the development of those intersubjective "objects." This would allow genealogical analyses a measure of intersubjective cogency or authority without those analyses being about underlying objective events. That is, Foucault's genealogical accounts would be about something other than his own beliefs yet not be about an objective reality he cannot invoke.

Deleuze makes the suggestive comment that "every point of view is a point of view on variation."[35] It is not my intention to further expound Deleuze's work. What I take from him is the idea that points of view may be interpretations of more than things and events. Perspectives may be taken on discursive components that are frequently used and referred to explicitly or implicitly. Through constant employment, these components gain a measure of autonomy in a discourse and come to constitute intersubjective objects of belief and attitudes. An example is stereotypes. Stereotypes are "variations" that are neither objects nor events, but they are not simply reducible to beliefs held by individuals. For one thing, stereotypes are present in books, plays, films, and art; for another, they figure prominently in discourse. Stereotypes are cultural components that in part define an ethos. A racial stereotype, for instance, is an intersubjective component of a culture to the extent that it can elicit different interpretive responses. A negative racial stereotype can provoke amused contempt on the part of some individuals or virulent antipathy on the part of others. The stereotype is not identical with the contempt felt by one individual and the antipathy felt by another.[36]

Foucault's and Deleuze's notion of intersubjective cultural components or objects of interpretation has a parallel in North American philosophical debate. Richard Dawkins facilitates a Darwinian account of culture by introducing the concept of "a new kind of replicator." Dawkins thinks there are cultural artifacts that are intersubjective and capable of cultural transmission comparable to genetic transmission. These ideational gene-like items contribute to the content of a culture and survive independently of particular individuals' beliefs and attitudes. Dawkins calls these cultural artifacts "memes," playing on the Greek *mimesis* (imitation). Examples of memes are "ideas, catch-phrases, [and] fashions," as well as practices such as "ways of making pots or of building arches."[37] Dawkins's contention is that "as genes propagate themselves . . . via sperm or eggs, so memes propagate themselves . . . via a process which, in the broad sense, can be called imitation."[38] Dawkins offers the example of how a scientist who has or hears a good idea passes the idea on to colleagues and students. The idea then is used in articles and lectures and "if the idea catches on, it can be said to propagate itself."[39] This "catching on" is Rorty's notion of "uptake" on a new metaphor or vocabulary and is analogous to natural selection.[40] Rorty maintains that "[m]emes are things like turns of speech, terms of aesthetic or moral praise, political slogans, proverbs . . . stereotypical icons, and the like." Memes "compete with one another . . . as genes compete" with one another, and different "batches of both genes and memes are carried by different human social groups."[41]

The point here is that a culture's discursive components or its memes are presented to its members in the process of enculturation and thereafter as realities on a par with the physical environment. Individual members of the culture form perspectives not only on their physical environment, but on their cultural environment as well. The components of the cultural environment are artifacts, such as stereotypes, and each of these components is an object of interpretation. Dawkins's memes and Deleuze's variations show how something can be a power-produced object of a perspective or an interpretation while not being either a thing or an event. Without individuals who hold things true there would be no memes or variations, as there would be no discourse, but memes or variations are not reducible to particular individuals' beliefs. The concept of an objective sexual nature is an example. For Foucault, objective sexual nature is a cultural construct, a power-produced artifact integral to the deployment of sexuality. The successful deployment of sexuality requires an underlying objective nature the manifestations of which can be construed as suppressed or distorted. Learned discourse propagates the idea that a sexual essence underlies our desires and acts and explains them. Members of our culture are taught about human sexual nature and form interpretations of what is presented to them as fact but actually is a discourse-sustained construct.

Memes and variations, then, are cultural artifacts or discourse-sustained intersubjective objects of interpretation. With this idea in place, we can describe how individuals appropriate a discourse's truths. Individuals appropriate the power-produced truths that are relative to and sustained in discourse when those individuals take those constructed truths as matters of fact and come to have beliefs about them and attitudes toward them. This understanding of how subjects appropriate truths does not reveal just that subjects come to have certain beliefs. It shows that just as subjects form beliefs about things and events, they form beliefs about cultural constructs. Subjects are surrounded by both physical objects and by cultural "objects" presented to them in myriad ways ranging from expert accounts to texts to advertisements to casual remarks. Subjects are inundated with multifarious presentations of "scientific facts" and "common knowledge" directly through formal and informal schooling. They are also swamped by indirect presentation of what "everyone knows" through implication, innuendo, and confirming or adverse reactions to things they say and do.[42] The bombardment of subjects' senses by the physical world is at least equaled by the barrage of cultural data that assails them. Subjects need to deal with cultural objects as much as with any physical thing or event that they encounter and must manipulate, navigate around, be present at, or avoid. Subjects appropriate the truths of their discourse in dealing with cultural artifacts as unproblematic givens. In dealing with them as with things and events, subjects treat cultural objects as so many more bits of reality. To the extent that this is the case, Foucault's tracings of the production of cultural artifacts assume an importance greater than psychological accounts of belief-formation.

This cultural-artifact account may be resisted because of the weight of our Cartesian epistemological tradition. Some find it hard to see what discourse-relative or power-produced truths could be except beliefs formed by particular individuals. They find it difficult to see how truths could be present in a discourse without simply being the beliefs held by discourse-participants. Consequently they construe power as a kind of pervasive imposition of beliefs. This is just the misinterpretation of power as covert or ideological distortion of "real" truth that Foucault rejects. However, once it is clear that power-produced truths are separable from beliefs in being intersubjective objects of interpretation, a space opens up between what individuals believe and the objects of (some of) their beliefs. We are able to separate power-produced truths from what subjects actually believe once we see how there is something "there" in discourse to form beliefs about. We then understand how acquiring beliefs about discourse's truths is the adoption of perspectives. It is then clearer how disciplinary techniques determine the beliefs acquired and the perspectives adopted and so produce particular Foucauldian subjectivities.

Four points should now be more understandable. One is how Foucault's criterial use of truth has to do with what counts as truth in a discourse. Another is how his constructivist use has to do with the production of truth in discourse. A third is how his perspectivist use has to do with the appropriation of truth by individuals. And the fourth is that subjectivities are shaped by power through constraints on individuals to acquire certain beliefs and to adopt certain perspectives. If these four points are clearer, it should be more evident how the criterial, constructivist, and perspectivist notions of truth fit together. However, there are two more pieces to the puzzle.

The Experiential Notion of Truth

Lawrence Kritzman observes that "Foucault was concerned, above all else, with the idea of experience."[43] Aside from the criterial, constructivist, and perspectivist notions of truth, Foucault has a fourth notion he characterizes by distinguishing between truth resulting from inquiry (*l'enquête*) and truth resulting from test or trial (*l'épreuve*). The contrast is between what is learned through investigation and what is realized in a challenging experience. If we do not read "insight" as discernment of objective truth, we can understand "realization" as insight gained from the cognitive dissonance and reflection that crises force on one. Truth so gained is truth that "does not belong to the order of that which is, but rather of that which happens: it is an event."[44] The examples Foucault offers are undergoing torture to establish innocence or trial by combat to establish rightness of action. A less dramatic but more useful example is experiencing the pressing need to understand occurrences that impugn much of what one believes and values, as in the loss of religious or political faith or betrayal by a friend.

The experiential notion of truth will seem very odd to traditional philosophers. It looks to be about changes of mind due to emotion rather than to reason. Experiential truth appears to be change or realignment of beliefs brought about by causal rather than rational factors, and so not philosophy's concern. Foucault himself describes experiential truth as "repugnant to both science and philosophy."[45] But the experiential notion is neither as philosophically irrelevant as it first appears nor as novel as Foucault would like. Experiential truth basically is the outcome or resolution of what Alisdair MacIntyre calls "epistemological crises." These are circumstances where individuals find themselves forced to question what they previously accepted unquestioningly. More specifically, the events that produce epistemological crises not only raise perplexities, they impugn the evidential criteria those individuals previously used to resolve doubt.[46] Resolving epistemological crises requires first deciding what to use as criteria for counting something as evidence. The result of forging and applying new evidential criteria in dealing with a pressing perplexity is just the sort of cognitive change Foucault claims is found in "limit experiences."

John Wisdom also considers a kind of truth that bears a striking resemblance to Foucault's experiential notion of truth. Wisdom explores the difference between "vertical" and "horizontal" reasoning. He stresses that in some cases, especially judicial ones, what is deemed to be "the truth" is not the result of deduction or discovery but of decision. Wisdom says that in these cases the process "is not a *chain* of demonstrative reasoning. It is a presenting and representing of those features of the case which *severally cooperate* in favor of the conclusion." Deciding the matter at issue is a process of "weighing the cumulative effect of one group of . . . items against . . . another group" rather than discerning facts.[47]

MacIntyre's epistemological crises and Wisdom's truth-establishing decisions dispel the initial oddness of Foucault's experiential truth that arises in "limit experiences." Putting the point in more mundane terms, sometimes truth is how things "come together." Sometimes things "come together" in certain ways because of decisions made rather than because of conclusions drawn or the results of successful inquiry. At first sight the experiential notion of truth looks too romantic and recalls Foucault's early and unproductive obsession with the purity of madness. But it is demystified by understanding how the cases MacIntyre and Wisdom consider actually work. The notion is further clarified by Foucault's acknowledgment that gaining experiential truth in a limit experience is not a "sudden illumination which makes 'the scales fall from the eyes.'"[48] Acquiring experiential truth may be an arduous process extending over a considerable period of time. It may also involve inquiry to support the deep rethinking of whatever suddenly became problematic and caused the epistemological crisis or limit experience.

We might note in passing that while he does not explicitly say so, there is little doubt that Foucault thinks of his own achievements in rethinking madness, penality, and sexuality as acquisition of experiential truth in limit experiences. There is even less doubt that he saw his work as providing others with the opportunity for limit experiences and acquisition of experiential truth. Speaking of his books, Foucault claims that truth "is not found in a series of historically verifiable proofs; it lies rather in the experience which [a] book permits us to have."[49] The relevance of this point is that it bears on the persistent problem posed by the ahistoricist tone of Foucault's genealogical pronouncements. We can think of Foucault as writing *Discipline and Punish* and *The History of Sexuality* to resolve his own epistemological crises. The catalyst for the first no doubt was Foucault's own involvement in penal reform. The catalyst for the second certainly was his marginalization due to his sexual orientation.[50] The texts show that Foucault resolved his crises by restructuring penality as imposition of control and sexuality as establishment of norms. The plight of the imprisoned looks very different seen as more a matter of programming inmates than exacting retribution from them. The sexual norms Foucault violated and even flouted look less threatening when seen as constructs. The point here is incidental, but it makes it easier to understand the assertive tone of both texts.

The experiential notion of truth has more to do with the appropriation of truth than with truth as such. Individuals appropriate a large number of discourse-dependent, power-produced truths in the process of being reared and enculturated and of participating in discourse. But unless lives are wholly placid and unremarkable, there will be times when encounters with new discourse-dependent truths will generate serious intellectual turmoil. For example, consider a young adult whose religious beliefs clash with some newly encountered idea or situation. A woman raised as a conservative Catholic may have her moral condemnation of abortion challenged by an unwanted pregnancy. A man raised as a fundamentalist Baptist may have his creationism challenged by exposure to Darwinian evolutionary theory. These are instances of major cognitive clashes and consequent changes in beliefs and attitudes. What is crucial is that the changes are perceived as hard-won achievements of insight occasioned by deeply disruptive intellectual trials. Individuals who embrace new truths after great agitation, indecision, and anguished reflection consider their hard-won new truths to be epiphanies or deliverances. In MacIntyre's terms, the wresting of new truth from deeply challenging bewilderment is adoption of new correctness-criteria and the consequent acceptance of new descriptions of how things stand. In Wisdom's terms, a profound decision is made about how something is to be construed. In Rorty's terms, it is the abandonment of one vocabulary and the adoption of another. In terms favored by Gadamer and

Ricoeur, it is a narrational change in which a subject's identity-defining narrative is altered by incorporation of a new perception, with all the adjustments that entails.

To better understand Foucault's experiential truth it must be seen that, though perceptive, MacIntyre's, Wisdom's, Rorty's, Gadamer's, and Ricoeur's accounts of experiential truth essentially are descriptive. Foucault's notion is normative. What is important for Foucault is that it is in a limit experience's clash of old and new ideas that we can adopt genuinely new perspectives. Otherwise we only change particular beliefs or make adjustments to beliefs that remain substantially unchanged. The rigidity of our belief structures, the inertia of intellectual habits, and power's ever-tightening control make limit experiences necessary. It is the intellectual's imperative to provoke limit experiences to achieve experiential truth because new thought is our only mode of resisting power. Occasions for experiential truth almost always *happen* to people; they befall individuals unprepared for them. Foucault thinks one should actively provoke such occasions. Some of his own attempts to do so are intellectual in nature, as in rethinking penality and sexuality, his treatment of madness, and his exploration of Greek and Roman sexuality.[51] A more methodological strategy is his practice of taking the most extreme stand on an issue to provoke argument.[52] More problematic efforts include experimentation with sex, sadomasochism, and drugs. Regardless of mode, Foucault takes it as axiomatic that intellectual life demands constant change: "Modifying one's own thought and that of others seems to me to be the intellectual's reason for being."[53] The job of the intellectual is "to shake up habitual ways of working and thinking, to dissipate conventional familiarities, to re-evaluate rules and institutions."[54] He says of his own work: "When I write, I do it above all to change myself and not to think the same thing as before."[55] The normative aspect of experiential truth is illumined by Deleuze's comment that Foucault offers "counterphilosophy."[56] Foucault's criterial, constructivist, and perspectivist notions of truth all have to do with power-produced truth. Experiential truth is in opposition to power's truth. Experiential truth wrung from the cognitive and emotional disruption of a limit experience offers the only counter to the ever-tightening grip of power.

If we could stop here, understanding Foucault's views on truth would be simpler than it is. His position would be wholly relativistic and, if the worse for that, at least it would be fairly straightforward. However, there is a fifth and rather elusive use of truth still to be considered.

The Tacit-Realist Notion of Truth

The fifth of Foucault's notions of truth is the tacit-realist use.[57] This is the use that critics think is inconsistent with Foucault's account of truth as produced by power.[58] This use occurs in comparatively few textual remarks, but that it occurs at all is what raises questions. The problem here is different from the question of whether Foucault directly or indirectly makes ahistoric truth-claims in or about his genealogical analyses. The remarks look to many philosophers as clearly inconsistent with a historicist account of truth—the criterial, constructivist, and perspectivist uses—because truth seems to be used objectively in them.

Perhaps the most notable example is Foucault's assertion that when he speaks of truth he does not mean "the ensemble of truths which are to be discovered and accepted." He states that instead what concerns him is "the ensemble of rules according to which the true and the false are separated and specific effects of power attached to the true."[59] Dreyfus and Rabinow render this passage a bit differently. They have Foucault saying that by truth he does not mean "those true things which are waiting to be discovered."[60] The difference in phrasing has some significance, as I consider below, but what matters is the contrast drawn. Foucault seems to be inconsistently contrasting power-produced truth or historical truth and objective or ahistorical truth. He reiterates the contrast in other remarks, as in comparing "the constraints of truth" with prohibitions developing "out of historical contingency."[61] It does sound as if here Foucault "intends to distinguish . . . objective, i.e., discovered, truth from his own use of the term."[62] The dilemma is that Foucault either is inconsistent or is only talking about ideologically or culturally distorted "real" truth despite his vehement denials.

I argue below that the contrast drawn has to do with what I am calling Foucault's tacit realism, but critics pounce on these and similar passages to interpret Foucault as inconsistently using or acknowledging ahistorical truth.[63] They then resolve the inconsistency by interpreting Foucault as concerned only with ideological distortions of truth. As we have seen, this is an interpretation Foucault rejects explicitly because ideology "always stands in . . . opposition to something else which is supposed to count as truth."[64] Foucault's account of truth as a product of power cannot be about ideological distortion since what ideology purportedly distorts is precisely the ahistoric truth his account opposes. However, this point only makes it likelier that the tacit-realist use is inconsistent.

To sort out the apparent inconsistency between the fifth and the first three uses of truth, we first have to recall a point made in Chapter 3. Foucault, like Rorty, does not offer a theory of truth. If we read him as doing so "we shall get [him] wrong." As Rorty says about the pragmatists, the point of his work is not to offer a competing theory of truth but to show that such theories are historical products pretending to ahistorical import.[65] Critics err if they think Foucault's criterial, constructivist, and perspectivist notions of truth are parts of a theory about the nature of truth. That reading is due more to their theory-biased expectations than to what Foucault says. The relations among Foucault's several uses of truth are not those holding among elements of a theory. Foucault's uses of truth are wholly contextual; nothing prior or extra-contextual determines anything about them. The five notions deal with the ways "true" or "is true" are used and work in different sorts of discussions. If ill-conceived cross-contextual comparisons are made, on the assumption that the uses are parts of a cohesive theory, then the several uses will look inconsistent with one another. Cross-contextual comparisons of uses of "true" wrongly assume that since "true" has the same *force* in different contexts, whatever is said to be true in those contexts must be true in the same way.[66] However, as Rorty points out, "'true' resembles 'good' . . . in being a normative notion, a compliment paid to sentences that seem to be paying their way." In other words, when we use "true" to describe a sentence we use "a term of praise."[67] The commendatory force of "true" may be acknowledged as the same across different contexts without postulating a theoretically explicable essence that explains the common force. The parallel is to "good." All sorts of things are described as "good," from meals to books to persons, but the criteria for judging meals, books, and persons good vary greatly.[68] There is no essential or core "being good" that a theory might discern and would explain how things as diverse as a point made in discussion and a bottle of wine are both good. Foucault's various uses of "true" need not have any more in common than commendatory force.[69] If that is all that they have in common, they will not be inconsistent in a philosophically worrying way.

A second clarificatory point introduces the idea of tacit realism. The appearance of inconsistency in Foucault's uses of truth is partly due to his terminology. He should not speak of "truths" when expressing disinterest in "the ensemble of truths which are to be discovered," because in this case he is not talking about truth. Referring to an ensemble of truths waiting to be discovered conflates linguistic truth, which is what he is discussing, and extra-linguistic states or how things are or the world. What Foucault dismisses in the passage is not truths about the world but the world. He is not interested in the world because his concern is with what governs objectification of the world or of what imposes itself on us. Foucault is making the same point Rorty makes in saying that while the world plays a causal role in our awareness of it, it plays no epistemic role.[70] In other words, like Rorty, Foucault is dismissing the world as "the ineffable cause of sense" and as not immediately relevant to what he wants to say about truth.[71] Rorty speaks of "the world" as either a vacuous notion or simply everything that "inquiry at the moment is leaving alone."[72] Foucault is leaving the world alone while trying to say something complicated about truth. This will seem paradoxical to many, but it is crucial to understanding Foucault to see that he is talking about truth without thereby talking about how things are. I pursue this point in Chapter 7 and argue that Foucault is a tacit realist. Rather than deny the world in describing truth as relative to discourse, as constructed in discourse, and as perspectival, he simply ignores it.

A third clarificatory point is that apparent inconsistencies in Foucault's tacit-realist use of truth may be due to the difference between his speaking as a genealogical analyst of discourse and his speaking as a participant in discourse. For instance, Foucault does not answer as a genealogist when asked if it is true that he visited Tunisia. In answering that it is true that he did, he speaks as a participant in discourse and in doing so he is not inconsistent with his criterial or constructivist account of truth. Foucault has as much right as anyone to use "true" in an ordinary way. However, one has to wonder what he has in mind when he does so. The question is whether the discourse-participant use of "true" entails that true sentences are true because they accurately portray the world. This is to ask if the correspondence theory of truth is a philosophical theory of truth or simply articulates what ordinary uses of "true" assume. If the latter is the case, Foucault's participant uses of "true" are not innocuous and likely are inconsistent with his relativism and constructivism. Many think this is the case, and argue that the entailed accurate portrayal of the world is what it *means* to say a sentence is true.[73] This point becomes more evident if we change the example. If Foucault is asked if it is true that water expands when it freezes, it is not clear that he can say that it is true even as a participant in discourse. Foucault might intend to say only that in our present regime of truth "Water expands when it freezes" counts as true. I pursue this in Chapter 7, and it suffices here to say that some cases of apparent inconsistency in Foucault's use of "true" may be resolved by understanding Foucault's discursive role.

The foregoing clarifications go some way toward dispelling the appearance of inconsistency in Foucault's tacit-realist use of truth, even if there are tough cases like the water one. However, the clarifications do not help with respect to Foucault sounding as if his genealogical claims are cogent because ahistorically or objectively true. This is the point on which Habermas and Hoy focus.[74] They do not see how Foucault can present his genealogical accounts as cogent and compelling while claiming that they are historical interpretations. May adds that Foucault owes us "an account of how it is that we can accept his inquiries as justified, and possibly as true," given the extent to which he problematizes established principles and histories.[75] It certainly is difficult not to read Foucault's contentions about penal practices and alleged suppression of sexuality as discernment and exposure of what was really going on. *Discipline and Punish* and *The History of Sexuality* do read like corrections of historical distortions rather than as merely intriguing interpretations. Despite clarifications, then, ambiguities remain in some of Foucault's uses of "true" and especially in his description and presentation of his genealogical accounts as compelling.

To be fair, Foucault does—more or less—acknowledge the problem. He asks "What historical knowledge is possible of a history which itself produces the true/false distinction on which such knowledge depends?"[76] Unfortunately, Foucault offers little in answer. In a somewhat different context he remarks that sorting out "the difficult relation with truth" must begin with "the way in which truth is found used inside an experience."[77] This is not much help. If resolution of the historicist ambiguity of genealogical accounts turns on what is found "inside an experience," it begins with the experiential impact of his ideas on Foucault himself. The question then becomes why Foucault expects us to find his genealogical accounts compelling. This is what prompts Rorty to complain that Foucault mistakenly proceeds as if his philosophical project must be *our* project by not respecting Rorty's own distinction between the public and private.[78] All Foucault should do is present his genealogies and hope that his readers will have similar productive experiences. What he should not do is make the claim, quoted in Chapter 5, that his books must assert what is true to be of value.[79] He also should not challenge his critics by asking whether any of them has shown that his genealogical accounts are "false [or] ill-founded."[80] To do so clearly is to imply that his genealogical accounts are true and well founded.[81] And Foucault should clarify his claim that genealogy is "a form of history which can account for the constitution of knowledges, discourses, domains of objects, etc."[82]

There is textual evidence that Foucault occasionally slips into an objectivist use of "true" different from troublesome but arguable uses of tacit-realist truth and ambiguities in the presentation of his genealogies. For instance, in one passage Foucault contrasts "the constraints of truth" with prohibitions that are "arbitrary in origin" or that develop "out of historical contingency."[83] He then characterizes only the historically contingent constraints in the way he describes power's production of truth. Another example is when he responds to the claim that whoever has the power to shape or "formulate" truth also has the power "to express it as he wishes." Foucault answers that doing so—that is, expressing the truth in some self-serving way—"does not mean however that what he says is not true."[84] The implication is that in various forms of indoctrination discourse-relative truth may coincide with what really is true.[85] Again, speaking of censorship and propaganda, Foucault says that "[n]othing is more inconsistent than a political regime that is indifferent to truth."[86] There are also some references to truths "about oneself" that strongly imply there is, after all, something about oneself that is not a product of power relations.[87] These passages confirm critics' view that Foucault must distinguish real and apparent truth. They argue that he "needs the distinction between what is true and what we take to be true" to unmask the power relations "he alleges determine our discourses about what we believe to be true or false."[88] Certainly the cumulative effect of these and other passages makes it difficult to argue that Foucault's inconsistency on truth is only apparent.[89]

A tempting but perhaps facile way to deal with Foucault's apparent inconsistencies is to read him as holding the common view that there are "hard" and "soft" truths: the truths of the physical sciences and the material world and the truths of the social sciences and politics. This interpretation distorts Foucault's views by undermining the radicalness of his relativism, constructivism, and perspectivism. Here we again can make a little headway by comparing Foucault with Rorty, who is unambiguous about how "true" and "truth" only commend sentences that "seem to be paying their way."

Rorty acknowledges that regardless of our beliefs, cultural constructs, and any amount of pragmatic consensus, "there is such a thing as brute physical resistance."[90] But acknowledgment of brute resistance is not a concession in the realist/irrealist debate, which Rorty sees as only an unfortunate legacy of Cartesian epistemology.[91] The concession does not qualify Rorty's rejection of the idea that what is true is true in virtue of some way the world is. As mentioned earlier, Rorty claims that the idea of brute physicality or "the world" is just the "vacuous notion of the ineffable cause of sense" or simply everything that "inquiry at the moment is leaving alone."[92] As indicated, the brute reality Rorty acknowledges has no epistemic role to play with respect to truth-claims. He insists on the purely linguistic nature of truth and is thoroughly Davidsonian in denying that anything makes sentences true.[93] For Rorty, as for Foucault, the world plays no role in the justification of the truth of sentences. Both agree with Sellars that "[s]emantical statements," such as saying that a sentence is true, "do not assert relations between linguistic and extra-linguistic items."[94] Saying of a sentence that it is true is not comparing the sentence to the world to justify its use. Only one proposition can justify another proposition.

To proceed we need to distinguish three things: Foucault's uses of "true" as a genealogist and as a discourse-participant, occasional straightforward mistakes, and the didactic tone of his genealogies. My concern here is only with the first of these, namely, Foucault's uses of "true" as a discourse-participant and as a genealogist. Some of these uses pose problems because they suggest that some things are true because of how the world is and not because of power. We also need to remind ourselves of two points. One is Sellars, Davidson's and Rorty's view that truth is wholly linguistic and that what establishes some sentences as true is not the world but other sentences. The other is that Foucault does not offer a theory of truth. Finally, we must take May's point that passages suggesting a distinction between power-produced and objective truth indicate Foucault's focus of the moment rather than inconsistency.[95] In the next chapter I will argue that Foucault's apparently inconsistent references to an "ensemble of truths which are to be discovered" are gestures toward what "inquiry at the moment is leaving alone."[96] This interpretation accords well with the focused, local nature of genealogical analysis. It also accords well with Foucault's rejection of power-produced truth as merely ideology's distortions and suppression of underlying truth. Finally, the interpretation fits with Foucault's abandonment of what he calls "naturalism." This was the idea that we might "rediscover the things themselves" and discern "behind the asylum walls, the spontaneity of madness; through the penal system, the generous fever of delinquency; under the sexual interdict, the freshness of desire."[97]

To close this section we can say that the tacit-realist notion of truth is best understood in terms of four interwoven factors. The first is that "true" and "truth" have commendatory roles irrespective of what might be said about how things are true. The second is that Foucault does not always speak as a genealogical critic. The third is that truth is wholly linguistic. The fourth is that genealogical analysis is limited to particular sets of truth-claims. Nonetheless, problems remain. Most notably, reference to "truths which are to be discovered and accepted" sounds as if there are truths that are not power-produced.[98]

Summing Up

Foucault uses "true" and "truth" in at least five distinct though interrelated ways. His criterial, constructivist, and perspectivist uses of truth depend primarily on whether his concern is with discourse-defining practices, the role of power relations, or the appropriation and value of truth. His experiential use of truth has to do with radical perspectival change and adoption of belief. The tacit-realist use seems to refer to things put aside as unproblematic, but raises questions about consistency. As worrisome is Foucault's presentation of his genealogies as having the cogency of discerned ahistorical truth. Nor is this problem posed only by what Foucault actually says. Rorty and others fear that in the final analysis genealogy cannot claim to expose the deployed nature of dominant truths, such as about penality and sexuality, without implying that it reveals hidden realities and suppressed truths.[99]

Foucault's five notions of truth do not constitute a theory of truth. The notions do not jointly describe a unitary way sentences are true, as does the theory holding truth to be a relation of correspondence to the facts. However, while Foucault is not offering a theory of truth, he is saying something new about truth. His notions of truth need not separately nor collectively constitute a theoretical account to provide a new perspective on truth. They constitute a pluralistic perspective that counters the traditional view of truth as monolithic and as the sort of thing that supports productive theorizing. For Foucault, truth does not support theorizing because it is neither diachronically nor synchronically monolithic. Truth has been different things at different times and is different things at the same time. Truth is historical and heterogeneous.

If Foucault offered only a pluralistic perspective on truth it could be argued that others have done the same. Rorty claims that Foucault offers nothing more than Dewey's pragmatic account of truth offers.[100] This is mistaken; the role of power is new. Foucault offers a novel account of the diverse nonsubjective and impersonal mechanics that produce different sorts of truths in disparate discourses and epochs.

To close this chapter something needs to be said about how the five notions of truth are integrated in Foucault's relativism. Foucault decidedly is a relativist though, contrary to appearances, he is not an extreme relativist in thinking that all views or claims are equally valid. As Krausz remarks, the "range of positions characterizable as relativistic is varied and heterogeneous." To better understand Foucault's relativism we need to articulate its "opposing concept" more exactly.[101] Barry Allen describes the "classical" conception of truth as having four elements. These are: "the priority of nature over language, culture, or [history]"; "the idea that truth is a kind of sameness . . . between what is said and what there is"; the "derivative character of the signs by which truth is symbolized"; and the unquestioned value of truth.[102] For Foucault, nature has no priority over language and discourse determines what nature is. Truth is not a sameness with anything; as a product of power it does not mirror anything. Signs are not derivative but primary; their uses constitute what they supposedly symbolize. And lastly, he questions the value of truth, calling the issue "one of the fundamental problems of western philosophy."[103]

Surprisingly, it is neither power nor truth as a product of power that lies at the heart of Foucault's opposition to the "classical" conception of truth. The role of power in the production of truth only arises when nature is subordinated to language and truth ceases to be a sameness of what is said and what there is. Power is an answer to a question, not a foundational idea.[104] The notion of power basically is a consequence of Foucault's rejection of the structuralists' view of discourse as unilaterally determining practice. It is when Foucault "thematizes" the reciprocal influence of practice on discourse that he needs power to explain how practices manufacture truth in discourse.[105] What is most central to Foucault's opposition to truth as traditionally conceived is denial that truth is a "sameness," a kind of representational isomorphism, "between what is said and what there is." As we will see in more detail in the next chapter, this is rejection of the idea that anything—the world or "the facts"—makes sentences true. This is the fundamental move. Foucault severs the connection between thought and language, on the one hand, and the disposition of the world, on the other. That connection is what traditional philosophy takes as the essence of truth. The consequence is that, as Rorty says of metaphors that have yet to be taken up, Foucault's rejection of truth as sameness "initially sound[s] crazy."[106] That is, we do not know what to make of the idea that something might be true but not be so in virtue of getting something right about how things are. It then looks to many as if in making truth wholly discursive, Foucault is denying the world. I pursue this issue in the next chapter, but to close consideration of Foucault's vision of truth, a little more needs to be said.

Foucault's five notions of truth are genealogical mappings of uses of "true" and "truth." They are in no way intended as theoretical definitions of truth. Foucault understands that efforts to define truth are doomed to fail. This is because if truth is defined in terms of any other property, for instance, utility, it still always makes sense to ask if a belief or sentence having the defining property is true.[107] Foucault has a good deal to say about truth, but what he has to say is all about *truths*, not about some defining property or relation discernable through theorizing. In this way, Foucault's treatment of truth is a Rortyan change of subject despite how much he does say about truth.[108] Foucault's concern is not with truth as a relation or property but with investigating how "true" and "truth" work in diverse contexts and how "true" and "truth" come to work as they do in those contexts.[109] However, Foucault is not doing linguistic pragmatics; his is not a purely empirical project. He is making philosophical claims about truth. His detachment of truth from how things are is not a heuristic device; he is not merely setting aside sentences' relation to the world. As Allen puts it, Foucault is arguing that "truth is manufactured internal to a given discourse, and has nothing to do with 'how things are.'" Truth does not have to do "with the identity or nature of a thing, apart from its inscription in a language-game."[110] The result is that Foucault is read as denying the world or how things are. This is a nearly inevitable consequence of failure to understand how a sentence, especially a descriptive sentence, could be true and *not* have to do with how things are. The idea that truth is how things are is too deeply ingrained in our intellectual tradition to allow Foucault's detachment of truth from the world without him seeming an irrealist. It must look to many as if Foucault is saying that the world is a construct of thought and language.

John Searle contends that the world or things being a certain way is a "Background" presupposition; that it is neither an opinion nor a postulation.[111] Searle argues that taking the world as objective and determinate is a condition of our thinking and doing most of what we think and do. This condition is so basic to thought and action that Searle finds it difficult to understand why "when we start doing philosophy we are . . . driven to deny things we all know to be true—for example, that there is a real world."[112] Foucault's view that truth is entirely discursive is read as denial of something we all know to be true. Even sympathetic exponents of Foucault's work try to understand Foucault's claims in a way that softens them. For example, May argues that we have to draw a distinction that "Foucault neglected in his epistemic inquiries: the distinction between justification and *truth in an ultimate sense.*"[113] However, this is not a distinction Foucault's work can accommodate. Ironically, the problem with May's claim is the same as Foucault's own when Foucault says he is not concerned with an ensemble of discoverable truths. Neither Foucault nor May can be referring to "ultimate" or discoverable *truth*. To do so is to conflate truth with extra-linguistic reality for the sake of asserting that there really is a way things are regardless of what we say or believe. And this is precisely to employ the traditional idea that truth just is how things are.

It may seem tempting to some, at this point, to resolve perplexities by having recourse to an established philosophical treatment of truth as discursive. One might follow up the similarities between Foucault and Rorty and explain Foucault's position as philosophical pragmatism. But three points preclude this move. First, it is problematic how close Rorty's neo-pragmatism is to that of the classical pragmatists, John Dewey, C. S. Peirce, William James, or contemporary pragmatists like W.V.O. Quine and Hilary Putnam. Certainly Rorty is quite distant from Peirce and Putnam. Similarities between Foucault and Rorty are not necessarily similarities between Foucault and other pragmatists.[114] Second, most pragmatists differ from Rorty in trying to rearticulate truth in terms of effectiveness and utility and oppose the traditional conception of truth primarily because of its metaphysical implications. They are "suspicious of the notion of *truth* because of its association with metaphysical absolutes outside experience."[115] Foucault would concur with this much, but he cannot accept the classical pragmatists' agreement on the value of truth. Truth is "a phase of the *summum bonum*" for Peirce. James is indignant at the charge that pragmatists deny truth, and insists they only want "to trace exactly why people . . . *always ought to follow it.*"[116] Finally, Foucault cannot accept Peirce and Dewey's faith in scientific method nor Peirce's notion of "concordance" at the end of inquiry, which Dewey endorsed. Foucault could not agree with Dewey's view of "scientific methods" as showing "intelligence operating in the best manner."[117] These differences between Foucauldian relativism and mainstream pragmatism highlight the distance between Foucault's view of truth and the best known and most plausible philosophical rejection of truth as objective. There is only one thing common to Foucault's and the pragmatists' view of truth. This is the idea considered earlier that "is true" has commendatory force that is detachable from theoretical claims about whatever explains that force.

Foucault's vision of truth has to be assessed on its own merits. As I have indicated and will stress further, the most serious obstacle to fair assessment of that vision is misconstrual of it as irrealist, as entailing denial of the world. The next chapter focuses on this point. To close this chapter it suffices to reiterate that what holds Foucault's five uses of truth together, what makes them all notions of truth, is their shared commendatory force. What separates the uses into five distinct notions are the contextual peculiarities of how each use of "is true" is justified and justifies other attributions of truth. All five kinds of attribution of truth commend sentences or beliefs regardless of context. But each attribution must meet criteria peculiar to particular contexts, and each attribution functions in a way peculiar to particular contexts. I now turn to the question of whether all this denies the world.

Notes

1. Foucault 1989:295.
2. Foucault 1980b:66.
3. Foucault 1989:314.
4. I offer this list well aware of Foucault's use of Jorge Luis Borges's "animal" list in *The Order of Things*.
5. In the first edition I called this the "relativistic" use.
6. Foucault 1980b:131.
7. Foucault 1980b:131.
8. Compare Burrell 1988; Hooper and Pratt 1993.
9. Foucault 1980b:93.
10. Foucault 1984b:17.
11. Foucault 1980b:118.
12. Clear examples occur in court, as when a judge or jury establishes that an act was, say, culpably negligent, thereby making a prosecutorial description true.
13. Foucault 1980b:131.
14. I return to this point in considering some remarks by Todd May.
15. Hacking 1981:29.
16. Nietzsche 1968a:267, my emphasis.
17. Nietzsche 1968a:330.
18. Nietzsche 1968a:267.
19. Krausz 1989:1.
20. Nehamas 1985:64.
21. Krausz 1989:1.
22. May 1993:80.
23. May 1993:79.
24. May 1993:79.
25. Nietzsche 1968a:298.
26. Foucault 1980b:117.
27. Bernauer and Rasmussen 1988:15.
28. See Allen 1991.
29. Foucault 1971:78; 1988b:107.

30. Foucault 1988b:107.
31. See Allen 1993, especially the first two chapters.
32. Deleuze 1993:20.
33. Deleuze 1993:20.
34. Nola 1994:37.
35. Deleuze 1993:20.

36. Deleuze's treatment of perspectivism and his attempt to describe the "varia-tions" that are the objects of perspectives likely have their roots in Foucault's own work. In *The Order of Things* and particularly in *The Archaeology of Knowledge*, Foucault addresses how concepts come to be constituted within discursive forma-tions. Foucault 1972, 1973.

37. Dawkins 1976:206.
38. Dawkins 1976:206.
39. Dawkins 1976:206.

40. Philosophers other than Rorty have availed themselves of Dawkins's memes, notably Daniel Dennett.

41. Rorty 1991c:4.

42. For instance, shows of surprise at ignorance or doubt or assumptions evident in comments and questions.

43. Kritzman 1988:xviii.
44. Foucault 1974, in Miller 1993:271.
45. Foucault 1974, in Miller 1993:270.
46. MacIntyre 1977.
47. Wisdom 1955:195.
48. Foucault 1989:304.
49. Foucault 1991a:36.
50. Miller 1993:56, 185–98, 255–57; Macey 1993:14–15, 86–87, 256–89.
51. Foucault 1965; 1986; 1988a.

52. Witness his infamous 1971 debate with Noam Chomsky. Miller 1993: 201–031.

53. Foucault 1989:303.
54. Foucault 1989:305.

55. Foucault 1991a:27. Some may strive to change themselves for the sake of cre-ativity or enhanced awareness, or to escape a stultifying orthodoxy. But for others the need for change is more pressing, as in the case of those trapped in a psycholog-ically debilitating gender role.

56. Deleuze 1984:149.

57. In the first edition I called this the "semi-objectivist" use. Note that it is my claim that Foucault uses truth in these five different ways. He nowhere draws the distinctions I have drawn.

58. E.g., Nola 1994:sec 5.6.
59. Foucault 1980b:132.
60. Dreyfus and Rabinow 1983:117.
61. Foucault 1972:217–18.
62. Nola 1994:39.

63. Even Rorty agrees that, in the end, genealogy cannot claim to expose the deployed nature of dominant truths without implying it reveals suppressed truths. Rorty 1986:41–9, 1991b.

64. Foucault 1980b:118.

65. Rorty 1982:161.

66. It may be assumed that all true statements are true in virtue of "corresponding to the facts."

67. Rorty 1982:xxv, 1991d:127. Rorty is referring to James's point that truth is "the name of whatever proves itself to be good in the way of belief." James 1978:42.

68. The criteria are largely incomparable. There is nothing in common between a good point made in discussion and a good peach tart.

69. Foucault is not likely to forget commendatory force since his Nietzschean concern about the value of truth has to do precisely with why "true" and "truth" have commendatory force.

70. Rorty 1982:xxv, 1991d:127. Like Foucault, Rorty also is charged with inconsistency in claiming that truth is only commendation of sentences while acknowledging that "there is such a thing as brute physical resistance." Rorty 1982:xxv; 1991d:81. But Rorty distinguishes between what causes our thoughts and beliefs and what justifies our truth-claims. He then follows Wilfrid Sellars and Donald Davidson in holding that only other sentences justify truth-claims.

71. Rorty 1982:15.

72. Rorty 1982:15.

73. John Searle, for one; see Chapter 7.

74. Habermas 1987b:273–74; Hoy 1986.

75. May 1993:71.

76. Foucault 1991b:82.

77. Foucault 1991a:36.

78. Rorty 1991a:198.

79. Foucault 1991a:36.

80. Foucault 1980b:87.

81. This passage can be read as saying only that Foucault is confident he has provided meticulously researched support for his genealogies of penality and sexuality. However, reference to proper research raises the same question about objectivity.

82. Foucault 1980b:117.

83. Foucault 1972:217–18.

84. Foucault 1984b:17.

85. Compare Nola 1994:39–41.

86. Foucault 1988b:267.

87. Foucault 1988b:240; 1983a:212, 214.

88. Nola 1994:39.

89. Foucault is not unique in seeming ambiguous about truth and puzzling us with pronouncements and modes of presentation apparently at odds with his avowed historicism. There is a similar ambiguity in Gadamer's hermeneutical work. There one finds uses of "true" and "truth" that sound objectivist in nature and at odds with Gadamer's hermeneutical principles. Gadamer 1975:267; Bernstein 1983:168.

90. Rorty 1982:xxv; 1991d:81.
91. Rorty 1991a:21–172.
92. Rorty 1982:15.
93. Davidson, D. 1985:194.
94. Sellars 1968:82.
95. May 1993:85–109.
96. Rorty 1982:15.
97. Foucault 1988b:119–20.
98. Foucault 1980b:132, compare Nola 1994:39–41.
99. Rorty 1986; 1991c.
100. Rorty 1982:xviii; 1991b, 1991c:3.
101. Krausz 1989:2, 3.
102. Allen 1993:9–10.
103. Foucault 1988b:107.
104. Admirers and critics alike give power too high a priority and so invite interpretive error.
105. Foucault 1980b:105; Dreyfus and Rabinow 1983:104.
106. Rorty 1991c:3. Compare Fodor 1987.
107. Putnam 1978:107–9; White 1970:125–26; Rorty 1991d:127; Prado 1987:54.
108. Rorty 1982:xiv.
109. See Foucault 1988b:107.
110. I am grateful to Barry Allen for his comments on an earlier version of Chapter 7. Where I cite him in this and the next chapter without title or year, I am quoting those comments.
111. Searle capitalizes "Background" to indicate he is using it in a semi-technical way. Searle 1999:10; see Searle 1995:129–137. Searle defines the Background as "the set of nonintentional or preintentional capacities that enable intentional states of function." Searle 1995:129.
112. Searle 1999:9.
113. May 1993:71, my emphasis. May also wrongly claims that Nietzsche's perspectivism is not integral to Foucault's thought. May 1993:79.
114. See Prado 1987:41–47.
115. Matson 1987:454.
116. Peirce 1931:para. #575; James 1907 in Thayer 1982:220, my emphasis.
117. Dewey 1938:345n, 535.

Chapter Seven

Truth and the World

Lumping Foucault "with . . . other French contemporaries . . . especially Derrida, is a disservice both to Foucault and to the important ideas that he can bring to North American philosophy."[1] Foucault's conception of truth is one such important idea. His pluralistic, discursive redescription of truth is worth serious consideration but is often ignorantly dismissed. Analytic philosophers do lump Foucault with Derrida and dismiss Foucault's work because they perceive him as an extreme relativist.[2] That is, they think that Foucault holds "that all claims involving truth . . . are on a par."[3] Rorty describes the extreme relativist position as holding that "every belief . . . is as good as every other" but adds "[n]o one holds this view." He maintains that "[e]xcept for the occasional cooperative freshman, one cannot find anybody who says that two incompatible opinions on an important topic are equally good."[4] However, those who dismiss Foucault also dismiss Rorty's own work as hopelessly relativistic. The fact is that mainstream North American philosophers are unprepared to take seriously those who take relativism seriously. They see any form of relativism as entailing extreme relativism and so as not meriting consideration.

Rorty is right that no one who is philosophically sophisticated holds the extreme relativist position. Certainly it is difficult to think that the author of *The Order of Things* and *The History of Sexuality* held that every belief or assertion is as good as every other and therefore does not deserve to be taken seriously. Foucault simply is not an extreme relativist; he does not think that all truth-claims are on a par. In Chapter 6 I tried to clarify Foucault's relativism by differentiating five ways he uses "true" and "truth." The point was not to try to show that Foucault is not a relativist but to show how he is not an extreme relativist, that his relativism is not self-vitiating. Foucault's concern is not to level truth-claims but to say how truth is relative to discourse in different and complex ways. Nonetheless, some of my intended readers will see my efforts as misdirected. They will remain unprepared to take Foucault's views seriously and especially to see those views as having any bearing on their own work. But the reason for this steadfastness is complicated; it goes beyond arguments about whether truth is relative to discourse or is a product of power. What drives dismissal of Foucault's work is not just relativism; it is also what relativism is perceived to entail. Foucault himself articulates the core of the problem.

In the context of discussing truth, Foucault puzzles an interviewer by using truth in some of the different ways outlined in Chapter 6, prompting the interviewer to ask if perhaps truth is not a construct after all. Foucault responds by saying, "[t]hat depends. There are some games of truth in which truth is a construct and others when it is not." He goes on to say a little about alternative descriptions, and it is in doing so that he makes the key point. Foucault says that giving alternative (genealogical) descriptions of events *"does not mean that there is nothing there and that everything comes out of somebody's head."*[5] Dismissal of Foucault's views on truth, and of his work generally, is motivated by commitment to realism and rejection of what is perceived as irrealism entailed by his relativism. That is, perception of Foucault as an extreme relativist is perception of him as one who denies the reality of a world independent of mind or language. It is this perceived denial of the real world that drives dismissal of his work. The moment Foucault says that truth has nothing to do with how things are, he is heard as saying that truth is wholly discursive and that discursive truth is all there is. He is taken as saying that everything comes out of our heads, that reality is mind-dependent or language-dependent. Foucault articulates this preclusive interpretive gloss by saying, "some draw the conclusion that I said that nothing exist[s]."[6]

In this chapter I pursue what I called Foucault's tacit-realist notion of truth with a view to showing that his relativism does not entail denial of reality independent of human consciousness. My aim is to bar easy dismissal of Foucault's work on the grounds that it is irrealist in conception or by implication. I use John Searle's articulation and defense of realism as my touchstone in considering Foucault's tacit realism.[7]

Searle defines realism as holding that "[t]he world (or alternatively, reality or the universe) exists independently of our representations of it."[8] This is the proposition that many think Foucault denies explicitly or implicitly. I contend that Foucault neither does deny nor intends to deny realism as Searle defines it. Moreover, the significance of this point goes beyond questions about the acceptability of Foucault's ontology. Its real thrust is that Foucault's relativism cannot be extreme relativism in Krausz's and Rorty's senses if Foucault is a realist in Searle's sense. Differently put, the dismissive interpretive slide goes from Foucault's discursive relativization of truth to extreme relativism to alleged irrealism. If it can be shown that Foucault is not an irrealist, his relativism will have to be reconsidered along the lines given in the last chapter.

The Specter of Irrealism

Foucault's relativization of truth to discursive practices and detachment of it from how things are looks to analytic philosophers as more than saying that "[s]emantical statements . . . do not assert relations between linguistic and extra-linguistic items."[9] He is taken as denying that things are any way at all and as asserting that there is nothing outside discourse.

Anti-relativism usually is rooted in correspondism or the theory that sentences are true in virtue of "corresponding to the facts" or accurately picturing how things are.[10] Correspondists are Foucault's most resolute opponents and invariably interpret his views as irrealist in nature. Correspondists read Foucault's relativization of truth to discourse as denial of independent reality. The way this works is as follows. For Foucault the conditions determining the truth of statements are "uniformly conventional, discursive, historical." These conditions "do not include 'how things are'" in the sense that states of affairs are not elements in what makes sentences true. But correspondists consider how things are, or states of affairs, as "truth-maker[s] par excellence."[11] For them, the conditions that determine the truth of sentences precisely are states of affairs. Therefore, they see Foucault's separation of truth from states of affairs as denial that there are states of affairs. Correspondism seems to have no place for states of affairs or the world except as what confers truth on sentences. Searle thinks it "intuitive" that true sentences are "made true by how things are in the real world."[12] The basic idea is that the world confers truth on statements much as objects photographed determine their own images on film. A true sentence's correspondence to some fact is seen as that fact making the sentence true. So if the truth-conferring role of the world is denied, the world is denied. If *being* true is being *made* true, any account of truth that excludes what makes sentences true must be denial of what makes sentences true, and that is the world.

A passage typical of those used to support the irrealist interpretation of Foucault is one where he writes of substituting "for the enigmatic . . . 'things' anterior to discourse, the regular formation of objects that emerge only in discourse."[13] This does sound as if Foucault is denying that there is anything beyond language. However, Foucault is not denying the world in this and similar passages, nor is he embracing irrealism by making the conditions of truth intra-linguistic. To say that objects emerge only in discourse is not to deny the world. It is to say that the things we find in the world are intralinguistic in the sense that what they are for us results from how we conceptualize them, how we *objectify* them.[14] Emergence in discourse is all about conceptualization and objectification. It has to do with how something comes to be what it is in virtue of how it is thought of and spoken about. We are intentional entities for whom the world is a collection of particulars of various sorts. But this is not to say, as many take Foucault to be saying, that we manufacture a language-dependent or mind-dependent reality. However real it is, the world is not a collection of *things*, of *objects*. The point is elusive but crucial, and it needs to be made carefully.

Speaking of revisionist accounts of truth like his own and Foucault's, Rorty says that such accounts are "usually met by changing the subject from truth to factuality."[15] The appeal is to "hard facts":

> When Galileo saw the moons of Jupiter through his telescope, it might be said, the impact on his retina was "hard" in the relevant sense, even though its consequences were . . . different for different communities. The astronomers of Padua took it as merely one more anomaly . . . whereas Galileo's admirers took it as shattering the crystalline spheres once and for all. But the datum *itself*, it might be argued, is utterly real quite apart from the interpretation it receives.[16]

It goes without saying that what caused the datum, the moons of Jupiter, is also real in the relevant hard sense. This appeal to factuality is the other side of the view that if the world is not used to establish the truth of statements, then it is in effect denied. The point of the change of subject to factuality is to stress that, whatever we make of or say about the datum or its cause, neither is a product of consciousness or language. Rorty goes on to say that the pragmatist responds to the appeal to factuality by rejecting idealism. What is important with respect to Foucault is how idealism is rejected. Rorty maintains that pragmatists reject idealism by acknowledging that "there is such a thing as brute physical reality."[17] Rorty himself acknowledges that "there is such a thing as brute physical resistance."[18] Notice that Rorty is careful to speak of brute "reality" and "resistance" and not of brute objects. This is because objects are never "brute" in the relevant sense. Something is an object only when conceptualized as a particular thing of a certain sort. What Rorty and the pragmatists acknowledge is the reality of the world, not a reality of objects as such. Objects emerge only in discourse. That is, some bit of the world is an *object* for us only when it is conceptualized as a particular thing: as a sailing ship or a bit of sealing wax, as a cabbage or a king. To say, then, that objects emerge only in discourse is not to deny mind-independent reality. It is to say that that reality does not consist of so many objects.

More indirectly, it is to say that that reality is epistemically irrelevant. "Factuality" or reality in itself is an epistemic dead-end because there is "no way of transferring this nonlinguistic brutality to *facts*, to the truth of sentences."[19] This is the Davidsonian point that nothing *makes* sentences true. However hard brute reality might be it is just *there*; it does not confer truth on statements.

Foucault is not concerned with brute reality. He neither denies it nor bothers to acknowledge it. In the last chapter I stressed that his tacit-realist use of truth indicates that brute reality simply is not at issue. To put the point in Rorty's terms about brute reality or resistance, regardless of our beliefs and any amount of consensus to the contrary, water expands in volume when it freezes. This is quite independent of discursive conditions that determine the truth of sentences about freezing water. But at one time we believed that water froze because it lost caloric fluid and now we believe that water freezes because of a reduction in mean kinetic energy. *That* is what concerns Foucault. What would matter to him in this example is how water emerged as something that either lost caloric fluid *or* kinetic energy. He is not interested in reaffirming that bad winters play havoc with external plumbing. Nonetheless, something is being denied in the emphatic description of truth as discursive and of objects as arising only in discourse. What, then, is Foucault denying?

Notice that in the passage about "'things' anterior to discourse," Foucault puts "things" within quotation marks. The quotes might be taken as "sneer quotes" and his use of them read as dismissive reference to "things" as what people believe exist but do not exist except as products of thought or language. This is how correspondists read the passage, if they even notice the quotes. However, the quotes are not "sneer quotes." Foucault is not talking about Rorty's brute reality or resistance or the world. The passage's context makes this abundantly clear. That context is the nature of Foucault's archaeological project. He says of archaeology—and could say about genealogy—that "there can be no question of interpreting discourse with a view to writing a history of the referent." That is, it is not his concern to somehow "neutralize" discourse in order "to reach what remains silently anterior to it."[20] It is tempting to think, as I once did, that what is being set aside precisely is Rorty's brute reality, that Foucault is dismissing the world as "the referent" or what is "silently anterior" to discourse. If this were so, making out the tacit-realist sense of truth would be easier. But Foucault is not concerned primarily with brute reality. Setting aside the world is more or less incidental. The remarks he makes about everything coming out of somebody's head and his having said that nothing exists basically are asides. He is ridiculing misinterpretations of his claims. He just does not take the charge of irrealism seriously. What Foucault is most concerned to do is to deny *essences* or *na-tures*. These are what he mainly is talking about in saying that objects emerge only in discourse, that we cannot give a history of the referent and that we cannot reach something that is silently anterior to discourse. Neither human sexuality nor madness nor any other nature is anterior to discourse. Learned discourse about sexuality or madness does not and cannot reach out and capture a "referent," an essential facticity that determines behavior.

When Foucault says he wants "to dispense with 'things'" he is saying that he wants to treat objects emergent in discourse "without reference to the *ground*, the *foundation of things*."[21] Here he is setting aside Rorty's brute reality or Searle's world, but above all Foucault is denying that the world contains essences that determine history, sexual behavior, madness, class struggle, and so on. What he wants to do is say how determining essences emerge as intentional focal points according to the "rules that enable them to form as objects of a discourse."[22] Power-produced essences are what are most centrally at issue.[23] This is evident in Foucault's own explicit abandonment of what he calls "naturalism" or the attempt to "rediscover the things themselves in their primitive vivacity." What is crucial is that the "things themselves" that Foucault is relinquishing as imaginary, as manufactured, are not the world but "the spontaneity of madness; . . . the freshness of desire."[24]

What Foucault does reject is Searle's view that the world confers truth on statements, that brute reality makes beliefs and sentences true.[25] As suggested in Chapter 6, in doing so Foucault is agreeing with Davidson that "[n]othing . . . no *thing*, makes sentences . . . true."[26] He is not making bizarre ontological claims about reality being mind-dependent. What Foucault is doing is rethinking what it is for something to be true; he is rethinking what it is to attribute truth to a sentence or to justify a sentence's truth. What makes Foucault's claims special is that he has a story to tell about precisely how something comes to be true. He has a story to tell about how power produces truth in the ways reviewed in the last chapter. But regardless of his relativism, constructivism, and perspectivism Foucault's contentions are not irrealist in nature.

The trouble is that both critics and adherents turn Foucault's denial of things or states of affairs *as truth makers* into denial of things or states of affairs *as such*. Part of the problem is that terms like "the world," "states of affairs," "how things are," and "the things themselves" are not understood in philosophical discourse as referring just to brute reality. These terms are understood as referring to the world as what confers truth on statements. Most philosophers side with Searle rather than Davidson and take true sentences as made true by states of affairs. They then see impugning the world's truth-conferring role as impugning the world itself. This perception explains historical resistance to alternatives to the correspondence theory of truth, such as holding statements true because they hang together with a favored set (coherentism) or are propitious tools (pragmatism). Both positions redefine truth as intralinguistic, so both are construed as irrealist in nature.

What Foucault says about truth admittedly is complicated and sometimes unclear. As we saw in Chapter 6, his contention that "there are different truths and different ways of saying [the truth]" results in at least five different uses of truth.[27] Again as we saw, the five uses of truth are not simply a matter of statements that share the quality of being true playing different roles in different contexts.[28] For Foucault, playing those roles is what makes those statements true. It is the roles played that make sentences true, so different roles produce different sorts of truth. Sentences or statements are not true other than in being used and accepted as they are. Relativization of truth to governed discourse first of all has to do with what counts as true and how it comes to be taken as true. That is why the criterial use of truth is pivotal in Foucault's work: it defines the universe of discourse as discourse itself. The criterial use detaches— or attempts to detach—truth from the world.[29] However, this detachment of truth from the world is not denial of the world but talking—or attempting to talk—about how statements are true without thereby talking about prelinguistic reality.[30] The constructivist use, which casts truth as produced by power, is a necessary complement to the criterial. Once the criterial use separates truth from how things are, the constructivist use is needed to say how what is true in a discourse comes to be true in that discourse.[31]

The Nietzschean perspectivist use is more problematic with respect to irrealist interpretation of Foucault's work.[32] It explicitly claims that "facts is precisely what there is not, *only interpretations.*"[33] This much is acceptable because it is in line with the point that brute reality does not contain *facts*, that facts are as much linguistic as truth is. But Nietzsche also tells us that a world that might be mirrored in thought and language "is not a fact but a fable."[34] Foucault seems to endorse this, saying that "if interpretation is . . . never-ending," it is so because "there is nothing to interpret."[35] However, Foucault's denial of anything to interpret is not as irrealist as it first sounds. What both Nietzsche and Foucault in effect are denying is the Kantian scheme/content distinction that Davidson denies. Nietzsche explicitly asserts that the Kantian opposition of the "'thing-in-itself' and 'appearance' is untenable."[36] In the same vein, Foucault immediately adds to his "nothing to interpret" remark that "[t]here is nothing absolutely primary to interpret."[37] For his part, Davidson disavows con-

tent as something "absolutely primary to interpret" in rejecting conceptual schemes and the content they supposedly organize. In denying that
there is anything to interpret, Foucault is concerned to deny what he calls
"conditional" transcendencies or what supposedly "is either transcendental in relation to the field of events or runs in its empty sameness throughout the course of history."[38] But as Davidson notes, rejecting the
scheme/content distinction, and so a noumenal or conditional content,
does not mean "we . . . give up the world."[39] On the contrary, it means
we "re-establish unmediated touch with the familiar objects whose antics
make our sentences and opinions true or false."[40]

As for those "familiar objects," a somewhat different but complementary
point is that what Foucault's perspectivism denies is not the world but ultimate commensurability or descriptive completeness. Nehamas's comment
that perspectivism denies that "there could ever be a complete theory . . . a
view that accounts for 'all' the facts" captures Foucault's view if we replace
"facts" with "points of view."[41] Even Searle admits "it is only from a point
of view that we represent reality."[42] But points of view need not all be rec-
oncilable. For one thing, we cannot purge interest and value judgments
from our awareness of the world. We are conscious of the world not only
as things and events of certain sorts, but also as things and events that in-
trigue, frighten, bore, concern, sadden, or elate us. The perspectivist use of
truth recognizes the diversity of viewpoints and denies that there could be a
comprehensive account—a theory or what Thomas Nagel calls "the view
from nowhere"—that would rationalize all viewpoints.[43] When Foucault
rejects "conditional" transcendencies he rejects any "ground" that would
enable integrating all viewpoints and showing them to be ultimately com-
mensurable.

The hard idea in Foucault's account of truth is that *being true* does not
have to do with the world or brute reality as such. That is what emerges
when we clarify that Foucault is not denying brute reality. But it is difficult
to grasp that sentences are true in virtue of wholly discursive factors and
not because they accurately portray states of affairs. It is much easier to
read Foucault's account of truth as discursive and power-produced as irrealist in nature, and his tacit-realist use of truth as his being inconsistent or
disingenuous.[44]

Foucault is neither inconsistent nor disingenuous about truth and the
world. He is concerned with truth as a purely linguistic or discursive phenomenon. He separates being true from the world. When he says that he is
not concerned with "the ensemble of truths which are to be discovered and
accepted," he is setting aside whatever relation sentences have to brute reality. As noted, the only denial in all of this is the claim that essences or na-

tures are linguistic and not part of brute reality. Foucault is concerned with "the ensemble of rules according to which the true and the false are separated and specific effects of power attached to the true."[45] Dreyfus and Rabinow's rendition of the first part of this passage is the better one. As noted in the previous chapter, they have Foucault say that he is not concerned with "true things . . . waiting to be discovered."[46] It would be better still if the passage read that Foucault is not concerned with "those things which are waiting to be discovered." As mentioned earlier, "true" does not belong in this remark; its use conflates truth and how things are. It runs together the linguistic and the prelinguistic; it confuses the truth of sentences with brute reality.

Davidson describes this error as the "common source" of the failure of correspondence theories of truth. The error is a consequence of "the desire to include in the entity to which a true sentence corresponds not only the objects the sentence is 'about' . . . but also whatever it is the sentence says about them."[47] In other words, the source of confusion is the projection of the truth of sentences onto brute reality itself. This is to take brute reality as naturally parceled up into "facts." But facts are things and events—bits of brute reality—that are parceled up by conceptualization and descriptive language. The world may be all that is the case, but it is *not* a collection of facts.[48] The world does not contain truths along with things and events; it simply is things and events. That is why it cannot confer truth on sentences; there is "no way of transferring . . . nonlinguistic brutality to . . . the truth of sentences."[49]

Foucault understands that brute reality is not composed of things and events *and truth*. He is investigating how we construct, objectify, and justify truth in discourse.[50] He is not raising an ontological question. Foucault's relativization of truth to discourse does not entail irrealism. Brute reality simply is not relevant to his investigation. My claim, then, is that the question of whether Foucault's account of truth is viable is a question that is not precluded by that view constituting or entailing an absurd denial of the obvious.

The core of Foucault's account of truth is the idea that the constraints on what we say are "not from the things, from their nature, how they are, but from [the] normative, conventional, discursive constraints of the language-game."[51] Even if it is understood that this idea is not and does not entail irrealism, the idea poses a serious problem. The crux of the problem is that Foucault's tacit realism is not robust enough to enable drawing a distinction we feel needs to be drawn. Though the distinction must be a fuzzy one, we think there is a crucial difference between two kinds of situations. On the one hand, a discourse or an economy of knowledge may sanction statements that attribute freezing either to loss of caloric fluid or to loss of mean kinetic energy. We have been through this sort of development before and understand how newly sanctioned statements displace previously sanctioned statements. We have stopped talking about the ether; we no longer explain erratic human behavior in terms of demonic possession. On the other hand, a discourse or economy of knowledge could sanction statements that describe water as contracting on freezing. We feel that this will not do, that there is a crucial and intuitively clear difference between incompatible theoretical descriptions and incompatible practical descriptions. Some would-be practical descriptions just do not work, such as describing water as contracting on freezing. If water contracted on freezing, our oceans would long since have solidified and life on earth would have ended shortly thereafter. We might go for some time describing planetary orbits as perfectly circular by saying a lot about epicycles, but no amount of talk would sustain an economy of knowledge that described water as contracting at thirty-two degrees Fahrenheit. But Foucault seems indifferent to the problem. To see how and why, we need to say a little more about his view of truth.

Setting the World Aside

I have described how Foucault uses truth in ways that are differentiated by the contextual peculiarities of intradiscursive justification or the "means by which each is sanctioned" in a regime of truth.[52] The differentiation of the five uses can be seen as an inevitable result of how being true "is not a property of sentences" but is instead "a relation between sentences, speakers, and dates."[53] Foucault's five uses of truth are prompted, if not necessitated, by the complexity of the relations between statements, speakers, and dates. These relations are not straightforward ones among so many utterances, utterers, interlocutors, and temporal contexts. The relations can remain straightforward only if we restrict ourselves to consideration of sentence meaning. What Foucault sees is that the relations, and sentence meaning itself, are determined by all the historical and contextual factors affecting speakers and their audiences. Foucault has no interest in sentence meaning as such. What interests him is how the relations between sentences, speakers, and dates are determined by all the conditions that shape utterances in particular contexts and at particular times. Those conditions are what Foucault describes when he inventories the components of regimes of truth and economies of knowledge and traces the productive role of power. But Foucault believes that to understand the production and role of truth he must loosen "the embrace, apparently so tight, of words and things."[54] That is, he needs to attend specifically to the language games we play. This requires putting the world aside or ignoring for the moment how much of our language games have to do with conceptualizing, objectifying, and describing how things are. First, it is only if words are loosened from things that we can see how some "things"—essences or natures—are manufactured in discourse rather than found in the world. Second, Foucault can best understand and describe how we hold something true and how holding something true shapes us as objects of study and as subjects of experience if he puts aside language's relation to the world. We might put the point this way: Foucault is not interested in the relation of sentences to the world, much less in denying the world; what he is interested in is how we relate to sentences.[55]

But another problem now arises. If loosening the embrace of words and things is not denying that the world is as it is regardless of what we say about it, then it may look as if loosening the embrace is focusing on what merely passes for truth.[56] This misperception is prompted by conflation of truth and the world. If truth continues to be thought to be in the world, and Foucault is understood as not denying the world, then it will look as if what he loosens is the embrace between "real" truth and apparent truth.

As stressed earlier, Foucault's genealogical treatment of truth is of truth itself, not of "something else which is supposed to count as truth."[57] Foucault's ignoring the world while he considers truth as a discursive phenomenon is not ignoring "real" truth while he focuses on what only passes for truth. What is set aside is brute reality, not truth; setting aside the world is not setting aside truth because truth is not in the world. The root of the misperception and of the conflation of truth and the world is what Davidson calls "the essential question" posed by true sentences. That question is whether a true sentence "is *the* . . . place where there is direct contact between linguistic theory and events, actions and objects, or objects described in non-linguistic terms."[58] Many philosophers take a true sentence to be the place where the envelope of language is thinnest and where we most directly touch the things themselves.[59] Foucault does not believe that a true sentence provides the closest possible connection with the world. He agrees with Rorty that we must "see sentences as connected with other sentences rather than the world."[60] Foucault's detachment of truth from things is implementation of Rorty's view that referring to the world in discussing truth is an unproductive gesture toward the "vacuous notion of the ineffable cause of sense." Setting aside the ineffable cause of sense or brute reality is not a bifurcation of truth into real truth and what passes for truth. There is only one kind of truth, and it is linguistic, discursive, and that is what concerns Foucault.

Doubts will persist. Separation of words and things, of truth and the world, is not a thought that is easily grasped. Even if we accept that Foucault's separation of truth and things is intended to enable understanding of how truth works in discourse once it is shorn of its correspondist baggage, we struggle with the idea. What is it that enables Foucault's separation of truth and things? The subtitle of *The Order of Things* says it all: "An Archaeology of the Human Sciences." Foucault's work on the development of institutions like the clinic, the asylum, and the prison, and of exclusionary categories like "madness," "deviancy," and "normalcy," is all about *us*. It is about how we have taken ourselves as objects of study and how we have manufactured truths about ourselves. But little of the content of the human sciences fits or fails to fit Davidson's familiar objects or Searle's real world or Rorty's brute reality. Fitting sentences to the world is the job of the physical sciences. Foucault is interested in the physical sciences only when their pronouncements encroach on the human sciences.[61] Foucault "inscribes" truth in discourse to deal with how sociologists, social psychologists, cultural anthropologists, educators, psychiatrists, penologists, vocational counselors, and others conjure up natures and essences. He wants to expose how they gerrymander human behavior into protean categories generated by those natures and essences. His objective is to comprehend how economies of knowledge function in order to understand how their disciplinary truths define and redefine us.[62] Achieving that comprehension has little to do with how things are in the world or the accuracy of descriptions such as of what happens when water freezes. Foucault neither has an interest in nor a need to deny the real world. To read him as if he does is to do one of the things his work is about, namely, to exclude something on the basis of imposed categories.

We can close this chapter by noting that Foucault's treatment of truth discloses a degree of complexity regarding truth that traditional philosophy ignores or obscures. The simplicity of truth is taken for granted. Even Davidson, who insists that being true is a complex interrelatedness of sentences, speakers, and dates, describes "the concept of being true" as "simple."[63] What make statements true for Foucault are their various roles in economies of knowledge. Truth "concerns . . . the historical circulation of statements" and statements circulate in different ways at different times, so statements are true in different ways and truth is complex.[64] What underlies perception of truth as simple is the correspondist idea that a statement's being true is that statement relating to the world by corresponding to a fact. This idea runs together truth and the world; it instantiates "the desire to include in the entity to which a true sentence corresponds . . . whatever it is the sentence says about them."[65] Foucault stresses the linguistic nature of truth and sets aside the world to show how statements are true in different ways. This is why "[w]hether we are analyzing propositions in physics or phrenology," our concern is not with those propositions' relations to the world. What concerns Foucault about true sentences is "their place within the discursive formation."[66] The result is that Foucault is read as saying that nothing exists outside of discourse and his work is dismissed as not serious philosophy.

Foucault is adamant that truth is internal to discourse, that it is produced in discourse, that it "has nothing to do with 'how things are.'"[67] But precisely because he is not making the mad claim that we spin the world out of language, he uses truth in what I dubbed the tacit-realist sense. Critics then write him off as inconsistent or disingenuous about truth. Foucault is neither. Like others he sees that truth is linguistic, that the world or brute reality does not contain truth or facts. Once this is seen it is possible to consider how truth works without necessarily referring to how things are. That is what Foucault is doing. He is *not* saying that "everything comes out of somebody's head" or that "nothing exists" outside of discourse.[68]

Notes

1. Munteanu 1998.

2. I do not care for the labels "analytic" and "Continental" because of the stereotypes they connote. However, it is undeniable that they mark significant differences. The best brief account I have seen of these differences is Giovanna Borradori's "The Atlantic Wall." Borradori 1994.

3. Krausz 1989:1. Krausz calls this "extreme relativism" in contrasting it with others that are viable. He points out (page 2) that the position is self-defeating because "the claim that each belief is as good as another is itself a nonrelativistic claim." The perception of Foucault as relativistic in this way, as holding, in effect, that it's absolutely true that truth is relative, is misguided. Whatever Foucault may have been, he was neither naïve nor stupid.

4. Rorty explains that "philosophers who get *called* 'relativists' are those who say that the grounds for choosing between . . . opinions are less algorithmic than had been thought." Foucault is certainly saying that. Rorty 1982:166.

5. Foucault 1984b:17, my emphasis. Compare Rabinow 1998:297 for a somewhat different translation of the passage.

6. Foucault 1984b:17. Foucault goes on to say:

I have been made to say that madness does not exist, although the problem was quite the contrary. It was a question of knowing how madness, under the various definitions that we could give it, could be at a certain moment, integrated in an institutional field which considered it a mental illness, occupying a certain place alongside other illnesses.

The reference here is to madness, not to the world generally, but Foucault nonetheless is denying irrealism in denying that he thinks madness is not a series of events regardless of how construed.

7. Searle is one of the most outspoken contemporary adherents of realism. I have begun a book comparing Searle and Foucault on the model of my comparison of Descartes and Foucault. Prado 1992.

8. Searle 1995:150.

9. Sellars 1968:82.

10. The most notorious problem with understanding truth as true statements "corresponding to the facts" is that we can neither identify nor differentiate facts on their own, so cannot compare statements to facts. Davidson, D. 1985:37–42.

11. Allen.

12. Searle 1995:xiii.

13. Foucault 1972:47. It is noteworthy that this passage occurs in *The Archaeology of Knowledge*, which antedates the major genealogical works.

14. One problem with putting things this way is that it sounds as if objects that emerge in discourse are the objects in a conceptual scheme that organizes a noumenal reality, but Foucault wants no part of a Kantian world-in-itself that contrasts with the world of our awareness. It is interesting that at least one commentator reads Foucault as not an irrealist on the basis that Foucault does accept a noumenal reality. May argues that what Nietzsche meant—and Foucault adopts—about there being only interpretations is that "the world is ontologically indeterminate" and supports any number of interpretations. May 1993:79.

15. Rorty 1991d:80.

16. Rorty 1991d:81. Rorty adds that

The way in which a blank takes on the form of the die which stamps it has no analogy to the relation between the truth of a sentence and the event which the sentence is about. When the die hits the blank something causal happens, but as many *facts* are brought into the world as there are languages for describing that causal transaction.

17. Rorty 1991d:81.

18. Rorty 1982:xxv.

19. Rorty 1991d:81.

20. Foucault 1972:47–48.

21. Foucault 1972:47–48.

22. Foucault 1972:48.

23. Recall that Foucault's primary concern is not with ordinary talk but with expert discourse, with the idioms of science, medicine, the judiciary, the academy. Dis-

ciplinary discourses that shape subjectivity and establish regimes of truth all involve theory-laden references to the world.

24. Foucault, 1988b:119–20.

25. Allen. Despite his disagreement with my reading of Foucault, Allen nonetheless stresses that Foucault is concerned to establish that "a thing . . . a substance, a reality . . . does not confer truth upon statements."

26. Davidson, D. 1985:194. This is essentially the point Sellars argued decades ago, maintaining that propositions are justified, not by the things themselves, but by other propositions. Sellars 1968:82.

27. Foucault 1989:314.

28. Davidson does think statements are true in the same way but play different roles.

> Satisfaction of closed sentences is explained in terms of satisfaction of sentences both open or closed, whereas it is only closed sentences that traditionally have corresponding facts. Since different assignments of entities to variables satisfy different open sentences and since closed sentences are constructed from open, truth is reached, in the semantic approach, by different routes for different sentences. All true sentences end up in the same place, but there are different stories about how they got there; a semantic theory of truth tells the story for a particular sentence by running through the steps of the recursive account of satisfaction appropriate to the sentence. Davidson, D. 1985:48–49.

29. A parallel might be to discussing photographs with respect to composition, degree of contrast, poses, effectiveness of sharp or diffuse focus, and coloration, without once referring to *likenesses*. We can easily imagine photographers or critics assessing photographs without at any time raising the question of whether they do justice to the people or things they picture.

30. I owe the term "prelinguistic" to E. J. Bond. It captures just the sense that brute reality is prior to any discourse rather than simply being external to discourse.

31. See pages 119–122.

32. Krausz's definition of relativism as holding that "cognitive, moral, or aesthetic claims involving . . . truth . . . are relative to the contexts in which they appear" includes perspectivism. Krausz 1989:1. However, as indicated in Chapter 6, perspectivism focuses on commensurability of viewpoints rather than the truth of statements. In this respect it appears more likely irrealist than other forms of relativism.

33. Nietzsche 1968a:267, my emphasis.

34. Nietzsche 1968a:330.

35. Dreyfus and Rabinow 1983:107.

36. Nietzsche 1968a:298.

37. Dreyfus and Rabinow 1983:107.

38. Foucault 1980b:117.

39. It will be thought that the picture I have been painting of objects being linguistic is at odds with Davidson's rejection of the scheme/content distinction. But as pointed out in Note 14, above, the point is that some bit of brute reality is a *this* or

a *that* only when conceptualized. This does not entail that what we conceptualize is a noumenal reality. Even Searle allows that our awareness of the world is always from some point of view. See Note 42, below.

40. Davidson, D. 1985:198. Notice that Davidson has no problem saying it is familiar objects "whose antics make our sentences and opinions true or false" despite telling us that "[n]othing . . . makes sentences . . . true." There is no inconsistency here. Davidson's denial that anything makes sentences true is rejection of what he describes as a "new entity" which determines the truth of sentences. This also clarifies why Davidson speaks of "objects."

41. Nehamas 1985:64.

42. Searle 1995:176.

43. Nagel 1986.

44. e.g., Nola 1994:sec 5.6.

45. Foucault 1980b:132.

46. Dreyfus and Rabinow 1983:117.

47. Davidson, D. 1985:49. Davidson adds that a "well-explored" result of this error is that "it becomes difficult to describe the fact that verifies a sentence except by using that sentence itself." Another result is that "the relation of correspondence . . . seems to have direct application to only the simplest sentences."

48. The *locus classicus* of the view rejected here is Wittgenstein's *Tractatus.* Wittgenstein 1922.

49. Rorty 1991d:81.

50. Rorty does not think Foucault offers anything new on truth, as we saw in Chapter 6.

51. Allen.

52. Foucault 1980b:131.

53. Davidson, D. 1985:43–44.

54. Foucault 1972:47.

55. The question of how we relate to sentences is not only about how we relate to the sentences that are current in a regime of truth or an economy of knowledge. The question is also about how we relate to sentences that were current in a regime or economy long since obscured or suppressed. This latter issue is what archaeology is all about and what genealogy's disruptive role is all about.

56. This basically is the familiar problem of reading Foucault as concerned with ideologically distorted truth.

57. Foucault 1980b:118.

58. Davidson, D. 1985:219–23.

59. This is the idea Dewey worked to defeat by stressing our manipulation of things. We are much closer to the things themselves when we work with and change them than when we describe them. The view that uttering truths is somehow more direct contact with the world is of a piece with what Dewey rejected as the "spectator" theory of knowledge.

60. Rorty 1982:15.

61. *The Order of Things* and other works are full of examples of how biologists and physicians extrapolate from their work on cells or glands to pontificate on attitudes and preferences.

62. What Foucault offers regarding economies of knowledge is relativistic, but it is not Krausz's "radical" relativism.

63. Davidson expresses the common view of truth's simplicity while dismissing as unproductive the idea that truth is correspondence to the facts: "the notion of fitting the facts, or of being true to the facts, adds nothing intelligible to the simple concept of being true." Davidson, D. 1985:193–94.

64. Allen 1999:69. Foucault's pluralistic relativization of truth is seen by some as denying truth not only in detaching it from the world but also in fragmenting its supposedly inviolable simplicity. Foucault was impatient with such charges, describing those who took him to be denying truth as "simple-minded." Foucault 1989:295.

65. Davidson, D. 1985:49.

66. Dreyfus and Rabinow 1983:117.

67. Allen.

68. Foucault 1984b:17.

Chapter Eight

Novel Construals and Cogency

Novelty always comes hard in philosophy, given philosophy's self-defining commitment to discerning timeless truth. Established ideas are taken as hard-won truths and are ardently defended and all the advantages afforded by incumbency are employed. Most relevant here is that challenges to established philosophical evaluatory methods and standards are met by applying precisely those same methods and standards to the challenges. When new ideas do succeed in displacing previously accepted ones, they are heralded as representing discerned deeper truths or truths formerly obscured. The new ideas then become as entrenched as those they displaced. Wittgenstein, a major philosophical innovator, predicted that if his project succeeded, the arguments he used would come to be no longer understood. His point was that after the success of his project, people would not appreciate "why all this needed saying."[1] Foucault's work was nothing if not innovative, and nearly two decades after his death much of what he said no longer seems to need saying. His conception of power relations now is thoroughly integrated into many disciplines. However, this is not true of mainstream North American philosophy. Foucault's innovations remain suspect and are little used or understood within that philosophical tradition. I have considered two related reasons for this in the last two chapters, namely, perception of Foucault as an extreme relativist and as an irrealist. In this last chapter, I focus on a question that poses a more serious obstacle to taking Foucault's work seriously than do misconceived charges of extreme relativism and irrealism. This is the question of cogency, or the question about how to evaluate Foucault's innovations for possible adoption.

Innovative Visions and Periods

Despite all the talk about postmoderism, ours is not postmodern age. We may not want our age to be postmodern, if that means that Derridean word

163

play and artistic excess are its defining characteristics, but as Hoy points out, "periodization" is a tricky matter.[2] We must already be beyond an intellectual era before we can characterize it meaningfully. To identify the conceptual and disciplinary principles and practices of an epoch we must already be using different principles and practices. Otherwise, there is insufficient distance to enable effective characterization. Many take Foucault's vision as being postmodern in the sense that its critiques periodize modernity or the modern era. However, perhaps as many take what he says as violating or flouting reasoned inquiry rather than as periodizing it. Certainly for most of my intended readers, reasoned inquiry still is pretty much what Kant considered it to be. There has not been a decisive periodization of modernity.[3] To put the point in Rorty's terms, for better or for worse we still have not come into a "postphilosophical culture."[4] This is why Foucault's novel construals, particularly his genealogies, meet with confident application of what they oppose or differently explain.[5] His historicization of rationality is met with charges of irrationality on the grounds that rationality can only be ahistorical. His relativization of truth meets with charges that he cannot be talking about "real" truth because he presupposes objective truth in making any claims at all. Some of this is mistaken, as I tried to show in the last two chapters, but what is significant is that it is mistaken more in degree than in kind. That is, the charge of extreme relativism, for instance, is mistaken because it ignores the complexity of Foucault's position on truth, not because extreme relativism has become "the truth of our time." The question of how cogent Foucault's proposals are, according to established standards, still is a real question and it may remain a real question.

Paradoxically, this is as it should be, at least with respect to genealogy. Genealogy would fail if evaluation of its effective histories were conducted in its own terms. Genealogy must remain marginal and oppositional. What genealogy offers always needs saying. Its analyses must always strike the orthodox as counterintuitive. Its arguments at first must seem not to be arguments at all because they violate accepted intellectual procedures. To be effective, genealogical analyses must *always* meet with application of what those analyses impugn. Genealogy is a problematizing attitude or stance that draws its life from what it investigates and opposes. Genealogy would be self-vitiating if it aspired to displace established philosophical principles and methods and to become codified and itself established as the dominant truth of an era.

Genealogy is like pragmatism in being mainly attitudinal. Rorty notes that pragmatism does not try to replace foundationalist epistemology, the philosophy of language, or any other sort of Capital-P Philosophy.[6] Underlying the attitudinal character of both genealogy and pragmatism is a realization that Rorty claims "ties Dewey and Foucault, James and Nietzsche, together." This realization was referenced in Chapter 2, and is that "[t]here is no . . . criterion that we have not created in . . . creating a practice, no standard of rationality that is not an appeal to such a criterion, no rigorous argumentation that is not obedience to our own conventions."[7] Genealogy is a readiness to continually problematize established truths through development of alternative accounts of targeted facts, concepts, principles, canons, natures, institutions, methodological truisms, and established practices. Genealogy cannot become the dominant truth of an age for it can only exist as opposition to orthodoxy cashed out in table-turning reconstruals of the familiar. Relying on convincing historical detail, genealogy provides startling, perspective-altering reversals and inversions of what passes as given and is unquestioned. That is how genealogy enables resistance to power's otherwise inexorable tendency to become ever more restrictive and confining.

Given the foregoing, it may look as if the cogency question cannot apply to genealogy—though it might well apply to archaeology and Foucauldian ethics. However, the cogency question applies to genealogy in a holistic way. That is, even if particular genealogies are always in opposition to established evaluatory standards, we need good reason to adopt the genealogical stance. More simply put, we need good reason to continuously roil the intellectual or disciplinary waters. Particular genealogies may not be rivals to established theories, but we need to justify producing them in the first place; we need to justify endorsement and promotion of genealogy.

As hinted, archaeology and Foucauldian ethics differ importantly from genealogy with respect to the cogency question. Archaeology and ethics are not primarily problematizing, as is genealogy. Both have positive content. This likely is why so many traditional philosophers see them, especially archaeology, as more familiarly philosophical. Unlike genealogy, archaeology appears to aspire to replace epistemology as a theoretical method for understanding knowledge. Foucauldian ethics are not theoretical, but offer a conception of the self as more autonomous and substantive than any found in *Discipline and Punish* or the first volume of *The History of Sexuality*.[8] The question of the cogency of Foucault's archaeological and ethical proposals may be more straightforward than the question of the cogency of his genealogies. Both involve claims that are independent of those they challenge or seek to displace, and those claims seem to admit of assessment using established standards. These differences make it necessary to say a little about what unifies the three modes of analysis to better understand application of the cogency question. Of particular interest is Foucault's shift from genealogy to ethics.

Unifying Factors: History

Foucault's archaeological, genealogical, and ethical analyses are unified by the fundamental role of historical research in each.[9] Thomas Flynn tells us that "[a]ll of Foucault's major works are histories of a sort."[10] Foucault himself describes his books as "work on the history of thought."[11] But as Flynn notes, the "challenge is to determine what sort of history [Foucault] does."[12] Certainly, Foucault is not, as many think, a familiar sort of intellectual historian. He contends that the history of thought is "not simply a history of ideas or of representations, but also the attempt to respond to this question: How is it that thought . . . can also have a history?"[13] This question encompasses issues such as how representation became problematic and how we made thought—and thus ourselves as thinkers—objects of scientific inquiry. These questions are not answered by intellectual history because they undercut that history in querying its possibility. Speaking of his archaeological mode of analysis, Foucault remarks that "such an analysis does not belong to the history of ideas." Instead it is "an inquiry whose aim is to rediscover on what basis knowledge and theory became possible; within what space of order knowledge was constituted."[14] Even genealogy's or "effective history's" meticulous historical research is not conducted for its own sake. Foucault describes genealogy as attempting to "emancipate" obscured knowledges from "subjugation." The point of this emancipation is, again, not for its own sake. Rather it is to make those knowledges "capable of opposition . . . against the coercion of a theoretical, unitary, formal and scientific discourse."[15] The sort of history being done, then, is of a special sort.

Foucauldian archaeological, genealogical, and—to a lesser extent—ethical histories have a common focus: the marginal and the subjugated. Foucault's histories are tracings of descent and emergence that concentrate on what established disciplines and traditional histories shun or obscure. His histories, especially his genealogies, are not passive tracings of the development of economies of knowledge, institutions, and practices. They actively seek out the accidental, the apparently trivial, the excluded. In this way, Foucault's histories are competing alternatives to established histories in the sense that they impugn and prompt rethinking of orthodox accounts just in being alternative accounts. Foucault makes the point by saying that whereas archaeology is the "analysis of local discursivities," genealogy consists of "the tactics whereby, on the basis of . . . these local discursivities," the newly emancipated knowledges are "brought into play."[16] Genealogy is best thought of as guerilla history. The objective is not merely to unearth and trace, but to provide alternity in an intellectually competitive way. The very existence of an alternative account poses a challenge to the essentialism and objectivism that characterize contemporary disciplinary inquiry. If our various disciplines claim to discern truth, genealogical redescriptions must be disproven, assimilated, or dangerously ignored. This is the force of Arac's point that defending a disciplinary subject against Foucault requires "redefining the subject."[17]

Archaeology is less concerned with providing alternity than with delineating and understanding it. Describing genealogy as having to do with the "antecedents of socio-intellectual reality, Gary Gutting describes archaeology as primarily concerned" with the conceptual structures subtending the reality."[18] Archaeology traces and charts the conceptual structures that enable, support, and define a socio-intellectual reality. By identifying and grasping the conceptual structure of a socio-intellectual reality, we understand an *episteme*, or what Wittgenstein might have called "a form of life."[19] In mapping *epistemes*, Foucault shows how disciplinary fields of inquiry became possible. In *The Order of Things* the focus is on "general grammar . . . natural history and . . . analysis of wealth" and their modern counterparts, linguistics, biology, and economics. Mapping the *episteme* that made these fields or disciplines possible and shaped their contours is doing history because Foucault is concerned with contingent "conditions . . . established in time."[20]

It is important that the historical elements most central to the development and definition of a socio-intellectual reality, and so what archaeology most directly maps, are not ideas or events but concepts. This is shown by the priority Foucault gives to concepts in defining disciplinary knowledge, which is the main subject of archaeology. Foucault defines disciplinary knowledge as in part a dynamic discursive context or "field of coordination and subordination of statements in which concepts . . . are defined, applied, and transformed."[21] Gutting concurs that much of Foucault's work "falls in the genre of 'the history of concepts.'" However, he points out that these are not ordinary concepts; they are concepts as "understood by . . . Georges Canguilhem."[22] These are not recognitional capacities but basic interpretive scientific ideas. The important difference has to do with derivation or inception. For Canguilhem, scientific concepts are not generated by theories. Canguilhem rejects the familiar positivistic understanding that scientific concepts are generated in the process of theoretically interpreting data. He thinks that scientific concepts precede theories and are diversely developed in disparate and even contradictory theoretical ways. A simple example is the concept of temperature arising as an understanding of hot and cold as a variable property rather than as, say, disparate intrinsic states of things or purely subjective reactions. Once the concept arises of temperature as a property that might be increased or diminished, gained or lost, the concept admits of varying interpretation. For instance, it may be interpreted as addition, depletion, or loss of caloric fluid, or it may be interpreted as intensification or abatement of mean kinetic energy.

In Canguilhem's view, a given concept will be longer-lived than the theories in which it is developed, which means that a concept's history will not be the same as the history of any given theory. The history of a concept may be studied with reference to various contemporaneous and succeeding theories in which that concept is employed and developed. Foucault takes up Canguilhem's view of concepts, but as with everything else, he rethinks the view in appropriating it. Foucault broadens the notion of a concept well beyond its scientific sense. Canguilhem considers concepts specific to disciplines. Foucault considers concepts as not only prior to theories, but also as prior to the disciplines in which theories are developed. This modification enables a more radical approach to the sort of conceptual history at the heart of archaeology. It allows Foucault to link and compare "apparently very different disciplines by showing similarities in their basic concepts."[23] The fruits of archaeological investigations then are not only the chronicling of theory and discipline development, but histories of the *epistemes* that define whole eras.

The Order of Things, the prototypical archaeological treatment of the human sciences, illustrates the conceptual history at issue in being a history of the concept of "man."[24] Foucault construes social-scientific disciplinary knowledges as turning on the advent and diverse development of the concept of "man" as something that is at once in the world and aware of the world. "Man" is described by Foucault as "that entity for which representations of objects exist" and that which "is both an object in the world and an experiencing subject."[25] However, whereas the human sciences that Foucault investigates take this concept as definitive of what it is to be human, he takes it as one among several possibilities. Whereas the human sciences take the concept as historical only in being temporal articulation of an ahistorical truth, Foucault takes it as being created at the end of the eighteenth century. Moreover, whereas scientists take the concept as gradually being better understood through research, Foucault takes it as in the process of decline. He tells us that "man is an invention of recent date. And one perhaps nearing its end." It is about to disappear "like a face drawn in sand at the edge of the sea."[26] This is mainly because thinkers like Hegel, Freud, and Saussure raised anew "the great problem of the sign and meaning" and problematized representation. The consequence is that "man is disappearing."[27]

According to Foucault, the turning point was Kant's investigation into the conditions of representation. For Descartes, representation is identical with thought; representation is ideas being before the mind. With Kant, our capacity to entertain representations of objects becomes problematic. His Copernican revolution recasts representation as an active operation, not just a passive receptivity. It then becomes important to understand how representation operates, what rules govern it, and the limits it may have. These questions soon overflow the boundaries of epistemology. They spawn many disciplines concerned with how we represent the world, how we represent ourselves, and how we are both things in the world and representers of the world. Archaeology's excavation of what shaped the present *episteme* investigates what concepts arose and developed so that modern disciplinary inquiry "orders all these questions around the question of man's being." The aim is to fathom how disciplinary inquiry came to conceive the project of understanding ourselves as the limning of a given nature and so "allows us to avoid an analysis of practice."[28]

Historical research and its focus on the marginal and subjugated may be described as a methodological unifying factor. A different kind of factor unifying Foucault's work is his concern with the subject, with subjectivity. This factor is most evident in his ethics. Sounding more as if he is describing archaeology, genealogy, and ethics rather than only genealogy, Foucault offers a characterization of genealogy as having three "domains." These are "an historical ontology of ourselves in relation to truth . . . an historical ontology of ourselves in relation to a field of power [and] an historical ontology in relation to ethics."[29] The concern of the first domain is how "we constitute ourselves as subjects of knowledge." The concern of the second is how "we constitute ourselves as subjects acting on others." The concern of the third is how "we constitute ourselves as moral agents."[30] Arnold Davidson considers this third domain of genealogy as a domain in its own right and not a part of genealogy.[31] Dreyfus and Rabinow are less sure, emphatically asserting that *"[t]here is no pre- and post-archaeology or genealogy in Foucault."*[32] However, while they are right with respect to temporal progression, Davidson's view seems correct with respect to focus and emphasis. Gutting's view is more holistic and he is dubious about Foucault's methodological consistency. Gutting thinks terms like "genealogy" are best understood as "retrospective (and usually idealized) descriptions of Foucault's complex efforts to come to terms with his historical material."[33] This approach is useful to deal with the tensions in Foucault's shift from genealogy to ethics. In any case, what matters is that Foucault answers the question of how we constitute ourselves as moral agents by providing an historical ontology. In doing so, he proceeds in the same way as in his archaelogical and geneaological projects. In the case of ethics Foucault investigates Greek and Roman ethical concepts and contrasts them with current ethical concepts.

The contrast problematizes our current law-centered conception of ethics, which Foucault calls "Christian."[34] The problematization is achieved in proper genealogical fashion by providing an alternative: the largely forgotten Greek conception of ethics as having to do with how best to live rather than with conformity to law. Foucault tells us that for the Greeks *ethos* was "deportment and the way to behave. It was the subject's mode of being and a certain manner of acting visible to others."[35] The Greek and Roman ethical project was the creation of not only a moral subject but of an admirable moral life. Significantly, this ethical project is reserved for a relative few. Greek and Roman ethics were for "the bearers of culture," those with the means to appreciate and "live a beautiful life, and to leave to others memories of a beautiful existence."[36] Ethics in this sense is not normalization of the many. This understanding of ethics might better be described from today's perspective as the aesthetics of self-development and life-management, rather than as the ethics of the self.

The history of concepts comes into Foucauldian ethics in his attempt to unearth, investigate, and build on what Foucault calls "techniques of the self." Foucault describes these techniques as having to do with "the freedom of the subject and the relationship to others, i.e., that which constitutes the very matter of ethics."[37] He maintains that the Greeks considered "the freedom of the individual as an ethical problem." In his view, "in antiquity the will to be a moral subject, the search for an ethics of existence, was principally an effort to affirm one's liberty and to give one's own life a certain form."[38] The ancient moral quest, therefore, was "essentially a search for a personal ethics" in contrast to the Christian conception of ethics "as obedience to a system of rules."[39] With Christianity, the will to be a moral subject and live a moral life was transformed into the will to live in accordance with divine law. The crucial question for the Christian is: What is God's will? This is a point often missed because Christian conformity to the law differs from antecedent Judaic conformity to explicit, putatively divine decrees and their intricate interpretations. Christian conformity is to the embodiment of the law in the figure of Christ. Being moral is still a matter of conforming, but to a paradigm rather than to rules. The paradigm is made available through parables, admonitions, and example rather than only decrees. This new understanding of ethical obedience is what Thomas à Kempis summarizes in his aptly titled *The Imitation of Christ*. There he informs the faithful that anyone seeking to achieve moral perfection and enlightenment "must endeavor to conform his life wholly to the life of Christ."[40]

Foucault paints a picture of the Greco-Roman conception of ethics as more fundamental than the Judeo-Christian conception. The basic question asked by Socrates, Plato, Epictetus, Aristotle, Epicurus, Seneca, and Marcus Aurelius is: How ought I to live? However, even if the answer was not given in terms of conformity to law or to example, it carried a commitment to truth. The best way to live was in accordance with a given nature: for instance, Plato's tripartite soul, Aristotle's rational essence, and Epictetus's determined universe. This sort of answer is not acceptable to Foucault, which is why his ethics do not merely endorse and emulate antiquity's ethical views. Foucault needs "techniques of management" and ethics that will enable us to best order our lives and recreate ourselves within power relations and "with a minimum of domination."[41] We cannot hope to escape power, but we can hope to follow the Nietzschean admonition to recreate ourselves and do it to the greatest degree possible within power relations. To do that, we have to understand and resist what we find detailed in *Discipline and Punish* and *The History of Sexuality*. In short, we have to understand and resist how in our social order "the individual is carefully fabricated . . . according to a whole technique of forces and bodies."[42]

What we find in *The Use of Pleasure* and *The Care of the Self* is an historical investigation into Greek and Roman techniques of the self, an investigation that could be described as archaeological or genealogical. The difference is in the objective. Unlike archaeology's attempt to trace and grasp a conceptual framework, or genealogy's attempt to map power relations, the aim is to recapture productive techniques of self-management. However, the point of the conceptual history or the attempt to "rethink the Greeks today" is not to merely emulate Greek and Roman ethics. Rather, it is to see to it "that European thought can get started again on Greek thought as an experience given once and in regard to which one can be . . . free."[43] The investigation centers on "how the experience of sexuality as desire had been constituted for the subject."[44] It should be noted, though, that sex and sexuality are purportedly only the means to understanding how the subject was shaped as a moral agent in antiquity. Foucault does not consider *The Care of the Self*, his book most centrally concerned with ethics, to be a book about sex or sexuality.[45]

The historical character of archaeology, genealogy, and Foucauldian ethics unifies them as domains of analysis. However, this unifying factor should not be misconstrued. It is important to keep in mind that Foucault eschews totalizing or essence-seeking history and disavows an interest in the past as such. He tells us his interest in the past is not a matter of "writing a history of the past in terms of the present" but rather is a matter of "writing the history of the present."[46] He describes his work as beginning "from a question posed in the present."[47] With respect to archaeology, the impetus is less to trace chronological development than to unearth the "deep structures that determine the limits and possibilities of knowledge for any given period."[48] The impetus to genealogy is feeling something is amiss, such as that penal reform has failed or that discussion of sexuality restricts rather than frees us. We then have to look hard at the sources and development of the key notions and ideas we take to be central to and definitive of what concerns us. That means doing not totalizing but "effective" history. In Foucault's words, we have to investigate "the historical conditions which motivate our conceptualization. We need a historical awareness of our present circumstance."[49] That awareness problematizes current truths by tracing their descent and emergence and by uncovering alternatives. We proceed by asking questions such as whether "the critical discourse that addresses itself to repression" really does "act as a roadblock to a power mechanism" or is integral to what it supposedly opposes.[50] We problematize the accepted, the obvious, the supposedly fundamental; we pursue what has been obscured or suppressed. We pay close attention to enabling accidents and coincidences; we discount established essentialist histories. In short, we trace the inception and development of concepts that were employed, that became established, and so became the dominant truth. The impetus to ethics is more positive. It is the desire or need to make oneself and one's life a work of art. This where subjectivity is most central to Foucault's thought. It is also where subjectivity is most problematic in conception.

Unifying Factors: Subjectivity

The unifying role of subjectivity is least important in archaeology and secondary to effective or nonessentialist history in genealogy. This is so despite Foucault's claim that "during the last 20 years" his main concern was less to analyze power than "to create a history of the different modes by which . . . human beings are made subjects."[51] The presentation of the ethical subject or self is, in fact, at odds with this last remark because rather than individuals being made subjects of certain sorts, individuals practicing Foucauldian ethics make or remake themselves.[52] The point is put to Foucault in an interview. The interviewer remarks that in his ethics, Foucault shifts from the "coercive practices" detailed in *Discipline and Punish* and *The History of Sexuality* to "practices of self-formation."[53] Unfortunately, Foucault does not address the issue raised. Instead, he speaks of being suspicious of the notion of liberation because it poses the risk of assuming a basic human nature to be liberated. The question he dodges is how the disciplined subject of the central genealogical works finds the wherewithal for self-determination. If "the individual is carefully fabricated . . . according to a whole technique of forces," how can one engage in practices of self-formation?[54] A related question is how subjects could ever know that they were succeeding in determining their own subjectivity as opposed to their subjectivity being determined by power relations.[55] This is not the place to pursue this matter, but a point can be made that may alleviate the tension.

Genealogy deals with practices that involve *populations*; for instance, prison inmates, psychiatric patients, and all of us insofar as we are sexual beings. The move to ethics is like refocusing on individuals as opposed to populations; it is like reading ourselves back into power relations. Refocusing on the individual may reveal a previously obscured measure of autonomy. There is no room for self-forming autonomy in genealogical analysis because its focus is the disciplining of substantial numbers of inmates, patients, students, soldiers, and so forth. However, ethics deals with the actions of particular people. That means allowing for the idiosyncrasies of individuals and the diversity of their responses to constraints on their actions. Power relations are not, after all, wholly deterministic. Recall that individuals are in power relations only insofar as they have options open to them. If their "comportments" are predetermined, then they are slaves and not subjects at all. It may be that there is room for something like autonomy in the range of possible responses to constraints on action. Nonetheless, there is a shift, and it can be differently construed. We can understand the new autonomy in the ethical works as a maturation of Foucault's understanding of power relations. Alternatively, we can construe it as resulting from a de-emphasis or even abandonment of power.[56] Or we can see the new autonomy as unexpectedly salvaged from the bleak accidental near-determinism of power. However, the shift from genealogy to ethics, from power-determined subjects to self-determining subjects, does raise the issue of the overall consistency of Foucault's work. That issue bears on the cogency question in this way. If historical method and subjectivity tightly unify archaeology, genealogy, and ethics, then the cogency question applies to the whole of Foucault's work. If the three domains are more separable, perhaps as stages in a progression, then the cogency question bears most directly on genealogy.

Cogency

The cogency question is one about why we might accept and adopt Foucault's novel construals, or what Gutting calls his "complex interpretive frameworks." Foucault presents his construals as polemicists present their theses, that is, as rationally compelling. His claims about the invention of madness, the institutionalization of illness, the manufacture of the penal disciplinary system, and the deployment of sexuality are all presented as cogent, that is, as intellectually compelling. In particular, Foucault presents his conception and account of power relations as fundamental to understanding human behavior and the emergence of subjects. The question is why we should accept what Foucault says. This is the question underlying Rorty's complaint, referred to earlier, that Foucault simply assumes that his philosophical project should be our philosophical project.[57] Many who are initially intrigued by Foucault's work falter in their pursuit of it when they begin to wonder why they should consider Foucault's accounts, analyses, and histories preferable to those he rejects. The trouble is that Foucault's historicism precludes assessment of his archaeological and ethical construals, and especially of his genealogies, as true or false. There is no broader context—as might be provided by ahistorical rationality—within which Foucault's construals can be evaluated. Evaluation can only be conducted in the terms of the discourses Foucault challenges. But since the point of his novel construals is to impugn the methods and standards of those discourses, evaluation is ineffective and pointless. If we cannot independently establish that those construals are rationally compelling, if we cannot judge them *true*, we are at a loss as to how to judge them more worthy of adoption than their competitors. Worse still, we must keep in mind that choosing between Foucault's construals and established ones might be a function of power relations and not our doing at all.

The question of the cogency of Foucault's claims poses a particularly serious problem for my intended audience, namely, philosophers in the analytic tradition. Their conception of philosophy requires that Foucault's accounts, analyses, and histories be assessable for truth-value. Even Taylor concurs on this point, though he is familiar with the European philosophical tradition and so apt to be more sympathetic to Foucault. Taylor characterizes Foucault as a "neo-Nietzschean" and demands to know where the argument is "that will show the . . . Nietzschean claim to be true." He insists that subordination of truth to power is a position that "has to show itself to be a superior construal." He further insists that the debate must be conducted in the language and according to the standards of those he calls the "defenders of critical reason."[58] In this, Taylor rejects a possible way of evaluating Foucault's construals that I consider below. Nola, a harsher critic, focuses on remarks that Foucault makes in *Power/Knowledge* about his analyses and Marxist and psychoanalytic theories. Nola asks on what grounds Foucault can claim "that theories which rival his own are false."[59] May is more sympathetic, but nonetheless presses the cogency question. He contends that because of "the radical questioning" that genealogy requires and fosters, Foucault owes us, but fails to provide, an account of why we should "accept his inquiries as justified and possibly true."[60]

Defenders of Foucault usually focus on truth's complexities, on renunciation of the foundationalist conception of justification, and on repudiation of the traditional idea that content and mode of presentation are separable.[61] I do not consider these efforts persuasive. Moreover, those efforts are dubiously compatible with Foucault's own position on the issue. Foucault thinks that the cogency of his proffered novel construals lies in four distinct things. First, archaeological reconstructions facilitate understanding of antecedent conceptual frameworks, thereby enriching our understanding and multiplying our intellectual and practical options. Second, genealogies are "gray, meticulous, and patiently documentary" and so are as historically accurate as any competing totalizing history. Third, genealogies of established practices and institutions reveal that social policies often actually serve precisely what they intend to change or reform. Fourth, reconsideration of temporally distant techniques of the self enables productive new contemporary practices.[62] The gist of these points is that Foucault's novel construals are more empowering and enabling than their competitors, while presenting events and developments more scrupulously than those competitors. Of greatest significance, for our purposes, is what is implied about the mode of evaluation alluded to above, namely, that assessment of Foucault's novel construals must be retrospective. That is, instead of his construals being assessed as possibly worthy of adoption prior to the fact, they are properly assessed as productive or not only after being adopted and used. To see how this works, we need to reiterate the point of Foucault's problematizing efforts.

When Foucault gives reasons for offering one or another of his novel construals, the reasons provided invariably are specific to one or another particular project. This is so whether we look in the books themselves or at his answers to interviewers' or interlocutors' questions.[63] When we look for remarks at a higher level of generality, we find reflections (some are quoted above) on the role of the intellectual and the enabling of novelty of thought. Foucault insists that the role of the intellectual is "to question over and over again what is postulated as self-evident, to disturb people's mental habits, the way they do and think things, to dissipate what is familiar and accepted, to reexamine rules and institutions."[64] Novel construals admit of justification only individually and in particular contexts. The general point of producing novel construals is to change habits of thought. The construals, then, are not theses to be evaluated first and only then adopted. They are goads to new thinking. As such, novel construals must be judged in light of the success or failure of their adoption.

What underlies this view is that the only way to enable resistance to power's subject-determining influence is to constantly "promote new forms of subjectivity."[65] When Foucault writes *Discipline and Punish* or *The History of Sexuality*, he does not provide truths "found in a series of historically verifiable proofs." Instead, he provides opportunities for experiences that each book "permits us to have."[66] Those experiences are empowering because "the effort to think one's own history can free thought . . . and so enable it to think differently."[67] In Rorty's more familiar terms, novel construals are new metaphors that enable fresh ways of thinking and speaking about accepted truths, established practices, and our very selves.[68] It is through new metaphors that an individual "escapes from inherited descriptions . . . and finds new descriptions." New descriptions enable one to "make a self" or redefine oneself "in terms which are, if only marginally, [one's] own."[69] In this view, the cogency question is misconceived because new metaphors "initially sound crazy."[70] They can only be judged as productive or otherwise after they have been employed. The point, then, is that the cogency of Foucauldian alternative construals of established truths, institutions, and practices has to do with how enabling or empowering they prove to be.

Gutting offers a defense of Foucault's novel histories that illustrates this retrospective approach to the question of cogency. He argues that Foucault offers construals intended to "give intelligible order to an otherwise meaningless jumble of individual historical truths." Gutting goes on to say that "[t]he facts are not irrelevant for Foucault, but the primary support for his position is not its demonstrable correspondence with them but its logical and imaginative power to organize them into intelligible configurations."[71] Gutting is concerned to defend Foucault against the charge that he is a bad historian because mainstream historians question or reject the details of his historical accounts.[72] The core of the defense is that Foucault's alternative histories have value despite sometimes getting the details wrong. Speaking of Foucault's history of madness, Gutting says that "[s]o far there have been no decisive tests of the fruitfulness of Foucault's complex interpretive framework. What is still needed . . . is an assessment of his overall picture . . . through detailed deployments of its specific interpretative categories."[73] The remark applies just as well to genealogical treatments of illness, penality, and sexuality as to madness. The value of Foucault's novel construals supposedly is useful interpretive novelty, and that is value to be assessed retrospectively.

The trouble with the focusing on retrospective assessment to deal with the cogency question is that doing so looks question-begging. The fundamental aim of constant intellectual innovation, of continually promoting "new forms of subjectivity," is to resist power's determination of us as certain kinds of subjects.[74] Appropriate evaluation of subjectivity-redefining genealogies, then, is not anterior assessment for truth-value. First, there is no fixed nature that we can appeal to regarding what subjects should be, in order for us to tell what account or history is true or most true. Second, power relations preclude that we could tell ahead of time that one or another account or history will prove most productive. Remember that what we do not know is "what what we do does." Genealogies have to be evaluated retrospectively for effectiveness in recasting subjectivity and enabling resistance. What makes all of this look question-begging is that subjectivity-redefining genealogies are needed, and can have value in enabling resistance to power, *only if Foucault is right about power.*

Some—Rorty, Foucault himself—argue that all evaluation, like all justification, is "internal" to a vocabulary or a discourse or an economy of knowledge. They insist that there is "no criterion that we have not created in the course of creating a practice."[75] In other words, we have no access to anything outside our thought and language that we can use as an objective standard. The world cannot serve as a standard because, as Rorty contends, there is "no way of transferring this nonlinguistic brutality . . . to the truth of sentences."[76] The claim that all evaluation is internal to a discourse or an economy of knowledge by itself raises huge questions. However, we have to add that evaluation is retrospective and that power relations determine or significantly influence subjectivity. If evaluation is internal, retrospective, and conducted by changing subjects, it appears illusory or impossible. Adoption of a particular novel construal not only changes the conditions of assessment, it also changes us as subjects, and so as evaluators of the construal's productivity. What emerges is the issue of self-knowledge and of understanding our choices and actions in a Foucauldian framework. This is an issue that affects not only the matter of evaluation of Foucault's construals but also that of the possibility of self-formation in

Foucauldian ethics. Hoy puts the point succinctly, saying that given Foucault's principles, "[g]enuine self-knowledge is in a sense impossible, since the self that we make appear to ourselves as an object of knowledge will never be identical to the self that is constructing that object." It seems inescapable that acceptance or rejection of any novel construal ultimately is a function either of power relations or of capricious "limit experiences." This conclusion seems unacceptable.

The question, then, is whether the cogency issue precludes taking Foucault's work seriously, even if doing so is not precluded by extreme relativism or irrealism. Some may even argue that the cogency question reveals that despite the complexities considered in Chapter 6, Foucault *is* an extreme relativist. I have argued that Foucault is not foolishly claiming that all claims or beliefs are on a par or absurdly contending that nothing exists other than language. However, he does historicize truth in the five complex ways discussed earlier. There is, then, no easy answer to the cogency question. The only option seems to be Gutting's view that what is called for is "assessment of [Foucault's] overall picture . . . through detailed deployments of its specific interpretative categories."[77] This is in line with Foucault's own attitude. Despite the polemic tone of his work, Foucault insisted that he would not tell others "where their truth is and how to find it."[78] He did not think it his place "to tell others what they have to do."[79] Instead, he offered an interpretive framework. He did not even promise it would prove productive. He offered it as an opportunity to recast one's subjectivity. My goal has been to win a hearing for Foucault on the part of those least prepared to take him seriously. If the cogency issue is thought decisive, rejection of Foucault's work may be merited. However, such rejection should be informed rejection; it should not be unreflective dismissal.

Notes

1. Wittgenstein 1980:43e.
2. Hoy 1991.
3. See Latour 1993.
4. Rorty 1982:xxxvii–xliv.
5. See, e.g., Hoy 1991, especially 20–21.
6. Rorty 1982:xxxvii–xliv.
7. Rorty 1982:xlii.
8. Compare Rorty 1986.
9. Compare Dreyfus and Rabinow 1983:104, O'Farrell 1989.
10. Flynn 1994:28.
11. Foucault 1989:294.
12. Flynn 1994:28.
13. Foucault 1989:294.

14. Foucault 1973:xxi.

15. Foucault 1976:85.

16. Foucault 1976:85.

17. Arac 1991:vii

18. Gutting 1994a12.

19. Wittgenstein 1953. However, as noted in Chapter 2, the enabling and supporting conceptual structures are not unidirectional determinants of practices. Recall that Foucault is a poststructuralist in that he understands the structures that subtend a socio-intellectual reality to be themselves historical and reciprocally affected by practice.

20. Foucault 1973:208.

21. Foucault 1972:182–83.

22. Gutting 1994a:7.

23. Gutting 1994a:9.

24. Compare Gutting 1994a:11–12. Note that in this discussion "man" does not admit of replacement with an inclusive term like "human" or "person." Not only is it the term Foucault uses, but more importantly the term is exclusive in denotation and connotation, as is evident from much of the history of the human sciences. I also decline to add "*sic*" here because the word is neither grammatically misused nor misspelled.

25. Gutting 1994a:11.

26. Foucault 1973:387.

27. Foucault 1989:6.

28. Foucault 1972:204.

29. Foucault 1983b:237.

30. Foucault 1983b:237.

31. Davidson, A. 1986:221.

32. Dreyfus and Rabinow 1983:104.

33. Gutting 1994a:6.

34. Foucault is not the only one with doubts about the grounds of contemporary ethics. MacIntyre characterizes contemporary ethics as an unworkable mix of Enlightenment moral autonomy and a categorical morality ultimately based on divine law. MacIntyre 1981:60; compare 2, 135, 201.

35. Foucault 1984b:6.

36. Foucault 1988a:45; 1983b:230.

37. Foucault 1984b:20.

38. Foucault 1984b:6; 1989:311.

39. Foucault 1989:311.

40. à Kempis 1894:1.

41. Foucault 1984b:18.

42. Foucault 1979:217.

43. Foucault 1989:325.

44. Foucault 1989:310.

45. Foucault 1983b:231.

46. Foucault 1979:31.

47. Foucault 1988b:262.

48. Ingram 1994:232. As noted earlier, archaeology carries something of the structuralist project of discerning determinants of practices. It also contains some

of Foucault's early ambitions to discern pure forms such as the "spontaneity of madness" prior to the institutionalization of mental illness. Foucault 1988b:119–20. We saw in Chapter 2 (in considering the shift from conceiving of signs as naturally resembling what they represent to a system of arbitrary symbols) that archaeology is intended to enable comprehension of a temporally or culturally distant conceptual framework. The similarities between Foucault and Gadamer are very close in this respect. Philosophical hermeneutics, as the theory of interpretation, shares with archaeology the cardinal concern with understanding alien interpretive schemes. But unlike Foucault's oppositional objective, Gadamer seeks a "fusing of horizons," a consolidation of a remote perspective on the world with our own. Gadamer 1976.

49. Foucault 1983a:209.

50. Foucault 1980a:10.

51. Foucault 1983a:208.

52. Bronwyn Singleton, whose work I supervised, pursues this tension in her *Foucault's Failure of Nerve: From Genealogy to Ethics*, the title of which says it all. Singleton 1998.

53. Foucault 1984b:2.

54. Foucault 1979:217.

55. See Hoy 1991:16 and below.

56. See, e.g., Hoy 1991:26.

57. Rorty 1991a:198.

58. Taylor 1987:483, 484.

59. Nola 1994:37.

60. May 1993:71.

61. Taylor 1984; de Man 1986; Bové 1988.

62. Foucault 1977:76.

63. See, for example, Foucault 1973:ix–xiv; 1979:23–24; 1980a:7–9; 1980b: 95–96; 1989; compare Gutting 1994a:2.

64. Foucault 1988b:265.

65. Foucault 1983a:216.

66. Foucault 1991a:36.

67. Foucault 1986:9.

68. Rorty 1991c:3; compare Frye 1983.

69. Rorty 1989:29,43.

70. Rorty 1991c:3.

71. Gutting 1994b:64.

72. See Gutting 1994b:47–48.

73. Gutting 1994b:67.

74. Foucault 1983a:216.

75. Rorty 1982:xlii. Recall, though, that Rorty expresses doubt that Foucault can make genealogy work without implicitly claiming it reveals something that is the case and that other histories obscure or distort. Rorty 1986:41–9, 1991b.

76. Rorty 1991d:81.

77. Gutting 1994b:67

78. Foucault 1986:8–9.

79. Foucault 1988b:265.

Bibliography

Foucault's works are listed with the publication dates of the English translations and not of the French originals. For that reason there are some apparent anomalies, as in the case of *The Archaeology of Knowledge* seeming to antedate *The Order of Things*. NOT ALL TITLES LISTED ARE REFERRED TO IN THE TEXT.

à Kempis, Thomas (1894). *The Imitation of Christ*. London: James Parker and Co. (Original translator believed to be Lady Margaret, mother of Henry VII; no later translator given.)

Allen, Barry (1991). "Government in Foucault." *Canadian Journal of Philosophy*, 21(4):421–40.

_____. (1993). *Truth in Philosophy*. Cambridge, Mass.: Harvard University Press.

_____. (1999). "Power/Knowledge." In Racevskis 1999.

Arac, Jonathan (ed.) (1991). *After Foucault*. New Brunswick, N.J.: Rutgers University Press.

Armstrong, Timothy (ed.) (1992). *Michel Foucault: Philosopher*. New York: Routledge.

Audi, Robert (ed.) (1996). *The Cambridge Dictionary of Philosophy*. Cambridge: Cambridge University Press.

Bartky, Sandra (1990). *Femininity and Domination*. New York: Routledge.

Baynes, Kenneth, James Bohman, and Thomas McCarthy (eds.) (1987). *After Philosophy*. Cambridge, MA: MIT Press.

Bell, Daniel (1992). "The Cultural Wars." *Wilson Quarterly*, Summer 1992, pp. 74–107.

Bernauer, James W. (1993). *Michel Foucault's Force of Flight: Toward an Ethics of Thought*. Atlantic Highlands, New Jersey and London: Humanities Press International.

_____. (1999). "Cry of Spirit." Foreword to Carrette (1999), pp. xi–xvii.

Bernauer, James W., and David Rasmussen (eds.) (1988). *The Final Foucault*. Cambridge, Mass.: MIT Press.

Bernauer, S. J. (1987). "The Prisons of Man." *International Philosophical Quarterly*, December 1987, 27(4):365–80.

Bernstein, Richard (1983). *Beyond Objectivism and Relativism*. Philadelphia: University of Pennsylvania Press.

_____. (1992). *The New Constellation*. Cambridge, Mass.: MIT Press.

Bloom, Harold (1973). *The Anxiety of Influence*. Oxford: Oxford University Press.

Borradori, Giovanna (1994). *The American Philosopher*. Chicago: University of Chicago Press.

Bouchard, Donald (ed.) (1977). Michel Foucault, *Language, Counter-Memory, Practice: Selected Essays and Interviews*. Trans. Donald Bouchard and Sherry Simon. Ithaca: Cornell University Press.

Bové, Paul (1988). "The Foucault Phenomenon: The Problematics of Style." Foreword to Deleuze 1988.

Boyne, Roy (1990). *Foucault and Derrida: The Other Side of Reason*. London: Unwin Hyman.

Bullock, Alan, and Oliver Stallybrass (eds.) (1983). *The Fontana Dictionary of Modern Thought*. London: Fontana/Collins.

Burchell, Graham, Colin Gordon, and Peter Miller (eds.) (1991). *The Foucault Effect: Studies in Governmentality*. Chicago: University of Chicago Press.

Burrell, G. (1988). "Modernism, Post Modernism and the Organizational Analysis 2: The Contribution of Michel Foucault." *Organization Studies*, 9(2):221–35.

Caputo, John (1983). "The Thought of Being and the Conversation of Mankind: The Case of Heidegger and Rorty." *The Review of Metaphysics*, 36 (1983): 661–85.

Carnap, Rudolf (1931). "Überwindung der Metaphysik durch Logische Analyse der Sprache." *Erkenntnis* (1931) 2. Reprinted in part in Murray 1978:23–34.

Carrette, Jeremy R. (ed.) (1999). *Religion and Culture: Michel Foucault*. New York: Routledge.

Cervantes, Miguel de (1963). *Don Quixote*. Baltimore: Penguin.

Code, Lorraine (1987). *Epistemic Responsibility*. Hanover, N.H.: Brown University Press (University Presses of New England).

_____. (1991). *What Can She Know? Feminist Theory and the Construction of Knowledge*. Ithaca: Cornell University Press.

Davidson, Arnold (1986). "Archaeology, Genealogy, Ethics." In Hoy 1986: 221–33.

Davidson, Donald (1973/1974). "On the Very Idea of a Conceptual Scheme." *Proceedings and Addresses of the American Philosophical Association*, 47(1973/74):5–20, also in LePore 1986.

_____. (1985). *Inquiries into Truth and Interpretation*. Oxford: Clarendon Press.

_____. (1986). "A Coherence Theory of Truth and Knowledge." In LePore 1986:307–19.

_____. (1989). "The Myth of the Subjective." In Krausz 1989:159–72.

Dawkins, Richard (1976). *The Selfish Gene*. Oxford: Oxford University Press.

Deleuze, Gilles (1984). "Nomad Thought." In D. Allison (ed.) (1984). *The New Nietzsche*. Cambridge, MA: MIT Press, pp. 141–49.

_____. (1988). *Foucault*. Minneapolis: University of Minnesota Press.

_____. (1993). *The Fold: Leibniz and the Baroque*. Minneapolis: University of Minnesota Press.

de Man, Paul (1986). *The Resistance to Theory*. Minneapolis: University of Minnesota Press.

Dennett, Daniel (1991). *Consciousness Explained*. New York: Little, Brown.

Dewey, John (1938). *Logic: The Theory of Inquiry*. New York: Henry Holt.

Diamond, Irene, and Lee Quinby (eds.) (1988). *Feminism and Foucault: Reflections on Resistance*. Boston: Northeastern University Press.

Dreyfus, Hubert, and Paul Rabinow (1983). *Michel Foucault: Beyond Structuralism and Hermeneutics*. With an Afterword by Michel Foucault. Brighton, Sussex: The Harvester Press.

Ehrenreich, Barbara, and Deirdre English (1973). *Complaints and Disorders: The Sexual Politics of Sickness*. New York: The Feminist Press, City University of New York.

Eribon, Didier (1991). *Michel Foucault*. Trans. Betsy Wing. Cambridge, MA: Harvard University Press.

Feyerabend, Paul (1978). *Against Method*. New York: Verso.

Fink-Eitel, Hinrich (1992). *Foucault: An Introduction*. Trans. Edward Dixon. Philadelphia: Pennbridge Books.

Flynn, Thomas (1989). "Foucault and Truth." *The Journal of Philosophy*, November 1989, 86(11):531–40.

_____. (1994). "Foucault's Mapping of History." In Gutting 1994a:28–46.

Fodor, Jerry (1987). *Psychosemantics*. Cambridge, Mass.: MIT Press.

Foucault, Michel (1965). *Madness and Civilization: A History of Insanity in the Age of Reason*. Trans. Richard Howard. New York: Random House.

_____. (1971). "Nietzsche, Genealogy, History." In Rabinow 1984:76–100. Also in Foucault 1977:139–64.

_____. (1972). *The Archaeology of Knowledge* (including *The Discourse on Language*). Trans. A.M. Sheridan-Smith. New York: Harper and Row.

_____. (1973). *The Order of Things*. New York: Vintage.

_____. (1974). "La maison de la folie." In Franco Basaglia and Franca Basaglia Ongaro (eds.) (1980). *Les Criminels de paix: Recherches sur les intellectuels et leurs techniques comme préposé à l'oppression*. Paris: Presses Universitaires de France, pp. 145–60. (French translation of text published in Italian, in 1975, as "La casa della follia.") Quoted in Miller 1993:270–71.

_____. (1975). *The Birth of the Clinic: An Archaeology of Medical Perception*. New York: Vintage.

_____. (1976). "Two Lectures." In Foucault 1980b:78–108.

_____. (1977). *Language, Counter-Memory, Practice: Selected Essays and Interviews*. In Bouchard 1977.

_____. (1979). *Discipline and Punish*. Trans. Alan Sheridan. New York: Pantheon.

_____. (1980a). *The History of Sexuality*, Volume 1. Trans. Robert Hurley. New York: Vintage.

_____. (1980b). *Power/Knowledge: Selected Interviews and Other Writings*. Colin Gordon (ed.) (1980). New York: Pantheon.

_____. (1983a). "The Subject and Power." Afterword to Dreyfus and Rabinow 1983:208–26.

_____. (1983b). "On the Genealogy of Ethics: An Overview of Work in Progress." In Dreyfus and Rabinow 1983:229–52.

_____. (1984a). "What Is Enlightenment?" In Rabinow 1984.

_____. (1984b). "The Ethics of Care for the Self as a Practice of Freedom." In Bernauer and Rasmussen 1988:1–20. Also in Rabinow 1997:281–301.

_____. (1986). *The Use of Pleasure*. Trans. Robert Hurley. New York: Vintage.

_____. (1988a). *The Care of the Self*. Trans. Robert Hurley. New York: Vintage.

_____. (1988b). *Michel Foucault: Politics, Philosophy, Culture: Interviews and Other Writings 1977–1984*. In Kritzman 1988.

_____. (1988c). *Technologies of the Self: A Seminar with Michel Foucault*. In Martin, Gutman, and Hutton 1988.

_____. (1989). *Foucault Live*. Trans. John Johnston, Sylvère Lotringer (ed.) (1989). New York: Semiotext(e).

_____. (1991a). *Remarks on Marx: Conversations with Duccio Trombadori*. Trans. James Goldstein, James Cascaito. New York: Semiotext(e).

_____. (1991b). "Questions of Method: An Interview with Michel Foucault." In Burchell, Gordon, and Miller 1991. Also in Baynes, Bohman, and McCarthy 1987.

Frye, Marilyn (1983). *The Politics of Reality: Essays in Feminist Theory*. Freedom, CA: The Crossings Press.

Gadamer, Hans-Georg (1975). *Truth and Method*. New York: Seabury Press.

_____. (1976). *Philosophical Hermeneutics*. Trans. David Linge. Berkeley: University of California Press.

Gane, Mike (ed.) (1985). *Towards a Critique of Foucault*. London: Routledge and Kegan Paul.

Gutting, Gary (ed.) (1994a). *The Cambridge Companion to Foucault*. Cambridge and New York: Cambridge University Press.

_____. (1994b). "Foucault and the History of Madness." Gutting 1994a:47–70.

Habermas, Jürgen (1987a). "Philosophy as Stand-In and Interpreter." In Baynes, Bohman, and McCarthy 1987:296–315.

_____. (1987b). *The Philosophical Discourse of Modernity: Twelve Lectures*. Trans. Frederick Lawrence. Cambridge, MA: MIT Press.

Hacking, Ian (1981). "The Archaeology of Foucault." *The New York Review of Books*. Reprinted in Hoy 1986:27–40.

Harding, Sandra, and Merrill Hintikka (eds.) (1983). *Discovering Reality: Feminist Perspectives on Epistemology, Metaphysics, Methodology, and Philosophy of Science*. Dordrecht, Holland: Reidel.

Hartsock, Nancy (1990). "Foucault on Power: A Theory for Women?" In Nicholson 1990.

Harvey, David (1990). *The Condition of Modernity*. Oxford: Blackwell's.

Hekman, Susan (1990). *Gender and Knowledge: Elements of a Postmodern Feminism*. Boston: Northeastern University Press.

Hooper, Keith, and Michael Pratt (1993). "The Growth of Agricultural Capitalism and the Power of Accounting: A New Zealand Study." *Critical Perspectives on Accounting*, 4:247–74.

Hopper, Trevor, and Norman Macintosh (1993). "Management Accounting as Disciplinary Practice: The Case of ITT Under Harold Geneen." *Management Accounting Research*, 4:181–216.

Hoy, David Couzens (ed.) (1986). *Foucault: A Critical Reader*. New York: Basil Blackwell.

_____. (1991). "Foucault: Modern or Postmodern?" Arac 1991:12–41.

Ingram, David (1994). "Foucault and Habermas on the Subject of Reason." In Gutting 1994a:215–61.

James, William (1978). *Pragmatism and the Meaning of Truth*. Cambridge, Mass.: Harvard University Press.

_____. (1907). "Pragmatism's Conception of Truth." In Thayer 1982:209–26.

Jones, W. T. (1969). *A History of Philosophical: Kant to Wittgenstein and Sartre, Volume 4*. 2nd ed. New York: Harcourt, Brace and World,

Kinsey, Alfred C. (1948) *Sexual Behavior in the Human Male*. Philadelphia: Saunders.

_____. (1953). *Sexual Behavior in the Human Female*. Philadelphia: Saunders.

Krausz, Michael (ed.) 1989. *Relativism: Interpretation and Confrontation*. Notre Dame: University of Notre Dame Press.

Kritzman, Lawrence D. (ed.) (1988). *Michel Foucault: Politics, Philosophy, Culture: Interviews and Other Writings 1977–1984*. Oxford: Blackwell's. Introduction, pp. ix–xxv.

Kuhn, Thomas (1970). *The Structure of Scientific Revolutions*. Chicago: University of Chicago Press.

Latour, Bruno (1993). *We Have Never Been Modern*. Cambridge, MA: Harvard University Press.

Lawson, Hilary (1985). *Reflexivity: The Postmodern Predicament*. London: Hutchinson.

LePore, Ernest (ed.) (1986). *Truth and Interpretation: Perspectives on the Philosophy of Donald Davidson*. New York: Blackwell.

Lyotard, Jean-François (1992). *The Postmodern Explained*. Minneapolis: University of Minnesota Press.

Macey, David (1993). *The Lives of Michel Foucault*. London: Hutchinson.

Machado, Roberto (1992). "Archaeology and Epistemology." In Armstrong 1992:3–19.

Macintosh, Norman B., Teri Shearer, Daniel Thornton, and Michael Walker (2000). "Accounting as Simulacrum and Hyperreality: A Poststructuralist Perspective." *Accounting, Organizations and Society*, 25(1):13–50.

MacIntyre, Alisdair (1977). "Epistemological Crises, Dramatic Narrative and the Philosophy of Science." *The Monist*, 60(4):453–72.

_____. (1981). *After Virtue*. Notre Dame: Notre Dame University Press.

_____. (1988). *Whose Justice? Which Rationality?* Notre Dame: University of Notre Dame Press.

Mackie, Marlene (1990). "Who Is Laughing Now? The Role of Humor in the Social Construction of Gender." *Atlantis*, 15(2):11–26.

Mahon, Michael (1992). *Foucault's Nietzschean Genealogy: Truth, Power and the Subject*. Albany: State University of New York Press.

Malpas, Jeffrey (1992). "Truth in the World." In *Donald Davidson and the Mirror of Meaning*. Cambridge: Cambridge University Press.

Marshall, Brenda (1992). *Teaching the Postmodern: Theory and Fiction*. New York: Routledge.

Martin, L. H., Huck Gutman, and Patrick Hutton (eds.) (1988). *Technologies of the Self: A Seminar with Michel Foucault*. Amherst: University of Massachusetts Press.

Matson, Wallace I. (1987). *A New History of Philosophy*. New York: Harcourt Brace Jovanovich.

May, Todd (1993). *Between Genealogy and Epistemology: Psychology, Politics, and Knowledge in the Thought of Michel Foucault.* University Park, PA: Pennsylvania State University Press.

Merquior, J. G. (1985). *Foucault.* Berkeley: University of California Press.

Miller, James (1993). *The Passion of Michel Foucault.* New York: Simon and Schuster.

Moulton, Janice (1983). "A Paradigm of Philosophy: The Adversary Method." In Harding and Hintikka 1983:149–64.

Munteanu, Vasile (1998). Review of *Starting With Foucault,* in *International Studies in Philosophy,* XXX/2:153–54.

Nagel, Thomas (1986). *The View from Nowhere.* New York: Oxford University Press.

Nehamas, Alexander (1985). *Nietzsche: Life as Literature.* Cambridge, MA: Harvard University Press.

Nielsen, Kai. (1989). *After the Demise of the Tradition.* Boulder: Westview Press.

Nielsen, Kai, and Hendrick Hart. (1990). *In Search of Community in a Withering Tradition.* New York: University Press of America.

Nietzsche, Friedrich Wilhelm (1968a). *The Will to Power.* Walter Kaufman (ed.) (1967). Trans. Kaufman and R. J. Hollingdale. New York: Vintage Books.

———. (1968b). *Thus Spoke Zarathustra.* In Walter Kaufman (ed. and Trans.) (1968). *The Portable Nietzsche.* New York: Penguin.

———. (1982). *Daybreak.* R. J. Hollingdale (Trans.) (1982). Cambridge: Cambridge University Press.

Nola, Robert (1994). "Post-Modernism, A French Cultural Chernobyl: Foucault on Power/Knowledge." *Inquiry,* 37(1):3–43.

O'Farrell, Clare (1989). *Foucault: Historian or Philosopher?* Houndmills, U.K.: Macmillan.

O'Hara, Daniel (1986). "What Was Foucault?" In Arac 1991:71–96.

Parfit, Derek (1984). *Reasons and Persons.* Oxford: Oxford University Press. See Chapters 14 and 15.

Peirce, Charles Sanders (1931). *The Collected Papers of Charles Sanders Peirce,* Charles Hartshorne and Paul Weiss (1931) (eds.). Cambridge, MA: Harvard University Press.

Polan, Dana (1982). "Fables of Transgression: The Reading of Politics and the Politics of Reading in Foucauldian Discourse." *Boundary 2,* 10(3):361–82.

Prado, C. G. (1984). *Making Believe: Philosophical Reflections on Fiction.* Westport: Greenwood Press.

———. (1987). *The Limits of Pragmatism.* Atlantic Highlands: Humanities Press.

———. (1988) "Imagination and Justification." *The Monist,* 71(3):377–88.

———. (1992). *Descartes and Foucault: A Contrastive Introduction.* Ottawa: University of Ottawa Press.

———. (1995). *Starting With Foucault: An Introduction to Genealogy.* Boulder, CO and San Francisco: Westview Press.

Putnam, Hilary (1978). *Meaning and the Moral Sciences.* London and Boston: Routledge and Kegan Paul.

———. (1987). "Why Reason Can't Be Naturalized." In Baynes, Bohman, and McCarthy 1987:22–44.

_____. (1988). *Representation and Reality.* Cambridge, MA: Bradford Books, MIT Press.

Rabinow, Paul (1984). *The Foucault Reader.* New York: Pantheon.

_____. (1997). *Michel Foucault: Ethics: Subjectivity and Truth, Essential Works of Foucault, Volume 1.* New York: The New Press.

_____. (1998). *Michel Foucault: Ethics: Subjectivity and Truth, Essential Works of Foucault, Volume 1.* New York: The New Press.

Racevskis, Karlis (1999). *Critical Essays on Michel Foucault,* New York: Hall and Co.

Rajchman, John (1985). *Michel Foucault: The Freedom of Philosophy.* New York: Columbia University Press.

Ramazanoglu, Caroline (ed.) (1993). *Up Against Foucault: Explorations of Some Tensions Between Foucault and Feminism.* New York: Routledge.

Ramberg, Bjorn (1989). *Donald Davidson's Philosophy of Language: An Introduction.* Oxford: Blackwell's.

Rée, Jonathan (1992). "Massacre of the Innocents." *Radical Philosophy* 62(Autumn):61–62.

Ricoeur, Paul (1992). *Oneself as Another.* Chicago: University of Chicago Press.

Rorty, Richard (1979a). *Philosophy and the Mirror of Nature.* Princeton: Princeton University Press.

_____. (1979b). "Transcendental Argument, Self-reference, and Pragmatism." In P. Bieri, *et al.* (eds.) (1979). *Transcendental Arguments and Science.* Dordrecht: Reidel.

_____. (1982). *The Consequences of Pragmatism.* Minneapolis: University of Minnesota Press.

_____. (1984). "Heidegger Wider den Pragmatisten." *Neue Hefte fur Philosophie,* 22 (1984):1–22.

_____. (1986). "Foucault and Epistemology." In Hoy 1986:41–49.

_____. (1989). *Contingency, Irony, and Solidarity.* Cambridge: Cambridge University Press.

_____. (1991a). *Essays on Heidegger and Others: Philosophical Papers,* Volume 2. New York: Cambridge University Press.

_____. (1991b). "Moral Identity and Private Autonomy: The Case of Foucault." In Rorty 1991a:193–98. See also Rorty 1982:203–08.

_____. (1991c). "Feminism and Pragmatism." *Radical Philosophy,* 59 (Autumn 1991):3–12.

_____. (1991d). *Objectivity, Relativism, and Truth: Philosophical Papers,* Volume 1. New York: Cambridge University Press.

_____. (1992). "Cosmopolitanism Without Emancipation: A Response to Lyotard." In Scott Lash and Jonathan Friedman (1992) (eds.) *Modernity and Identity.* Oxford: Blackwell's.

Russell, Bertrand (1945). *A History of Western Philosophy.* New York: Simon and Schuster.

Ryan, Alan (1993). "Foucault's Life and Hard Times." *The New York Review of Books,* 40(7):12–17.

Ryle, Gilbert (1929). "Sein und Zeit." *Mind,* 38:355–70.

Sawicki, Jana (1991). *Disciplining Foucault.* London: Routledge.

_____. (1994). "Foucault, Feminism, and Questions of Identity." In Gutting 1994a:286–313.

Schurmann, Reiner (1989). "Power and Truth in Foucault's Philosophy." *The Journal of Philosophy*, November 1989, 86(11):540–47.

Searle, John (1983). "The World Turned Upside Down." *The New York Review of Books*, October 27, 1983:74–79.

_____. (1995). *The Construction of Social Reality*. New York: The Free Press.

_____. (1999). *Mind, Language and Society*. London: Phoenix (imprint of Orion Books.)

Seigel, J. (1990). "Avoiding the Subject: A Foucauldian Itinerary." *The Journal of the History of Ideas*, April 1990, 51(2):273–99.

Sellars, Wilfrid (1968). *Science and Metaphysics*. New York: Humanities Press.

Sheridan, Alan (1980). *Michel Foucault: The Will to Truth*. London: Tavistock Press.

Shumway, David (1992). *Michel Foucault*. Charlottesville: University of Virginia Press.

Singleton, Bronwyn (1998). *Foucault's Failure of Nerve: From Genealogy to Ethics*. Master's thesis, Queen's University, Kingston, Ontario.

Staten, Henry (1984). *Wittgenstein and Derrida*. Lincoln: University of Nebraska Press.

Szeman, Imre (1993). "Foucault, Genealogy, History." *Problématique*, 3(Fall): 49–73.

Taylor, Charles (1984). "Foucault on Freedom and Truth." In Hoy 1986:69–102.

_____. (1987). "Overcoming Epistemology." In Baynes, Bohman, and McCarthy 1987:464–85.

_____. (1989). *Sources of the Self*. Cambridge, MA: Harvard University Press.

Thayer, H. S. (ed.) (1982). *Pragmatism: The Classic Writings*. Indianapolis: Hackett Publishing.

White, Alan (1970). *Truth*. Garden City: Anchor.

Williams, Bernard (1983). "Auto-da-Fe." *The New York Review of Books*, April 28, 1983.

Wisdom, John (1955). "Gods." In Antony Flew (ed.) 1955. *Logic and Language* (First Series). Oxford: Blackwell's, pp. 187–206.

Wittgenstein, Ludwig (1922). *Tractatus Logico-Philosophicus*. London: Routledge and Kegan Paul.

_____. (1953). *Philosophical Investigations*. New York: The Macmillan Company.

_____. (1980). *Culture and Value*. G. H. Von Wright (ed.) Trans. Peter Winch. Chicago: University of Chicago Press

Index

Printed in the United States
41224LVS00006B/81